Cognitive-Behavior Therapy for Those Who Say They Can't

Cognitive-Behavior Therapy for Those Who Say They Can't is a comprehensive aid for people who stifle their personal freedom, creativity, and autonomy by telling themselves they "can't" do things such as: take risks; make commitments; control their anger or fear; avoid intrusive thoughts; tolerate disappointment; accept challenges, make decisions, and more. This accessible workbook concisely explains how to identify, refute, and replace "I can't" with uplifting and liberating virtues. Worksheets include systematic exercises on coping with shame, rational–emotive imagery, reframing, mindfulness, behavioral planning, and taking risks. Each chapter tackles a particular type of self-defeating "I can't" and is complete with an assessment inventory that helps users/clients identify which chapter/s they need to work on.

This workbook provides essential self-help for those struggling with disempowering thoughts and can also be used by mental health professionals in working with their clients.

Elliot D. Cohen, Ph.D., is president of the Logic-Based Therapy & Consultation Institute, with training centers in the United States, India, and Taiwan. He is a professor at Florida State College of Medicine, Ft. Pierce Regional Campus.

Cognitive-Behavior Therapy for Those Who Say They Can't

A Workbook for Overcoming Your Self-Defeating Thoughts

Elliot D. Cohen

Routledge
Taylor & Francis Group

NEW YORK AND LONDON

Cover image: © Getty Images

First published 2022
by Routledge
605 Third Avenue, New York, NY 10158

and by Routledge
4 Park Square, Milton Park, Abingdon, Oxon, OX14 4RN

Routledge is an imprint of the Taylor & Francis Group, an informa business

© 2022 Taylor & Francis

The right of Elliot D. Cohen to be identified as authors of this work has been asserted in accordance with sections 77 and 78 of the Copyright, Designs and Patents Act 1988.

Library of Congress Cataloging-in-Publication Data
A catalog record for this title has been requested

ISBN: 9780367473907 (hbk)
ISBN: 9780367472337 (pbk)
ISBN: 9781003035282 (ebk)

DOI: 10.4324/9781003035282

Typeset in Minion Pro
by Newgen Publishing UK

Contents

Foreword for Therapists

This book is a companion workbook to the Routledge CBT book, *Cognitive-Behavior Interventions for Self-Defeating Thoughts: Helping Clients to Overcome the Tyranny of "I can't."* The latter book provides a comprehensive, logic-based, language-oriented, neuro-psychological theory that is consistently applied in this *Workbook*. I have endeavored to present its content nontechnically and in a user-friendly manner without sacrificing the scientific framework from which it derives.

The *Workbook* is also constructed to serve as an independent resource. It is not merely a collection of worksheets with brief directions and sparce discussion of the concepts it introduces. To the contrary, it presents a standalone, thorough, nontechnical, practical articulation of the ideas that it introduces to users. Nevertheless, there is considerable latitude for therapists to incorporate their own videos, guides, bibliotherapy, and other resources into the mix. For example, while I suggest bibliotherapy, including movies and literature, I also inform the reader that therapists may wish to add their own wares. So, the book is also intended to be user-friendly to therapists who are using this book for their clients.

The approach is also not the ordinary CBT approach because it helps clients/users to identify and construct the premises and conclusions of their emotional reasoning (reasoning that generates emotions such as anxiety, fear, anger, guilt, and depression) and gives them the tools to carefully inspect and assess these premises and conclusions.

Another aspect that is far flung from the usual garden variety CBT treatment is its systematic use of empowering wisdom of great sages to build support for guiding virtues (Serenity, Courage, Temperance, Self-Respect, Prudence, Patience, Decisiveness, etc.) that counteract irrational, perfectionistic demands, catastrophizing, and self- and other-damnation. As such, it seeks to build cognitive–behavioral–emotive habits of resilience through application of condensed, focused philosophical gems of wisdom associated with ancients such as Plato, Aristotle, Epictetus, and Epicurus to moderns like Nietzsche, Buber, Sartre, and Frankl, to name just some.

Such empowering wisdom is not restricted to Western thought, however, because the treatment also draws on the wisdom of Buddhist and Hindu thinkers such as Thich Nhat Hanh, the Dalai Lama, Lao Tzu, and Indian sage, Patanjali, among others. My work across Eastern and Western cultures (from Taiwan and India to Europe and the States) has pointed to a common set of ideas that resonate multiculturally and I have attempted in this *Workbook* to use these ideas to help a wide and diverse range of clients/users attain feelings of empowerment and consolation to neutralize irrational thinking/feelings that spawn self-destructive emotions and behavior. Further, the treatment also systematically helps clients/users creatively bring their own positive constructions of wisdom to bear on their challenges.

This *Workbook* is intended to help clients/users work on their affect, not just cold cognition. In fact, the theory that supports it views cognition involved in emotion as a flow of images and interoceptive (visceral) feelings that, in the case of negative emotions, have painful valences. So, separating feeling from cognition, treating the latter without systematically addressing the former is artificial at the very least. Accordingly, this *Workbook* includes in its therapeutic bag of interventions, cognitive–affective imagery and various types of meditation.

The approach adopted here is based on Rational-Emotive Behavior Therapy (REBT), the first type of cognitive-behavior therapy, invented by my late mentor, Albert Ellis. Ellis well perceived the importance of replacing self-destructive language and logic with constructive language and rationality. Thus, this *Workbook* seeks to help clients/users cultivate logico-linguistic habits conducive to happiness.

In particular, it focuses on helping clients/users give up disempowering uses of "I can't" and supporting language such as perfectionistic and absolutistic "musts" and "shoulds," catastrophic terms ("awful," horrible," and "terrible"), and personally damning language such as "failure," "loser," and "screwup." It helps clients/users see just how they are destroying the quality of their lives by making inferences that disavow their capacity to accept freedom and responsibility for their thoughts, feelings, and actions. In this context, it helps clients/users overcome self-disabling inferences to "I can't" including ones that thwart rational risk-taking, generate and sustain low frustration tolerance and low anger control, phobias, dysfunctional dependency, and obsessive thinking. This clearly covers a broad range of clients who seek psychotherapy.

I assembled this *Workbook* because there has been a blatant gap in practical counseling materials that systematically address the disempowerment of "I can't" and its cognate vocabulary. Consequently, if this treatment helps your clients and others find a lighted path to empowerment and positive change where there was once a dark, self-stultifying "I can't," it will have accomplished its ultimate goal.

Elliot D. Cohen, Ph.D.

Preface for Users

HOW THIS *WORKBOOK* CAN HELP *YOU*!

Are you stifling your freedom and happiness by telling yourself that you **can't** accomplish any, or all, of the following things?

- Make positive changes in your life, or change old destructive habits;
- Take reasonable risks;
- Make life affirming commitments;
- Overcome intense fears known as phobias;
- Control your anger;
- Avoid debilitating rumination or obsessive thinking;
- Forego immediate, short-term gratification for the sake of long-term happiness;
- Tackle meaningful projects that may be difficult or challenging;
- Avoid overdependence on others;
- Make decisions instead of procrastinating or otherwise putting them off.

If these or related items are on your list of "No can do's," you are not alone! All or most of us, at least sometimes, are "*can't*stipated," that is, we use the four-letter word "can't" to keep ourselves from satisfactorily coping with life. Unfortunately, some of us do this more often than others and succeed in wrecking our own lives as well as those with whom we live and work. If this sounds like you, then this *Workbook* can help you identify the "I can't" thinking that may be undermining your personal happiness and your relations with others and give you the tools to overcome it!

These little words, "I can't," so prevalent in ordinary language, may be working their harm without your even knowing it! But once you see exactly how it may be undermining your freedom and happiness, you are in an excellent position to do something about it. The key to this understanding lies in becoming more sensitive to the language you use to make judgments about reality. You see, human beings have a well-developed symbolic language to think and communicate with one another. This is both a blessing and a curse. It is a blessing because, among other things, we can use language to keep ourselves as well as loved ones out of danger; acquire and retain knowledge; draw logical conclusions; share life experiences and knowledge with others; and express deep affections, including love and compassion, verbally as well as behaviorally.

But language can also be used in ways that defeat these constructive purposes and create barriers to them. For example, unlike your dog or cat, you may tell yourself such things as these:

- I *must* gain the approval of others; therefore *I can't* make my own, independent decisions.
- I *must* be certain (or near certain) before I act; therefore, I *can't* take any chances.
- I *have to* get what I want now; therefore, I *can't stand* to wait.
- It would be an *awful thing* if our relationship didn't work out; therefore, I *can't* make a commitment.
- If I fail, I'll be *a complete failure*; therefore, I *can't* do it.

Notice how such tyrannical uses of "I can't" involve *inferences* to or from other words that make absolutistic, demands ("must," "have to"), negative self-ratings ("complete failure"), and catastrophic assessments ("awful thing").

So, in the first instance, from your judgment that you *must* gain the approval of others, you infer that you are incapable of deciding for yourself, and therefore, give up personal freedom and autonomy.

In the second instance, from the demand that you *must* be certain, you infer that you *can't* take any chances. As a result, you may allow potentially positive opportunities to pass you by.

In the third instance, from the demand that you *must* have immediate gratification, you infer that you can't wait, and, as a result, substitute short-term pleasures for long-lasting ones.

In the fourth, you catastrophize about how *awful* it would be if a prospective relationship didn't work out and infer from this that you *can't* commit to it, thereby sustaining a potentially lifelong, self-defeating fear of making commitments.

In the fifth, from the possibility of failing at something, you infer that *you* (as a person) would be a *complete failure*; from which you further infer your incapacity to do things you could fail at, which are most human undertakings; thereby depriving yourself of the opportunity to succeed and flourish.

It is precisely in these ways that use of the word "can't" curtails freedom. It sustains or creates self-defeating thinking, behavior, and emotions by falsely declaring your *incapacity* to think, act, or feel differently. After all, if you *can't* take risks, then you *won't* take them; and if you *can't* make your own decisions then you won't even try! If you *can't* postpone immediate gratification, then how could you ever hope to reap the fruits of hard work or make important contributions to humanity! And if you can't make commitments to a relationship then how can you ever hope to enjoy the intimacy of a relationship based on trust, mutuality, and love.

But all these cases involve irrational word games that you play with yourself. In these word games, you make *inferences* about your life, the lives of others, and the world that can have profound bearing on your freedom and happiness. The tyranny of language is real, and the words "I can't," combined with a family of language used to make absolutistic demands, negative self-ratings, and catastrophic assessments, can go undetected as they subtly undermine your freedom and happiness. The good news is that you are the one who plays these games with yourself, others, and the world; and it is therefore *you* who can do something about it!

Yes, you can indeed liberate yourself and gain your freedom from this silent subversion. And here's how: This *Workbook* will show you how to substitute rational goals (which I call "guiding virtues") for your irrational, self-defeating "I can't" thinking, and give you exercises to help you practice these virtues. So, for example, instead of telling yourself that you can't make your own decisions, you can work toward greater *Authenticity*. Instead of telling yourself you can't take risks, you can cultivate *Courage* in the face of uncertainty. Instead of telling yourself you can't wait, you can work on *Patience*; and instead of telling yourself you can't do things you might fail at, you can work on *Self-Respect*.

This *Workbook* can help you to advance toward these guiding virtues, among others, making them second nature, by practicing them. This is the positive thinking side of doing away with your self-destructive, unrealistic "I can't" word games. It involves learning to make more realistic inferences using a positive set of vocabulary. As you will see, this is also an opportunity to become acquainted with the wisdom of some of the greatest minds in history, who have provided much learned counsel about how to aspire to the guiding virtues.

For example, the ancient Stoic philosopher, Epictetus, reminds us that it is our judgments about events that stress us out, not the events themselves. So, if you stop demanding perfection, you can gain greater Tolerance and Patience when others are not treating you how you would prefer. Likewise, 18th-century philosopher Immanuel Kant would remind you that you are not an object or thing that has value only to the extent that you are useful. To the contrary, your value as a *person* is inalienable, so when you make a mistake or fail at something (as you inevitably will) you still retain your worth and dignity as a person. And French existentialist Jean-Paul Sartre reminds you that in life one reckons with probabilities, not certainties, as part of "the human condition." So, being courageous means confronting the probabilistic nature of reality without attempting to hide behind a never-never-land of certainty.

It is heartening to know that you are not alone on your journey toward overcoming your self-defeating "I can'ts." You will be well served by the sagely counsel of such great minds; and, of course, you will have yours truly, as your guide.

I look forward to working with you!

Elliot D. Cohen, Ph.D.

Introduction: Getting Started!

As discussed in the Preface, your use of "I can't" may be stifling your freedom and wrecking your life without your even realizing it! This is because you may be "*can't*stipated." That is, you may be in a stubborn habit of unreflectively using the words, "I can't" to draw negative inferences (conclusions) about your *capacity* to manage your life. And it's not rocket science to figure out what happens when you tell yourself you can't do something: You don't!

So, here's the plan. I will show how to identify and overcome six different ways you may be stifling your capacity to live a happy, productive life by telling yourself you can't. Because not all six ways necessarily apply to you, this *Workbook* is arranged so that you only need to do the work that relates to your case.

SETTING GENERAL GOALS

More specifically, let's set three related, general goals:

1. Increase your awareness of how you are using "I can't" (or synonyms such as "I'm incapable" or "I'm unable") and related disempowering language to undermine your capacity to manage your life;
2. Help you give up these disempowering uses of language and, instead, reframe reality in terms of a new, forward-looking, self-affirming vocabulary; and
3. Use this new way of looking at reality (yourself, others, and the world) to build habits that increase your freedom to manage your life.

LANGUAGE IS KEY

Notice I have formulated the above set of goals in terms of the language that you use. This is important because the way we human beings *think* about reality is a function of the language we use to interpret it; and, of course, the way we think influences the way we *feel* and how we *behave*. For example, if you tell yourself that you are worthless because you screwed up at work and therefore can't do anything right, then guess what? Yes, that's right! You will *feel* worthless, and act as though you are—for example, not make any positive effort, or even self-sabotage.

The way you feel can also influence the language you use, which can, in turn, amplify or change your feelings, and your behavior. So, you do poorly at work. You associate doing poorly at something with a feeling of unworthiness; which leads you to tell yourself what a "failure" you are; which leads you to become unsociable, grumpy, and whiny.

DOI: 10.4324/9781003035282-1

Notice also that I have spoken of "related disempowering language" in Goal 1. This is important because people rarely use the words "I can't" in isolation from other disempowering words. As discussed in the Preface, this family of language includes words that make absolutist demands ("must," "must not," "shouldn't"), negative self-ratings ("complete failure," "worthless"), and catastrophic assessments ("awful," "horrible," and "terrible").

IDENTIFYING DISEMPOWERING INFERENCES

Such language of disempowerment is often used in the *inferences* people make when they use self-defeating types of "I can't." Inferences are conclusions that people derive from premises. Premises are what people use to try to prove or justify their conclusions. For example, here is an inference that uses language of disempowerment:

> It would be so awful if I asked her out and she turned me down.
> *Therefore*, I can't bring myself to ask her for a date.

This is an example of a catastrophic use of "I can't" where the speaker infers "I can't …" from a premise that uses the word "awful" to catastrophize about (exaggerate the badness of) getting turned down. And, of course, if the speaker *can't* bring himself to ask her out, he won't. So, the speaker uses such language to needlessly place restrictions on the freedom to forge meaningful intimate relationships!

DISEMPOWERING INFERENCE SYNDROMES

Disempowering language tends to beget further disempowering language. One prevalent strain of this is the *demanding approval-self-damnation syndrome*. Suppose you tell yourself that you *must* get the approval of others, and then you don't get that approval. You may then infer that you are an *unworthy person, a reject*, or worse; and then further infer that you *can't* do anything right. Thus:

1. I *must* get the approval of others
2. I didn't get this approval
3. So, I'm *worthless*
4. So, *I can't* do anything right.

In Premise 1, you demand approval; then because you don't get this approval (Premise 2), you infer that you are worthless (Premise 3); and finally conclude that you *can't* do anything right. As a result *you* only succeed in stifling your own freedom!

Another virulent strain is the *achievement-self-damnation syndrome*. In this case, you demand that you perform perfectly, or near perfectly, at some activity, and then tell yourself that if you aren't perfect at it, then you *can't* do it. For example, a student once told me this as a justification for attempting to cheat on an exam when I caught him and confronted him:

> I must not fail at anything I try to do
> If I try to pass the exam I might fail
> So *I can't* even try.

I instructed the student to study hard for the next exam (the final exam), and during the exam asked him to sit in the front row where I could monitor him. He ended up getting the highest score in the class on the final! The student obviously had strong aptitude but his catastrophic "I-can't" thinking kept him from actualizing it.

GETTING READY TO WORK

Overcoming such self-imposed, self-defeating restrictions on personal freedom takes considerable work. Simply refusing to say "I can't" will not itself stop you from acting and feeling as though you can't. You may realize that it is irrational to tell yourself that you can't, but old habits don't die easily. You may still be acting or feeling like you can't.

REFRAMING YOUR DISEMPOWERING SELF-TALK

To make genuine constructive change, you will need to make *behavioral* changes while working on the way you speak to yourself (self-talk). You will need to *reframe* the language of your self-talk in a more realistic way ("It's not that I can't; it's rather that I am choosing not to"). Then, you can put your actions where your mouth is; that is, change your behavior to align with your new self-talk. Indeed, the more you consistently *practice* thinking and acting in this more realistic manner, the more comfortable you will begin to *feel* about it.

SETTING REALISTIC EXPECTATIONS

Accordingly, in this *Workbook*, you will find practice exercises and worksheets to help you make such constructive cognitive, emotional, and behavioral changes. However, let's be honest from the start about what you can hope to accomplish through your hard work. You will never be perfect; there will always be room for improvement; positive change will take time and perseverance; and there can be *no guarantee* that your life will change for the better. On the other hand, it is highly unlikely your ability to manage your life will improve without putting in this effort; whereas, in doing so, you have a reasonable shot at making healthy strides toward the above-mentioned goals.

What makes such change "healthy"? It is because human beings tend to be happiest when they have a sense of freedom of thought and action. However, this cherished human value can be denied not just by external physical constraints (for example, imprisonment or poor physical health). The denial of freedom can also arise from mental constraints you needlessly impose on yourself. The tyranny of "I can't" is a chief way in which this ingredient of human happiness can be subverted.

THE FIVE CATEGORIES OF *I CAN'T*

This self-imposed tyranny stifles freedom in five self-defeating ways defined in Table I.1.

In other words, you can be *can't*stipated in five different ways: behaviorally, emotionally, volitionally, cognitively, and impulsively. As such, each of the six types of "I can't" to be examined in this *Workbook* are classified under one of these five broad categories.

SIX TYPES OF *CAN'T* STIPATION

Keeping Table I.1 in mind, look at Table I. 2. It identifies and classifies each of six types of self-defeating "I can't" under one of the four general categories distinguished in Table I.2 which provides an explanation, and gives an example.

TABLE I.1
Five self-defeating uses of "I can't"

Category of I Can't	Self-Defeating Result
1. Behavioral	Sustains or creates self-defeating behavior
2. Emotional	Sustains self-defeating emotions and prevents self-control
3. Volitional	Sustains weakness of will or obstructs the exercise of willpower
4. Cognitive	Sustains or creates self-defeating thoughts
5. Impulsive	Sustains or creates self-destructive impulses (fear or desire)

TABLE I.2
Six types of *can't* stipation

Type of Can'tstipation	Category	Dysfunction	Illustration
1. Risk-Aversion	Behavioral	Obstructs rational risk-taking	"I can't afford to take any risks"
2. Low Frustration Tolerance	Behavioral	Creates and sustains low frustration tolerance (LFT)	"I can't stand (don't have patience for) difficult things"
3. Low Self-Reliance	Behavioral	Creates and sustains dependency on others	"I can't make my own decisions"
4. Low Anger Control	Emotional	Keeps you in a constant state of self-defeating anger	"I can't help being pissed by that nasty comment"
5. Phobia	Impulsive	Sustains intense irrational fear	"I can't stand being in crowded places"
6. Obsessive Thinking	Cognitive	Sustains unwanted, painful thoughts	"I can't get that horrible thought out of my mind"

So, do any of the six types of *can't*stipation identified in Table I.2 fit your profile? Exercise I.1 can help you address this important question.

EXERCISE I.1

Think about the ways you use the words, "I can't." Which of the six types of "I can't" distinguished in Table I.2 fits the way you use these words? To help with this question, please take the following inventory:

For each of the below statements, indicate your level of agreement with it by circling one of the four choices. If you are not sure which of two choices apply, circle the higher number.

1. I can't help getting very angry when people treat me badly. Because it feels so wrong when I think of how badly they've treated me, I feel powerless over my anger toward them: (4) agree strongly, (3) agree, (2) agree somewhat, (1) do not agree.

2. I have an extreme fear of doing a certain thing(s) or being in a certain situation(s). So, I tell myself I can't do this thing(s) or be in this situation(s); and it's negatively impacting my life: (4) agree strongly, (3) agree, (2) agree somewhat, (1) do not agree.

3. I feel like I can't stand waiting very long for things, even if I want them a lot, so I easily give up on things that take a lot of time, or just don't pursue them.

4. I can't stand doing things that are unpleasant even if I need to do them to get something I really want. So, I give up on these things and try to do other things that give me more immediate pleasure.

5. I tell myself I can't do things when I find them difficult or challenging. I easily get frustrated and give up on them: (4) agree strongly, (3) agree, (2) agree somewhat, (1) do not agree.

6. I tell myself I can't do things when I feel uncertain about their outcomes. This creates a lot of anxiety for me when making decisions, especially important ones: (4) agree strongly, (3) agree, (2) agree somewhat, (1) do not agree.

7. I tell myself I can't do certain things when I think there's a chance I might mess up and make myself look foolish. This creates a lot of anxiety for me when making decisions, especially important ones: (4) agree strongly, (3) agree, (2) agree somewhat, (1) do not agree.

8. I tell myself I can't do certain things when I think there's a chance they might go wrong and ruin my life. This creates a lot of anxiety for me when making decisions, especially important ones: (4) agree strongly, (3) agree, (2) agree somewhat, (1) do not agree.

9. I can't make decisions on my own. I get very anxious that I might make a mistake, so I look to my significant other, or someone else I confide in, to tell me what to do: (4) agree strongly, (3) agree, (2) agree somewhat, (1) do not agree.

10. I feel like I need other people's approval to feel good about myself and tend to rely on others to tell me what to do.

11. I keep thinking about the possibility of something extremely bad happening to me or a loved one. I don't know that it will actually happen but I'm not certain it won't happen and can't get it out of my mind: (4) agree strongly, (3) agree, (2) agree somewhat, (1) do not agree.

12. I keep ruminating about the possibility of my doing something very bad. I don't think I will do it but I'm not really sure, and I just can't stop thinking about it: (4) agree strongly, (3) agree, (2) agree somewhat, (1) do not agree.

EXERCISE I.2

You are now ready to identify major ways in which you may be *can't* stipating yourself. Table I.3 will help you to accomplish this important first step. Please refer to your responses to the questions in the *Can't*stipation Inventory to complete the second and third columns of Table I.3.

TABLE I.3
Your *can't* stipation types with confidence ratings

If you agree strongly, agree, or agree somewhat with inventory question/s	Then you may have a problem with this type of can'tstipation: (Place a check (√) on each line next to the name that applies)	Indicate the strength of your agreement by placing a 4 (agree strongly), 3 (agree), or 2 (agree somewhat) in this column
6, 7, or 8	Risk-Aversion___	
3, 4, or 5	Low Frustration Tolerance ___	
9 or 10	Low Self-Reliance ___	
1	Low Anger Control ___	
2	Phobia ____	
11 or 12	Obsessive ___	

Congratulations! You now have identified the type of self-defeating "I can't" you use, as well as how confident you are that you use it!

OVERCOMING YOUR "I CAN'T" WITH ITS GUIDING VIRTUES

Having identified the ways you *can't*stipate yourself is a major step toward increasing your freedom. This is because the language of "I can't," including words that often accompany it, such as "unworthy," "incompetent," "awful," "mustn't," is *disempowering*. This language can keep you trapped in the same self-defeating habits of inertia. In contrast, there is a set of positive words that refer to ideals or "virtues" that point away from the latter disempowerment towards behavioral, emotional, and cognitive empowerment. I refer to the latter as "guiding virtues." They set particular goals that can liberate you from the tyranny of "I can't"!

In fact, for each of the six types of self-defeating "I can't" there is a set of guiding virtues that counteracts it. Table I.4 shows the set of guiding virtues for each type.

So, for example, if you tend to use the risk-aversive type of "I can't," that is, tell yourself that you can't take risks, then your guiding virtues are Decisiveness, Courage, and Foresightedness. This means that you would need to work toward these virtues as your particular goals.

SNAPSHOTS OF THE GUIDING VIRTUES

Table I.5 provides descriptions of each of the guiding virtues:

Exercise I.3 now gives you directions for setting up a list of *your* types of *can't*stipation with their guiding virtues.

TABLE I.4
Types of *can't*stipation with their counteractive guiding virtues

Type of Can'tstipation	Its Guiding Virtues
1. Risk-Aversion	Decisiveness, Courage, Foresightedness
2. Low Frustration Tolerance	Patience, Perseverance, Prudence
3. Low Self-Reliance	Decisiveness, Authenticity, Self-Respect
4. Low Anger Control	Courage, Respect for Others, Temperance
5. Phobia	Foresightedness, Courage, Continence.
6. Obsessive	Serenity (Peace of Mind), Respect for Life, Self-Respect

TABLE I.5
Definitions of the guiding virtues

Guiding Virtue	Description
1. Courage	• Confronting adversity without under- or overestimating the danger. It means fearing things to the extent that it is reasonable to fear them and, in the face of danger, acting according to the merits of the situation.
2. Respect for	• Self Unconditional, self-acceptance based on a deep philosophical understanding of human worth and dignity. • Others Consistently extends this profound unconditional respect for human worth and dignity to other human beings • Life Acceptance of life as possessing worth and meaning despite the inevitability of problems of living.

TABLE I.5

Continued

Guiding Virtue	Description
3. Authenticity	• Autonomously and freely living according to your own creative lights as opposed to losing yourself on a bandwagon of social conformity.
4. Prudence	• A grasp of what is in your power and what is not, including an appreciation of what things in your power are worth attaining; along with the skill to deliberate well about means to attaining them.
5. Foresightedness	• Making generalizations and predictions that are probable relative to available evidence.
6. Decisiveness	Realistic trust in your ability to accomplish the goals you set; and preparedness to take rational risks to accomplish these goals under less-than-ideal conditions.
7. Perseverance	Tenacious persistence, within rational limits, in striving for reasonable goals with keen awareness that perseverance can be key to accomplishing them.
8. Patience	Willpower to sacrifice short-term, fleeting pleasures for more long-term, lasting ones, with appreciation that good things often involve hard work and overcoming obstacles.
9. Temperance	Taking responsibility for, and exercising control over your emotions without making excuses, and without first having to overcome irrational emotional tendencies.
10. Tolerance	Willpower to entertain and accept alternative perspectives, or ways of doing things, even if one does not agree with them, without over- or under-reacting.
11. Continence	Willpower to constrain physical desires or aversions, neither over- nor under-doing them.
18. Serenity (Peace of Mind)	Allowing thoughts to freely enter and exit conscious awareness without catastrophizing, damning, or demanding perfection in conceiving, pondering, or dismissing them.

EXERCISE I.3

Look over the type/s of *can't*stipation you placed a check next to in Table I.3 (Exercise I.2). Also, take note of the strength of agreement you have indicated for each in the third column of this table. Now, in the column labeled "Your constipation type/s" in Table I.6, list each type on a separate line. Please list them in the order of your strength of agreement. For example, if you identified risk-aversion and low-self-reliance as your *can't*stipation types, and you strongly agree with the first and simply agree with the second, then please list risk-aversion first. If your strength of agreement is the same, for example you strongly agree with both risk-aversion and low self-reliance, then list them in any order you wish, keeping in mind that the order you in which you list them will determine the order you will be working on them.

Now, using Table I.6, find the guiding virtues for each type of *can't*stipation you have listed, and write them down in the space provided next to their respective type of *can't*stipation. For example, write Decisiveness, Courage, and Foresight next to risk-aversion.

Congratulations! Many people who *can't*stipate themselves never even get to the point of knowing what they are doing to stifle their own freedom. You now have an idea of what you may be doing to hold yourself back, create needless anxiety, stress yourself out, or otherwise preempt your own prosperity.

TABLE I.6
Your *can't* stipation types with their counteractive guiding virtues

Your Can't stipation Type/s	Your Guiding Virtue/s
1.	1.
2.	2.
3.	3.
4.	4.
5.	5.
6.	6.

Exercise I.4 now gives you an opportunity to reflect on the significance of your guiding virtues for your life.

EXERCISE I.4

1. The virtue/s you have listed in Table I.6 are ones you will be working on in the *Workbook*. Accordingly, please read carefully the descriptions of your guiding virtues as provided in Table I.5 and give them some thought. This should give you an idea about what it may take to make progress toward these constructive goals.

2. How might possession of each of these virtues potentially improve your life? For example, what things would you do differently if you were more courageous or more authentic? What challenges do you foresee in developing these virtues? Write down your reflections in the space below. Use additional paper if necessary:

Preliminary Reflections about My Guiding Virtues

I hope that this exercise has opened your eyes to some exciting possibilities that may await you in working toward your guiding virtues!

YOUR GUIDING VIRTUES ARE IDEALS

Notice that your guiding virtues are ideals. This is part of the excitement of reaching for them. It's because the sky is the limit, and you can keep getting better and better! This also means that they can never be actualized 100% in your lifetime. Instead, they are life-long projects for which there will always be room for improvement. Much like a skillful musician or craftsman, you will always be challenged to become more and more skillful. The more you practice, the more the virtues can become part of you, like any other habit. But don't fall into the trap of demanding that you be perfect. This is not humanly possible, and remember, you are a fallible human being!

THE POSITIVE, EMPOWERING LANGUAGE OF GUIDING VIRTUES

One of the most salient features of the guiding virtues is the positivity of the language with which they are associated. The words that refer to the virtues themselves are quite *empowering or uplifting*. For example, the word "Courage" *feels* uplifting when you even say it to yourself. Try it! So too do "Decisiveness," "Foresightedness," "Self-Respect," "Authenticity," and the other guiding virtues. *This is very important because thinking in terms of virtue words and associated language can help you to feel and do better.*

GETTING EMPOWERING WISDOM FROM THE GREATEST MINDS IN HISTORY

So how do you know what to do to become more courageous, more authentic, prudent, unconditionally self-accepting, and so forth? This *Workbook* will tap into some of the greatest minds in history to give you direction. For example, what empowering wisdom can a great sage like Roman Emperor Marcus Aurelius give you about controlling yourself if you happen to have an anger control problem? "[I]t is not men's acts which disturb us," admonishes this highly respected Emperor, "but it is our own opinions which disturb us. Take away these opinions … and thy anger is gone." For instance, what disturbs you is rather the judgment that this person who did something wrong to you is a "rotting, stinking piece of garbage who deserves hell and damnation." But to learn how to "take away" such an "opinion" requires work. It also requires a *cognitive-behavioral plan*.

CREATING A COGNITIVE-BEHAVIORAL PLAN

This plan will consist of a list of cognitive and behavioral changes (changes in the way you think and act), which you intend to make in the immediate or not-so-distant future using your empowering wisdom to guide your judgment. "I will reframe my thinking, avoiding the use of inflammatory language like 'rotting, stinking piece of garbage'; I will seek a more rational approach to dealing with wrongdoing by others." Implementing your plan is then the next step in the process of making constructive change.

WORKING ON YOUR COGNITIVE-BEHAVIORAL PLAN

Here is where you have an opportunity to begin building virtuous habits, instead of *can't*stipating yourself. This consists of *assignments* that will help you to implement your cognitive-behavioral plan. There are several different types of assignments you may be assigned in this *Workbook*:

Refuting and Reframing

This general type of assignment involves practicing refuting your *can't*stipating thinking (showing that it's irrational); and then reframing (constructively rethinking or reinterpreting) it in terms of some empowering wisdom from your sages. For example, suppose you mess up on a project at work for which you volunteered, and your boss discovers the mistake and tells you to check your work more carefully next time. Your tendency may be to say to yourself, "Now I'm really screwed! He must think I'm an idiot! I should never have volunteered to do this assignment in the first place. Never again!" However, you catch yourself in this self-defeating thinking, and speak sternly to yourself. "Wait a minute! There's always some risk of messing up no matter what I do. So, does this mean I should never do anything? Of course not! It's just part of life's learning process! No pain, no gain!"

Cognitive-Behavioral Assignments

These assignments can help to strengthen healthy habits. One form is a *shame-attacking* exercise in which you intentionally stage an event that puts you in a position where others disapprove of you. For example, in working to overcome low self-reliance (which involves demanding approval of others), you can do something strange like walking a banana on a string down a crowded street,[1] while passersby look at you as though you were insane. Before, during, and after doing this, you work on refuting and reframing your thinking. "So, what does it really matter what's going on in their heads. Why should it even bother me. Anyway, I am proving to myself that I can be my own authentic person, not some cog in a machine!"

Another form is a *risk-taking exercise*. This involves doing something that has relatively low stakes, but high risk. For example, in working on overcoming risk-aversion, you might engage in gambling a small amount of money, win, lose, or draw. Again, you would practice refuting and reframing your *can't*stipating thinking before, during, and after engaging in gambling. "So what if I lose this money? It's not much money anyway so I can think of it as paying to get some entertainment, like going to a movie or a nightclub. All things in life are, in a sense, a gamble, so how else can we live except to take risks!"

Still other behavioral assignments may involve *tackling a major behavioral challenge* such as acting on one of your goals obstructed by *can't*stipating thinking; and, before, during, and after tackling it, refuting and reframing your thinking.

Cognitive–Affective Imagery

Some assignments involve engaging in a cognitive–affective form of *guided imagery* that can help change negative feelings to positive ones. This involves getting in touch with painful feelings and replacing them with uplifting, empowering ones.

"Oh my God! What if I lose my job! It really *could* happen. It would be so awful! I just couldn't take that. No! I would just lay down and die!!" Indeed, telling yourself this could work you up into having a very strong, visceral negative feeling of gloom and doom reverberating inside you.

Well, that's exactly what you will first be asked to do in your imagery exercise: Make yourself *feel* this negativity by imagining yourself being told by your boss that you are no longer employed. Then, in concert with some empowering wisdom you have gotten about how to be courageous in the face of adversity, you tell yourself to change your imagery to a very positive, uplifting, inspiring one; for example, imagining triumphing over your adversity by finding new meaning and purpose in your life as a result of this life-altering experience.

By regularly practicing this exercise, you can eventually overcome the intense negative feeling so that you no longer experience it when you imagine losing your job (or whatever the object of your emotion may be).

Meditation

In these assignments you learn how to control the flow of negative images that lead to needless anxiety, depression, anger, guilt, or other unnecessary, self-disturbing emotions.

These assignments may include *mindfulness* training in which you focus on your breathing or some other object of consciousness while gently keeping other thoughts from disrupting your focused attention.

Another type of meditation is compassion-based meditation in which you build respect for self, others, and (eventually) the world by focusing on the target, while silently repeating some kindness such as "may you be happy" and/or "may you be free from suffering." This may also include imagery such as imagining light emanating from your heart to others. It usually starts with more friendly targets and gradually progresses to less friendly and less familiar ones, and eventually to all beings.

Bibliotherapy

Still other assignments involve *bibliotherapy*, that is, partaking in various forms of media to inspire and empower you. Bibliotherapy may include a certain movie, video, song, artwork, literary work, or self-improvement resource. This *Workbook* offers suggestions, but you have the opportunity to select something yourself, or discuss the selection with your therapist if you have one.

THE GENERAL APPROACH TAKEN IN THIS *WORKBOOK*

Accordingly, this *Workbook* provides worksheets and other exercises that can help you to overcome your self-defeating *can't*stipation and make progress toward your guiding virtues. Each chapter addresses one of the six types of *can't*stipation so you can concentrate on the chapters that pertain to you. The chapters are divided into six parts. Table I.7 provides a description of each part.

Your Next Step

Congratulations on having read through this introduction and completed all the exercises in it! This preliminary work is a necessary first step before moving on. The next step is to work on overcoming the type of *can't*stipation you have listed on line 1, Table I.6, in Exercise I.3. Accordingly, please go now to the chapter in this *Workbook* that covers it and start reading and working through the exercises and worksheets it contains. Table I.8 lists the chapter number where each of the six types of *can't*stipation is examined.Table I.8

TABLE I.7
Main parts of each chapter

Chapter Section	Description
1. Goals of the Chapter	Describes the particular goals to accomplish by working through the chapter and its exercises.
2. The Nature of [the specific] I-Can't Thinking	Discusses important aspects of the type of *can'tstipation* addressed in the chapter.
3. Examining Your [specific] I-Can't Thinking	Helps you to identify the language you use to *can'tstipate* yourself, and helps you to refute this thinking, that is, show that it is irrational.
4. Embracing Your Guiding Virtues	Prepares you to use these uplifting, empowering virtues to overcome your *can'tstipation*.
5. Empowering Wisdom from the Sages on Becoming Virtuous	Gives you uplifting or consoling insight from some of the world's greatest minds for cultivating your guiding virtues.
6. Creating a Cognitive-Behavioral Plan	Helps you identify ways you can apply this empowering wisdom to overcome your *can'tstipation*.
7. Working on Your Cognitive-Behavioral Plan	Provides you with exercises to build the cognitive-emotive-behavioral skills to *implement* your plan.

Chapter in which each *can'tstipation* type is treated

For This Type of Can'tstipation	Go to Chapter #
Risk-Aversion	1
Low Frustration Tolerance	2
Low Anger Control	3
Phobia	4
Low Self-Reliance	5
Obsessive Thinking	6

After you have satisfactorily worked through the first type of *can'tstipation* you listed on the first line of Table I.6, you will be ready to work through the second type you listed on the second line of Table I.6 (if you listed a second type), and so on.

How often has your internal voice, telling you that you "can't," kept you from making potentially worthwhile advances in life? How often have you said to yourself, I wish I could be different; not be so dependent; not be so afraid to take risks; not have so little willpower to persevere; not be so hotheaded, not be so obsessive? The truth is *you can*!

If you are like many others who want to be free of these self-imposed, self-defeating chains you wear, then it is worth the energy you expend to gain your freedom.

You have the capacity. Now it is time to get to work!

NOTE

1 I owe this example to Dr. Albert Ellis.

1

Overcoming Risk-Aversion

As you have seen in the Introduction to this *Workbook*, risk-aversive *can'tstipation* is a behavioral type of *can'tstipation* that obstructs taking rational risks. This can prevent you from *doing* things that can bring greater personal and interpersonal happiness. Instead, you settle into the same old routine because it feels "safe" and do little or nothing to make constructive changes in your life.

1. GOALS OF THE CHAPTER

Accordingly, the goals of this chapter are to:

1. Increase awareness of your risk-aversive thinking and the language you are using to obstruct taking reasonable risks.
2. Refute this thinking.
3. Identify guiding virtues that counteract your risk-aversive thinking.
4. Identify empowering wisdom from great sages on how to seek these virtues.
5. Use this learned counsel to construct a cognitive-behavioral plan for increasing your virtues.
6. Work on your plan, including taking some reasonable risks.

2. THE NATURE OF RISK-AVERSIVE THINKING

This type of *can'tstipation* is associated with anxiety about the *possibility* of bad things happening as a result of taking risks. Such risk-taking may include:

- Engaging in behavior that opens you up to being rejected or negatively judged by others;
- Doing something that carries the possibility of making a serious mistake (for instance, on an important work assignment);
- Making a life decision that carries the possibility of ending up alone (for instance, as a result of ending a relationship or getting a divorce);
- Engaging in behavior in which you can lose something of value (money, friendship, a job);
- Making commitments that may not work out (such as starting an intimate relationship);

DOI: 10.4324/9781003035282-2

- Doing things that have a relatively small risk of dying or being seriously injured (such as air travel,;
- Putting yourself in a situation where others could possibly betray you, or otherwise not do their part;
- Trying new things or unchartered territory (such as dining out at a new restaurant, changing jobs, learning to play a musical instrument, or taking dancing lessons).

So, instead of risking these consequences, you tell yourself you can't take the risk. For example, consider the reasoning by which risk-aversive people like you might keep themselves from making constructive change:

- If I get up in front of all those people to speak, I might mess up and
  everyone might laugh at me.
  So, it could be a *fiasco*!
  So, I can't do it.
- If I fly in a plane, it could crash and leave my children orphans.
  So, flying could be *a horrible mistake*.
  So, I just *can't* take such risks.[1]
- If I give her a (engagement) ring, what if the marriage doesn't work!
  So, it could be a *disaster*!
  So, I *can't* make this commitment.
- If I divorce my (physically and emotionally abusive) husband, I might never find someone else and be alone for the rest of my life.
  So, it could be a *catastrophe*!
  So, I *can't* go through with it.
- If I ask her to have sex with me, what if I *can't* have an erection!
  So, I could make an *ass* out of myself.
  So, I really *can't* do it.
- If I ask her out, she might turn me down.
  So, it could be *devastating* for me!
  So, I *can't* ask her out!
- If I tell her I have HIV, she will probably leave me.
  So, telling her could be *the worst mistake I could ever make*.
  So, I *can't* tell her.
- If I eat out in restaurants, I could contract a disease from dirty dishes and die.
  So eating out is a *terrible idea*!
  So, I *can't* eat out.

In cases like these you imagine bad things happening, which *feels* threatening to you, which leads you to catastrophize about them by using strong emotional language; this language, in turn, makes you *feel disempowered*, and leads you to conclude, "I can't do it."

Now, look at this disempowering language:

- "fiasco"
- "horrible mistake"
- "disaster"
- "catastrophe"
- "awful"
- "devastating"

- "the worst mistake I could ever make"
- "terrible idea."

These words pack an emotional punch! In each of the above cases they are used to rate imagined, negative outcomes as 100% or nearly 100% bad. So, on a bad scale of 1 to 10, where 10 is 100% bad, you are maxing out at a 9 or 10 when you use such language to assess the consequences of your actions. And, in speaking in such absolutistic, negative terms, you set yourself up to declare, "I can't do it!"

It's the negative *possibility* that feels threatening!

Notice that in all of the examples provided above, there is a level of uncertainty about whether things will work out or not. You don't know *for certain* that you won't mess up if you make a speech before a class or other group of people; that the plane won't crash if you book a flight; that your marriage won't go south if you commit to it; that you will have an erection; that the person you ask out on a date won't turn you down; and so on. So, there is possibility, not certainty in this mundane world of ours; no guarantees that things won't take a turn for the worse. And it is this very fact that can make us feel uncomfortable, to a varying degree, about making decisions and acting on them.

Folks who feel threatened by risks, tend to demand certainty about the outcomes of their acts. A key point here is that none of us know *for sure* that bad things won't actually happen. Unfortunately, those who are risk-aversive run these negative events in their imagination *as if* they were happening to them, catastrophize about them, and thereby chill themselves off from taking the risk. What they *demand* is *certainty* that they will reap the benefits of acting without incurring the risk. What *feels threatening* to them is this risk because it contradicts their demand for certainty.

Accordingly, your chain of reasoning, when more fully expanded, may take the following general form:

1. I *must* be certain my actions will not have bad outcomes.
2. But I am *not* certain doing this won't have (such and such) bad outcomes.
3. So, doing this could be a *catastrophe.*
4. So, *I can't* do it.

In Premise 1 you demand certainty, and in Premise 2 you perceive that you don't have the certainty you demand. This leaves you in a conflicted state of suspended anxiety which you top off with language like "Oh my God, this is awful, horrible, and terrible. How can I really make this commitment and keep it!" You thereby trap yourself in a never-never-land of waiting for the ideal moment when reality and absolute certainty converge, and you can act with absolute assurance. So, you may put things off, procrastinate, and, in the end, make your decision by indecision; that is, wait too long, and forfeit your window of opportunity.

Of course, you have sometimes taken risks, even serious ones. Right? Indeed, everybody does, like it or not. Sometimes the risk of inaction is just too high, such as when you need surgery to rectify a serious or life-threatening health condition. Still, you may want to consider how much needless anxiety you may have put yourself (and those who love you) through before you finally accept the risk.

As for the "must" in Premise 1, it is based on a *felt need for certainty* (a feeling deep inside you). Such a feeling stems from past negative experiences. For example, you may have experienced rejection and it felt bad. A representation of this feeling itself (not just the event of being rejected) is then stored in your brain's memory circuits (specifically, in somato-sensory structures in the forebrain) and this feeling is, in turn, associated with the felt need for certainty about future outcomes. So, when you imagine being turned down by someone you are considering asking out on a date, the feeling of rejection you have stored up runs in your imagination and activates that "No way!" feeling in your gut, which feels like you *need* assurance it won't happen again!

Exercise 1.1 is an icebreaker to help you get more in touch with the feelings going on inside you when you tell yourself you can't take risks.

EXERCISE 1.1

Write down your answers to the following questions in the space provided. Use separate pieces of paper if necessary:

1. When you are about to do something that you have not regularly done in the past, what goes through your mind? What feelings do you experience?

```



```

2. Think of something you recently wanted to do but decided against it because you didn't want to take the risk. Rerun in your mind how you felt when you decided not to do it. Try your best to describe this feeling that moved you to not do it.

```



```

3. Think of something you would very much like to do but have not yet done. Now think of something bad that might happen if you do it.

    a. Place a check next to any of the following words that describe what you are feeling. Feel free to add some of your own ideas to this list that might better capture how you feel.

- Conflicted ____
- Threatened ____
- Fearful ____
- Anxious ____
- Powerless ____
- Hopeless ____
- Trapped ____

b.   When faced with such situations, how do you usually resolve them?

```
┌─────────────────────────────────────────────────────────────┐
│                                                               │
│                                                               │
│                                                               │
│                                                               │
│                                                               │
└─────────────────────────────────────────────────────────────┘
```

c.   Are you satisfied with the way you usually resolve them? Explain.

```
┌─────────────────────────────────────────────────────────────┐
│                                                               │
│                                                               │
│                                                               │
│                                                               │
│                                                               │
└─────────────────────────────────────────────────────────────┘
```

The Self-Defeating Nature of Your Risk-Aversive Thinking

Because the future is not entirely predictable, it is human to experience some anxiety in confronting it. Unfortunately, your risk-aversive thinking can manufacture intense anxiety, which you resolve by concluding, "I can't." The self-defeating result of this syndrome is that you don't make constructive changes in your life that you would like to make. Instead, you hide your proverbial head in the sand.

3. EXAMINING *YOUR* RISK-AVERSIVE THINKING

In this section you will have the opportunity to examine the nature of your own risk-aversive thinking. So, what does *your* risk-aversive thinking look like? Exercises 1.2 through 1.4 will help you to answer this question.

EXERCISE 1.2

Let's start by briefly describing at least two and as many as five things you would like to do but are telling yourself you can't do because of the perceived risks. **At least one of these things should be something you can do short term and would like to work on first**, such as asserting yourself in some way you want, but have been afraid to do; for example, giving a presentation in class that you are afraid to give; trying out a new restaurant you are apprehensive about trying; or whatever else you can easily fulfill in the short term.

```
┌─────────────────────────────────────────────────────────────┐
│   1.                                                          │
│                                                               │
│                                                               │
│   2.                                                          │
│                                                               │
└─────────────────────────────────────────────────────────────┘
```

3.

4.

5.

EXERCISE 1.3

Now, make a list of the catastrophic language you are using to convince yourself that you can't take the risks involved in each of the cases you listed in Exercise 1.2. Note that this disempowering language can include language you may be using to negatively rate yourself, for instance, "make an ass of myself" or [show] "what a stupid idiot I am" (if that's what you are doing to make yourself afraid to do the thing in question) as well as language to negatively rate the consequences themselves.

Your Catastrophic/Disempowering Language List

With the above filled in, you have a list of at least some of the disempowering words you tend to use to draw regrettable inferences about what you think you can't do. These are word usages that you will need to retire from your vocabulary!

EXERCISE 1.4

Next, for each of the cases you listed in Exercise 1.2, write down your risk-aversive thinking (chain of reasoning leading you to say you can't) using the language you identified in Exercise 1.3. To formulate each of your cases, please follow the below form:

1. I *must* be certain that if I [insert here what you are afraid to do], it won't happen that [insert here a description of what you fear could happen].

2. But I'm *not* certain that won't happen.
3. So, if I [insert here again what you're afraid of doing] it could [insert here your catastrophic disempowering language].
4. So, I *can't* do it.

For example, suppose you once told yourself you couldn't take the risks of going back to school because you might not be able to juggle taking care of the kids and taking courses, and might end up failing your courses, which you would rate as "awful" (a 10 on the bad scale)—then your thinking would look like this:

1. I must be certain that if I <u>go back to school</u>, it won't happen that <u>I'm not able to handle school and the kids and end up failing my courses</u>.
2. But I'm not certain that won't happen.
3. So, if I <u>go back to school</u>, it could <u>be an awful mistake</u>.
4. So, I *can't* do it.

Now it's your turn to formulate *your* risk aversive thinking:

Case	Your Risk-Aversive Thinking
1	1. 2. 3. 4.
2	1. 2. 3. 4.
3	1. 2. 3. 4.
4	1. 2. 3. 4.
5	1. 2. 3. 4.

Refuting Your Risk-Aversive Thinking

Now that you have formulated the thinking you are doing to *can't*stipate yourself, it's time to look at it carefully with an eye to showing just how irrational it truly is. This step is known

TABLE 1.1

Example of refutation of Premises 1 and Conclusions 3 and 4 of risk-aversive thinking

Part of Risk-Aversive Thinking to Be Refuted	Ask Yourself This Question to Refute the Given Part of Your Risk-Aversive Thinking
Premise 1: I must be certain that if I accept the promotion at work, it won't happen that I do a really bad job.	*Where is it written that I must be certain that I won't do a really bad job?*
	Answer: Nowhere except in my head!
Premise 1 again	*Are the strong preferences of others always satisfied? If not, then why do yours have to be?*
	Answer: No one's preferences *need* to be satisfied!
Premise 1 again	*Am I even being consistent when I demand certainty that the promotion will work out?*
	Answer: There are a lot of things I do that are not certain. I took my current job even though I was not certain I would last at it let alone get offered a promotion.
Conclusion 3: So, if I accept the promotion at work, it could be a disaster!	*So, what if things don't work out as I would prefer? Does that really make it a catastrophe, like a 9 or 10 on the bad scale?*
	Answer: You can always imagine something so much worse, like a tsunami or earthquake. Doing poorly at a job wanes in comparison!
Conclusion 3 again	*What's the practical outcome of not accepting the promotion?*
	Answer: You prevent yourself from advancing your career!
Conclusion 4: So, I *can't* accept it.	*Is it really that I can't accept this promotion or is it rather that I just don't choose to? Answer: Unless I lack free will like some preprogrammed machine, I can accept the promotion!*

as *refutation* in cognitive-behavior therapy. It can help you to appreciate exactly why your thinking is irrational!

To illustrate, let's suppose this is how you are thinking:

1. I must be certain that if I accept the promotion at work, it won't happen that I do a really bad job.
2. But I'm not certain that won't happen.
3. So, if I accept the promotion at work, it could be a disaster!
4. So, I *can't* accept it.

Using the above reasoning as an example, Table 1.1 provides examples of some rational questions you can ask yourself in refuting the irrational parts of your risk-aversive thinking. These irrational parts are Premise 1 and Conclusions 3 and 4 of your risk-aversive thinking:

It's now time for you to refute your own risk-aversive thinking.

EXERCISE 1.5

Asking yourself the questions provided in Table 1.1 (as relevant), refute Premise 1 and Conclusions 3 and 4 of each of the risk-aversive thinking chains you have constructed in Exercise 1.4. Write down the premise or conclusion and your respective refutation in the columns provided in Table 1.1A.

TABLE 1.1A
Refutations of my risk-aversive thinking

My Risk-Aversive Thinking	My Refutation
Chain 1:	
Premise 1:	My Refutation of Premise 1:
Conclusion 3:	My Refutation of Conclusion 3:
Conclusion 4:	My Refutation of Conclusion 4:
Chain 2:	
Premise 1:	My Refutation of Premise 1:
Conclusion 3:	My Refutation of Conclusion 3:
Conclusion 4:	My Refutation of Conclusion 4:
Chain 3:	
Premise 1:	My Refutation of Premise 1:
Conclusion 3:	My Refutation of Conclusion 3:
Conclusion 4:	My Refutation of Conclusion 4:
Chain 4:	
Premise 1:	My Refutation of Premise 1
Conclusion 3:	My Refutation of Conclusion 3:
Conclusion 4:	My Refutation of Conclusion 4:
Chain 5:	
Premise 1:	My Refutation of Premise 1
Conclusion 3:	My Refutation of Conclusion 3:
Conclusion 4:	My Refutation of Conclusion 4:

4. EMBRACING YOUR GUIDING VIRTUES

Guiding virtues can help you to move beyond your irrational "I can't" to do and feel better. These virtues or idealistic goals can provide an exciting challenge for you to make positive, forward-looking changes in your life!

The guiding virtues of risk-aversive thinking are *Courage, Foresightedness,* and *Decisiveness.* Embracing these virtues can counteract your tendencies to demand certainty, base predictions on disempowering feelings and language, and procrastinate or

TABLE 1.2
Definitions of your guiding virtues

Guiding Virtue	Description
1. *Decisiveness*	Realistic trust in your ability to accomplish the goals you set; and being prepared to take rational risks to accomplish these goals under less-than-ideal conditions.
2. *Courage*	Confronting adversity without under- or overestimating the danger; and fearing things to the extent it is reasonable to fear them and, in the face of danger, acting according to the merits of the situation.
3. *Foresightedness*	Making predictions about the future that are probable relative to the available evidence.

otherwise fail to take reasonable risks. *These virtues can replace your disempowering language with the language of probability and reasonableness instead of certainty and necessity; and promote positive feelings about your ability to confront the future instead of feelings of powerlessness.*

Before proceeding, please carefully review the definitions of these virtues in Table 1.2. These are the ideals to which you are strongly encouraged to aspire! As ideals, they are never 100% attainable, and you will therefore never be perfect; but they set standards of excellence toward which to strive in getting better and better!

Decisiveness

Notice the definition of Decisiveness speaks in terms of being realistic. It is plainly unrealistic to think you can't accomplish goals that involve reasonable risks; and it is unreasonable to demand that you be certain things will work out before undertaking them. This is a recipe for stagnating!

Of course, it doesn't mean that you should act capriciously. The key here is to do your homework, examine the evidence, make your decision, and act on it. Waiting for the ideal situation before acting will only lead to inaction because the situation is not going to be ideal or perfect, now or in the future. There is risk inherent in whatever you may do in this material world of ours, and to demand that you eliminate it before acting is unrealistic. Moreover, deciding is not the same thing as acting because you can decide to do something and still not do it. Being decisive means that you also *act* on your decision.

How decisive are you? Exercise 1.6 can help you reflect on this question.

EXERCISE 1.6

1. When faced with a decision that involves risks, how do you usually deal with the situation? Do you sometimes decide to do things but end up not doing them? If so, give some examples and describe some of the things you tell yourself to avoid acting.

2. Do you sometimes just not reach a decision in the first place? If so, discuss some of the things you tell yourself that leads you not to decide in the first place.

Courage

Here is where Courage comes in. Being courageous means you are not ordinarily overcome by fear when it is rational *to act*. This does not mean going to extremes, however. There are some things that are reasonable to fear. For example, it is not courageous to needlessly risk your life; or invest your savings in a company with a shady history.

When we face hard times as all or most of us do, having Courage means dealing with the situation as best we can, realizing that there is not a perfect answer to difficult questions. Yet, under these less-than-ideal circumstances, having Courage portends the willingness to rationally confront the outcome, even if it is not what you hoped it would be. Thus, the courageous person tends to perceive such outcomes as opportunities to learn and grow. So maybe you took on more than you can handle, and now you know better how to navigate the course of your commitments better going forward. A courageous person also tends to view such misfortune on a relative plain. The loss of a job can be unfortunate, still not as bad as loss of life or limb. So, absolutistic terms such as "the worst thing that could happen" do not refer to anything actual, since things could conceivably be worse, even very bad situations!

Accordingly, being courageous implies four key tendencies:

1. Fearing things to the extent that it is reasonable to fear them.
2. Perceiving evil as a relative concept rather than an absolute one.
3. Taking reasonable risks in order to live well.
4. Learning from and deriving positive value from your misfortunes.

So, how courageous are you? Exercise 1.7 can help you reflect on this question.

EXERCISE 1.7

1. Briefly assess your own tendencies in relation to each of the four key tendencies of a courageous person. Give an example for each.

1.

2.

3.

4.

Foresightedness

Now, notice the definition of Foresightedness says "[making/accepting] predictions about the future that are probable relative to available evidence." A person who possesses this virtue tends to cope effectively with challenges arising in the material universe, which is a place where there are degrees of *probability*, not certainty. So instead of demanding certainty as you confront your practical life issues, you are invited to accept "degrees of probability" as a way of coping with the uncertainty of the world.

Accordingly, let's get clear about what we mean when we talk about probability. Actually, in ordinary life situations, we are not talking rocket science when we talk probability. We are talking instead about the *reasonableness* of beliefs. Mathematicians have methods to put numbers on how reasonable it is to believe something, but we rarely use numbers in everyday life.

Instead, when we say that a belief is *probable*, we mean simply that it would be unreasonable *not* to believe it (Chisholm, 1957). For example, it is probable that it will rain sometime in the next week or two during the rainy season in Florida. This means that it would be unreasonable *not* to believe it will rain.

On the other hand, to say that a belief is *improbable* means that it is unreasonable to believe it. For example, it is improbable that you will win the lottery. That is, it is unreasonable to believe that you will win the lottery.

However, in many everyday contexts we often entertain beliefs that are neither probable nor improbable. These are beliefs that it would neither be *unreasonable* to believe nor unreasonable *not* to believe (Chisholm, 1957). For example, it would not be unreasonable for you to believe, or not believe that a cure for cancer will be discovered in the next year.

When a belief is *im*probable, it is usually irrational to *act* on it. On the other hand, when a belief is *probable*, it is usually rational to act on it. For example, it would be rational to take an umbrella along with you during the rainy season in Florida.

But, when a belief is neither probable nor improbable, you may act on it or not depending on what the stakes are. For example, it would not be a good idea to invest your life savings in a certain stock because it was not improbable that it will go up in value. Given such high stakes you would rather want it to be probable that the stock will go up in value; in other words, that it would be unreasonable to believe it won't go up in value. But, still, you might invest a smaller amount in the stock even if you just had a "hunch."

In contrast to probability, to say that a belief is *certain* means there are no conditions under which it could fail to be true. So, while it is certain that a triangle has three sides, no belief about events in this material world of ours is ever certain. For example, it is uncertain that your marriage will be successful; your plane won't crash; or your new job will work out. On the other hand, these things may be probable, which is ordinarily good enough reason to take the risk.

Of course, some things can be probable and still not come to pass. So, you may be highly qualified for the job; it may seem to be just what you are looking for; and yet it might still not work out. But if you don't try things, you automatically disqualify yourself from succeeding. Unfortunately, this is the plight of many who are risk-aversive.

Beliefs are always probable *relative* to evidence. As this evidence changes your beliefs could cease to be probable; and beliefs that were not probable could become probable. For example, suppose you are considering whether to try a certain restaurant. A casual acquaintance of yours tells you that this restaurant serves very good salads, which is just what you are looking for. So, you are about to make a reservation when your significant other asks you to check out the reviews first. So, you google the restaurant and start seeing a bunch of negative reviews speaking about how the salads often contain cockroaches. This would send the probability rating plummeting for most of us!

At the end of the day, however, there is just so much checking you can do. Once you do your due diligence it is time to make your decision, and then to act on it. Otherwise, in trying to "make sure" you make the right decision, you'll create needless stress for yourself and others, and defeat the very point of dining out in the first place, namely, a pleasant dining experience.

Now try your hand at Exercise 1.8, which will give you some practice distinguishing between beliefs that are probable, just not unreasonable, and improbable.

EXERCISE 1.8

1. Provide three examples of predictions about the future which you believe are probable (that is, it would be unreasonable not to believe them). Describe the evidence you have for believing each.

1.

2.

3.

2. Provide three examples of beliefs you have that are not probable but are instead just not unreasonable. Describe the evidence you have for believing each.

1.

2.

3.

3. Now provide three predictions that are improbable, which you now believe or have believed. Describe the evidence you have that makes each improbable.

1.

2.

3.

As you can see, the virtues of Decisiveness, Courage, and Foresightedness "hang together" so that in working on one of them, you are effectively working on the others. Thus, to be decisive you would need to be courageous, and to be courageous you would need foresight to rationally assess the probability of danger.

    Let's get to work on these virtues in Exercise 1.9, starting with some preliminary self-reflections.

EXERCISE 1.9

1. How do you think embracing these virtues could change your life?

```



```

2. Do you know anyone who embraces these virtues? How does this impact their lives and the lives of those around them?

```



```

3. Would you like to be more like these people? Why, or why not?

```



```

5. EMPOWERING WISDOM FROM THE SAGES ON PURSUING THE VIRTUES

Your guiding virtues have been endorsed by some of the greatest minds in recorded history, and it is possible to derive some very useful insights from these sages. Below you will find some of this wisdom condensed into virtue-guiding insights. This can help you to form a worldview that can be quite powerful in offsetting the tendency toward risk-aversive thinking!

Courage

Empowering Wisdom from Aristotle:

- *Exercise moderation in feeling fear or confidence.*
- *Regulate your feelings and actions according to the merits of the case, not according to irrational fears.*

The ancient Greek sage, Aristotle, gives you a general guideline for attaining courage:

> Courage is moderation ... with respect to feelings of fear and confidence .... The courageous
> man regulates both his feeling and his action according to the merits of each case and as reason
> bids him.

This means that courage avoids the extremes of being over-fearful/confident and under-fearful/confident. So, it is okay to be fearful, or not confident, about taking *unreasonable* risks. The key here is not to panic or become overconfident, but to exercise *rational* judgment about the risks.

Empowering Wisdom from Nietzsche:

• *Seek new meaning and purpose in life, even in your suffering; and grow stronger through life challenges!*

You have already seen that it is usually irrational to act on improbable beliefs, especially when something major is at risk such as your life savings or your life. However, the most challenging, and apparently the most commonplace, cases are those in which it is neither probable nor improbable that acting on your belief will accomplish your goal. So, should you then sit on the sidelines of the arena of life, afraid to act?

Nineteenth-century German philosopher Friedrich Nietzsche (1913) puts a different spin on the matter:

> Man, the bravest animal and the one most inured to suffering, does not repudiate suffering in
> itself: he wills it, he even seeks it out, provided that he is shown a meaning for it, a purpose of
> suffering.

Nietzsche is here telling you that, instead of catastrophizing risk, you can reframe it as an opportunity to find new meaning and purpose in life. So, yes, in this vast domain of uncertainty that straddles the probable and the improbable, you might fall on your face. Nevertheless, it can be edifying to learn what it is like to be down.

So, fearing the negative judgments of others, being alone, upsetting the status quo, and the other perceived bogey men may be to miss the lessons learned through suffering through such things. In one's suffering, one can come to appreciate the value of things more when they come. For instance, the doctor who finds his calling through his own personal bouts with health owes his success to his suffering. It can help you to appreciate the plights of others who suffer misfortune, which can make you a better friend and colleague. You can later use what you have learned to your advantage in making subsequent choices ("Well I know that this doesn't work, so I better try a different approach").

So, to catastrophize about these possibilities is to underestimate their potentially valuable lessons in the mainstream of things. This does not mean that you should intentionally throw yourself in harm's way, but it should open your eyes to overreacting to the inherent risks in living.

Empowering Wisdom from Ralph Waldo Emerson:

- *Knowledge is the antidote to fear, the encourager that takes fear out of the heart*
- *You can conquer when you know how!*

In his essay entitled, "Courage," American philosopher, Ralph Waldo Emerson (1904) says:

> Knowledge is the antidote to fear—Knowledge, Use and Reason, with its higher aids. The child is as much in danger from a staircase, or the fire-grate, or a bath-tub, or a cat, as the soldier from a cannon or an ambush. Each surmounts the fear as fast as he precisely understands the peril and learns the means of resistance. Each is liable to panic, which is, exactly, the terror of ignorance surrendered to the imagination. Knowledge is the encourager, knowledge that takes fear out of the heart, knowledge and use, which is knowledge in practice. They can conquer who believe they can.

Emerson is telling you to assess and manage risks using knowledge instead of allowing "the terror of ignorance surrendered to the imagination" to overwhelm you. In other words, he is admonishing you to base your assessment of risks and how to manage them, not on irrationally creating catastrophes in your imagination, but instead *on evidence*. So you use knowledge to determine what the risks truly are and how to avoid or mitigate any unnecessary risk, and then you act on it. But this will "take the fear out of the heart" only for those "who believe they can"—in other words, only if you give up your "I-can't"!!

Empowering Wisdom from Karl Popper:

- *Accept trial and error as your only opportunity to learn new things!*

In turn, British philosopher, Karl Popper (2001), tells you how to acquire such knowledge:

> To solve ... problems, the sciences use fundamentally the same method as common sense employs, the method of *trial and error*. To be more precise, it is the method of *trying out* solutions to our problems and then discarding the false one as erroneous .... this procedure seems to be the only logical one.

(p. 3)

So, Dr. Popper is telling you that the only way you can solve your problems is to risk making mistakes. According to Popper, human beings solve their problems by trying things out based on what they already know, and if it works, well and good. If it doesn't then they have also learned what won't work and can try something different next time. So, having Courage involves *learning through a process of trial and error, and using this knowledge to solve your problems.* Otherwise, you won't learn, and you won't solve your problems!

Exercise 1.10 now gives you an opportunity to do some preliminary reflection on the empowering counsel offered by Aristotle, Nietzsche, Emerson, and Popper.

EXERCISE 1.10

Discuss briefly your approach to risk-taking and how you could use the positive counsel offered by Aristotle, Nietzsche, Emerson, and Popper to be more courageous about taking risks.

Foresightedness

Empowering Wisdom from Bertrand Russell:

- *Observe regularities to boost the probability your predictions will come true.*

Rivet your attention on the part of the definition of Foresightedness that says, "predictions about the future—are probable relative to the available evidence." British philosopher Bertrand Russell (2013) fleshes this out:

> The fact that two things have been found often together and never apart does not, by itself, suffice to prove demonstratively that they will be found together in the next case we examine. The most we can hope is that the oftener things are found together, the more probable it becomes that they will be found together another time.

> (Ch. 6)

The first thing to notice is that Russell is telling you that the probability of a belief increases (or decreases) depending on the available evidence to support it. To say that a belief becomes more probable (based on the available evidence) means that it becomes more reasonable, or less unreasonable, to believe it.

Second, he is telling you that such evidence may consist in the frequency in which two things have been found together in the past. Suppose you notice that the future has consistently resembled the past in a certain respect; for example, you notice that every time you eat a certain food, you develop a rash. This constant conjunction will increase the probability that the two things will be found together in the future. But this probability will never rise to certainty. You could have overlooked some other relevant factor that accounts for the constant conjunction. For example, it is possible that, each time you have eaten the food in question, you have also eaten another food to which you are allergic. And even if you eliminate this possibility, there is still no guarantee that you will eliminate the risk of an allergic response sometime down the road. That's just how life is. No guarantees!

But "no guarantees" does not mean no way to gauge reasonable risks. This is where probability comes into play. You can use the regularity of things to guide your judgments about whether risks are rational or not, and thus get a probability boost, even though you won't get certainty. But that's okay!

Empowering Wisdom from John Stuart Mill:

- *When two things resemble in one or more respects, if something is true of the one, barring any relevant differences, it's probably true of the other.*
- *So, if others can succeed, and my case is relevantly similar, barring any relevant differences, I can too!*

British philosopher, John Stuart Mill (1882), was the first to carefully dissect reasoning that compares things for the purpose of making predictions. He says this:

> Two things resemble each other in one or more respects; a certain proposition is true of the one; therefore it is true of the other .... [I]t is clear [however], that every dissimilarity which can be proved between them furnishes a counter-probability of the same nature on the other side.
>
> (pp. 394–395)

For example, do you recall this risk-aversive thinking?

1. I must be certain that if *I go back to school*, it won't happen that *I'm not able to handle school and the kids and end up failing my courses.*
2. But I'm not certain that won't happen.
3. So, if I *go back to school*, it could *be an awful mistake.*
4. So, I **can't** do it.

Instead, following Mill's method, you could think like this. "I know a lot of moms who have managed to successfully juggle the same responsibilities and I am at least as intelligent as them, so why couldn't I do the same!"

As you can see, you predict that you will manage, based on a comparison of yourself to the other moms. Of course, if you could point to some relevant respect in which your case was different from the other moms, then this might lower the probability of success (say, you also have an aging parent whom you care for). But this might simply mean figuring out a way to compensate for this difference (such as asking your partner to share the responsibility). In short, quite often, where there's a will there is a way to increase the probability that you too will succeed! The first step is to drop the self-defeating risk-aversive thinking and apply instead the comparative thinking method of Mill and the regularity standard of Russell!

Exercise 1.11 now gives you an opportunity to do some preliminary reflection on the learned counsel offered by Mill and Russell.

EXERCISE 1.11

Discuss briefly your own approach to risks and how you could use the learned counsel offered by Russell and Mill to increase your Foresightedness regarding risks.

Decisiveness

Empowering Wisdom from Jean-Paul Sartre:

- *Act on probabilities, not certainty, because no God, no scheme, can adapt the world and its possibility to your will.*
- *You are no more than the sum of your actions so define yourself positively by doing things!*

Existential philosopher, Jean-Paul Sartre (2007), points to the inescapable nature of living according to probabilities:

> When we want something, we always have to reckon with probabilities. I may be counting on the arrival of a friend. The friend is coming by rail or streetcar; this supposes that the train will arrive on schedule, or that the streetcar will not jump the track. I am left in the realm of possibility … The moment the possibilities I am considering are not rigorously involved in my action, I ought to disengage myself from them, because no God, no scheme, can adapt the world and its possibility to my will.
>
> (p. 29)

Sartre is admonishing you to base your actions on probabilities instead of demanding certainty because probability, not certainty, is part of "the human condition," that is, a condition we human beings cannot escape. So, you can demand certainty all you want but not even God is going to give you what you want. You have no choice but to *accept* probabilities. So, you are living in "bad faith," that is, lying to yourself, if you tell yourself you *can't* take risks; for whatever you do, or don't do, carries risks!

Now, for a person to accept probabilities means to actually *act* on them. Sartre declares, "He exists only to the extent that he realizes himself, therefore he is nothing more than the sum of his actions" (p. 10). So while you can make excuses for not doing things ("It just wasn't the right time"), in the end you will only succeed in defining yourself negatively as "a broken dream, aborted hopes, and futile expectations; in other words ... negatively, not positively" (p. 38). To actually make something (positive) of yourself, you need to *do* things with your life, and this requires actually taking risks!

You can say, *I could-a, would-a, should-a* done this or that; for example, "I could-a been a rich man today if I took that job offer." But this won't, in reality, *make* you a rich man!

So, take Sartre's advice: No reality except in action! It's the only way to actually make something *positive* of yourself. And this means taking risks!

Empowering Wisdom from William James:

- *Have faith that you can successfully make it, and your feet shall be nerved to its accomplishment.*
- *Mistakes are part of life; be lighthearted about them!*

This American pragmatist tells you that you can be your worst enemy by stressing yourself out about the possibility of making mistakes. Suppose, says James (1912),

> you are climbing a mountain, and have worked yourself into a position from which the only escape is by a terrible leap. Have faith that you can successfully make it, and your feet are nerved to its accomplishment. But mistrust yourself, and launching yourself in a moment of despair, you roll in the abyss.
>
> (ch. 4)

However, while most everyday life decisions are not such cliff hangers, many risk-aversive folks perceive them as though they were. They treat the possibility of making a mistake as though it would be the end of the world; and by catastrophizing about making a mistake rather than taking a healthier, more "lighthearted" approach to it, they mistrust themselves to make these decisions, and, in a "moment of despair," condemn themselves to "roll in the abyss."

So, here's Dr. James' pragmatic prescription for a new lease on life: Fess up to the fact that an inescapable part of human life is making mistakes, and instead of catastrophizing about making them, reframe your outlook with faith and trust in yourself ("I can do this!"). This way, you won't defeat your own purposes by needlessly stressing yourself out; and, consequently, you'll feel better, and tend to do better!

Exercise 1.12 now gives you an opportunity to do some preliminary reflection on the learned counsel offered by Sartre and James.

EXERCISE 1.12

Discuss briefly your own approach to risks and how you could use the learned counsel offered by Sartre and James to become more Decisive in confronting risks.

Perhaps you have a favorite sage of your own who you think gives positive advice on how to be more courageous, exercise greater foresight, or become more decisive. Exercise 1.13 below gives you an opportunity to add them to the list!

EXERCISE 1.13

1. Do you have a favorite sage of your own who offers empowering wisdom on how to be more courageous; more foresighted; more decisive? If so, formulate the insight below. (Even if you don't know the name of the person from whom the advice comes, that's still okay).

Additional Empowering Wisdom for Courage

Additional Empowering Wisdom Foresightedness

Additional Empowering Wisdom for Decisiveness

Compiling a Master List of Empowering Wisdom

Aristotle, Emerson, Nietzsche, and Popper have given you language to formulate their learned counsel that can go on a list of empowering wisdom to inspire Courage. For instance, for each of the formulations in the Courage column of Table 1.3, focus, one at a time, on the formulations with your mind's eye, and key into how it *feels. Does the language make you want to be more courageous in taking risks*!? If yes, keep it on your list of empowering wisdom; if not, take it off or change the language!

Similarly, for each of the formulations in the Foresightedness column of Table 1.3, focus, one at a time, on the language with your mind's eye, and key into how it *feels. Does it make you feel more secure or empowered to make predictions about the future?* If yes, keep it on your list of empowering wisdom; if not, take it off or change the language!

TABLE 1.3

Empowering wisdom regarding Courage, Foresightedness, and Decisiveness

Courage	Foresightedness	Decisiveness
Aristotle:_	**Russell:**	**Sartre:**
Exercise moderation in feeling fear or confidence.	Observe regularities to boost the probability your predictions will come true.	Act on probabilities, not certainty, because no God, no scheme, can adapt the world and its possibility to your will.
___ Regulate your feelings and actions according to the merits of the case, not according to irrational fears.	**Mill:**	___You are no more than the sum of your actions so define yourself positively by doing things!
Nietzsche:	When two things resemble in one or more respects, if something is true of the one, barring any relevant differences, it's probably true of the other.	**James:**
Seek new meaning and purpose in life, even in your suffering; and grow stronger through life challenges!		Have faith that you can successfully make it, and your feet shall be nerved to its accomplishment.
Emerson:	So, if others can succeed, and your case is relevantly similar, barring any relevant differences, you can too!	___ Mistakes are part of life; be lighthearted about them!
Knowledge is the antidote to fear, the encourager that takes fear out of the heart		
___ You can conquer when you know how!		
Popper:		
Accept trial and error as your only opportunity to learn new things!		

Finally, for each of the formulations in the Decisiveness column of Table 1.3, focus, one at a time, on language with your mind's eye, and key into how it *feels. Does it make you feel more empowered to make and act on decisions?* If yes, keep it on your list of empowering wisdom; if not, take it off or change the language!

Have you found the counsel in Table 1.3 to have a positive feeling of empowerment or uplift? Language use is an important part of why the counsel of the philosophers can help us to feel more inspired to take risks.

Exercise 1.14 gives you the opportunity to adapt the counsel in Table 1.3 to work for you.

EXERCISE 1.14

This exercise will help you to "tweak" Table 1.3 to provide a **master list of wisdom that is especially empowering for you**.

Please modify Table 1.3 in responding to the following instructions:

1. For each of the three guiding virtues, place a checkmark in front of each learned counsel you intend to use. Your selections should resonate with you, that is, feel uplifting, consoling, or otherwise empowering to you.

2. If you are not satisfied with the formulation of any of the counsels in Table 1.3, on a separate piece of paper, please rewrite it using language that resonates with you. For example, when I think of Nietzsche's counsel on dealing with life challenges by finding new meanings, I think of the words "empower" and "triumph." You are free to reformulate or tweak the sages' counsel using any language that is empowering to you!

3. Please also add any empowering insights to Table 1.3 that you may have formulated in Exercise 1.12. Again, it is important that the language you use is empowering *for you*.

4. Now, congratulate yourself! You now have a master list of wisdom that is empowering for you!

6. CREATING A COGNITIVE-BEHAVIORAL PLAN

Are you ready to harness the empowering wisdom of the sages to build a plan of action for approaching risk-taking? This is an exciting venture because it will open new avenues of freedom for you!

Suppose you have told yourself that you can't take risks because you might fail, and that this would be a terrible thing. Now maybe you have wanted to change your job but could never get up the nerve to seek another job.

So, you resolve to be more *courageous* in the future by

- taking a moderate approach—trying to avoid the extremes of being over or under-confident by trying to secure a new job *before* you quit your present one;
- using knowledge as an antidote to your fear by researching the job market so you know where and how to concentrate your search efforts.
- Reframing as a learning experience any possible mistakes you may make in your quest for suitable employment.

To exercise Foresightedness, you decide to

- look for consistent patterns in the past such as a high or low rate of job satisfaction, turn-over rate, etc. in the field;
- explore the qualifications of successful job applicants and compare them with your own qualifications.

To be more *decisive* you,

- accept probabilities rather than certainty by putting in job applications based on your market investigation;
- reframe this venture as an exciting opportunity to positively define yourself through your actions!
- instead of needlessly stressing yourself out about the possibility of making a mistake, reframe your outlook with faith that things will work out, and trust in your ability to prosper no matter what the consequences of this exciting new venture.

Now it's your turn to build a plan of action based on the learned counsel you have received. Exercise 1.15 can help with this!

EXERCISE 1.15

1. Choose a short-term goal from the ones you described in Exercise 1.2, which you are now willing to try to achieve. Recall you were asked to include at least one short-term goal. Restate this goal in the space provided below:

```


```

2. Now, restate the risk-aversive thinking you formulated in Exercise 1.4 that has blocked you from attempting to achieve this short-term goal.

My Risk-Aversive Thinking
1.
2.
3
4.

Using your empowering wisdom, the remainder of this exercise will help you to construct the elements of a cognitive-behavioral plan to overcome Conclusion 4 of the above risk-aversive thinking!

3. Using the counsel offered by Aristotle, Nietzsche, Emerson, and Popper, or any insights you may have added in Exercise 1.13 for becoming *more courageous*, what cognitive-behavioral changes would you make to overcome your risk-aversive thinking? For example, what changes would Dr. Popper tell you to make in the way you are presently *thinking* about making mistakes? What would you *do* differently according to Sartre? List at least three cognitive-behavioral changes you plan to make based on this advice:

1.
2.
3.
4.
5.

4. Using the empowering wisdom offered by Russell and Mill, or any other insights you may have added in Exercise 1.13 for becoming *more foresighted*, what cognitive-behavioral changes would you make to overcome your risk-aversive thinking? List at least two:

1.

2.

3.

4.

5.

5. Using the empowering wisdom offered by Sartre and James, or any other insights you may have added in Exercise 1.13 for becoming *more decisive*, what cognitive-behavioral changes would you make to overcome your risk-aversive thinking? List at least three:

1.

2.

3.

4.

5.

6. Now, congratulate yourself! You have just constructed a cognitive-behavioral plan!!

7. WORKING ON YOUR COGNITIVE-BEHAVIORAL PLAN

You will now have an opportunity to begin to build your habits of Courage, Foresightedness, and Decisiveness, instead of defaulting to your self-defeating habit of risk-aversive thinking.

Cognitive–Affective Imagery

As you know, when risk-aversive people think about taking risks they tend to *feel* threatened by the lack of certainty, which leads them to catastrophize about taking the risk, and then they tell themselves they can't. "It could be the worst mistake I'll ever make. Oh my God! No way I can do this!" Imagery exercises can help you change such negative feelings to positive, uplifting, empowering ones! Exercise 1.16 will help you to set up and practice cognitive–affective imagery.

EXERCISE 1.16

1. Choose a formulation from the Courage column of your master list of empowering wisdom (see Exercise 1.14) that is especially empowering, uplifting, or consoling for you. Keep it in the back of your mind at this point.

2. Refer to the risk-aversive thinking you identified in Exercise 1.15, which is blocking a *short-term goal* you also identified in Exercise 1.15.

3. Now here are instructions for doing cognitive–affective imagery. If you are working with a therapist, the therapist can provide guidance until you get the hang of it and can do it on your own. If you are not being assisted by a therapist, then please read these directions carefully now, memorize them (three steps), and then follow the three-step sequence laid out for you below:

- Step 1: Focus your mind exclusively on your risk-aversive thinking (as identified in Exercise 1.15). Keep going over it in your mind like you did when you first decided you couldn't accomplish your goal. Keep it up until you feel that negative visceral threatening feeling, the clashing of your felt need for certainty with the realization that what you fear so much could actually happen. Let yourself resonate with the feeling of powerlessness that emerges, and that "No way! I can't do this!" feeling.
- Step 2: At the peak of feeling this intense negative feeling, shift your focus of mind exclusively to the empowering wisdom that you have selected for feeling empowered to become courageous. Let yourself feel the uplift, the empowerment to confront the uncertainty; toward transcending the fear; toward feeling the freedom to take control.
- Step 3: Once you have fully brought yourself to resonate with the positivity of the experience, gently shift your attention to reflecting on your experience and what you have learned or discovered from it.

4. Try to reserve a time each day to practice your guided imagery exercise. Next time, however, choose a word or phrase from the Foresightedness column of your master list of empowering wisdom that is especially empowering or uplifting for you.

5. Similarly, the subsequent day, repeat the exercise except this time choose learned counsel from the Decisiveness column of your master list of empowering wisdom.

6. Practice regularly, shifting between learned counsel for cultivating each of the *three* guiding virtues.

7. What have you learned or discovered about yourself from your experience practicing your cognitive–affective imagery? Write down your reflections below:

> *My Reflections about My Experience:*
>
>
>
>
>
>
>
>
>
>
>
>
>
>
>

Great work!!

Refuting and Reframing

It is useful to refute and reframe the irrational premises and conclusions of your self-defeating thinking. As discussed in the Introduction to this book, reframing involves placing your negative thinking in a more positive light. Exercise 1.17 will help you to work on practicing refuting and reframing your risk-aversive thinking.

EXERCISE 1.17

1. Refer again to the risk-aversive thinking you identified in Exercise 1.15, which is preventing you from dealing rationally with the situation you also identified in Exercise 1.15. Look carefully at Premise 1 in your risk-aversive thinking, the premise that *demands certainty*. In Exercise 1.5, you have already refuted this premise so you can see how irrational it truly is. Think about this refutation until it resonates with you, that is, you get the "I get it" feeling that this premise is truly irrational. If this doesn't happen, then go back to Exercise 1.5 and find a refutation that *does* resonate with you. Write down your refutation in Table 1.4 in the refutation column for Premise 1.

Now, select some empowering wisdom from one or more of your sages (it could even be an insight you added in Exercise 1.13), and use it to reframe your demand for certainty. Use Table 1.4 to write down your reframing of Premise 1 in the reframing column for Premise 1.

TABLE 1.4
Refuting and reframing your risk-aversive thinking

Part	Refutation	Reframing
Premise 1		
Conclusion 3		
Conclusion 4		

2. Just as you have done for Premise 1, refute and reframe Conclusions 3 and 4 of the risk-aversive thinking you identified in Exercise 1.15. Use Table 1.4 to write down your refutation and reframing for each of these respective conclusions of your risk-aversive thinking.

Engaging in a Risk-Taking Exercise

This type of assignment can help you to work both cognitively and behaviorally on your risk-aversive *can't*stipation. Exercise 1.18 provides directions.

EXERCISE 1.18

1. Choose a low-stakes action to perform that has a low probability of success. For example, you could play the slot machines with a small amount of money or engage in a similar low stakes gambling activity; ask someone out on a date who does not appear to like you; apply for a job that requires credentials you clearly lack; dine out at a restaurant that is notorious for bad service; or take some other risk you are disinclined to take notwithstanding the relatively low stakes. Describe this activity in the space provided below:

2. Next, calendar a time you intend to perform the chosen act. Then, practice refuting and reframing your thinking about it using the empowering wisdom from your sages on how to be courageous or decisive now.

3. Next, prior to, during, and after actually performing the act, practice refuting and reframing your thinking about it using your learned counsel.

4. After performing the action, reflect on your experience below. How did you feel when you were engaging in the act? Was the act successful or not? If yes, what did you learn about risk-taking? About yourself? If not, what did you learn about risk-taking? About yourself?

Congratulations on completing your risk-taking exercise! Feel free to repeat it as many times as you like!

Getting Some Bibliotherapy

Movies about risking the odds to accomplish a noble goal or to finding personal happiness or fulfillment are quite popular in the public sphere. For example, one movie to inspire Courage and Decisiveness is the movie, "42" (2013), about Jackie Robinson, the first African American baseball player in the Major League. Imagine you are in a racist society, entering an athletic arena where you are the only black person and roadblocks are placed at almost every turn; yet you persist and succeed against all odds. That is a wonderful tale, and it's true! Exercise 1.19 provides an opportunity for you to receive some bibliotherapy.

EXERCISE 1.19

1. Select a movie or literary work that has the theme of exercising Courage to accomplish a valued goal in the face of substantial risks. If the Jackie Robinson story discussed here sounds like something with which you would resonate (assuming you have not already seen it), then feel free to take in this movie. Here is a link to the trailer: www.youtube.com/watch?v= iP3G4E2ael8.

Alternatively, if you are working with a therapist then you may find it useful to discuss other movies or literature with the therapist. If you are using this Workbook as a self-help tool, you are also free to find a suitable movie to inspire Courage.

2. Once you have viewed (or read) your bibliotherapy, write your reflections down below. What words would you use to describe the feelings it evoked? Has it helped to prepare you for your own personal goals that you have described in Exercise 1.2? Write down your reflections in the space provided below:

Acting on Your Goal

This is the final stage of your process of working on your cognitive-behavioral plan. It involves doing all the things you listed in your cognitive-behavioral plan, which you developed in Exercise 1.15, which includes actually acting on your goal. For example, if your goal is to apply for a new job, to exercise Foresightedness, you will research the job market, look for consistent patterns of job satisfaction, turnover, etc., and compare your qualifications to those specified in job descriptions to identify suitable employment. You will exercise Decisiveness by perceiving such job-seeking as an opportunity to define yourself positively as you pursue new and exciting avenues in your life, so you will *actually* put in your application for a particular job(s); while courageously seeing potential mistakes as an opportunity to learn; and refuting and reframing any of the self-defeating lines of thinking that have previously *can't*stipated progress toward achieving this milestone in your life.

Exercise 1.20 provides instructions.

EXERCISE 1.20

1. Review the cognitive-behavioral items on your behavioral plan created in Exercise 1.15.

2. Review the refutation and reframing of Premise 1 and Conclusions 3 and 4 of your risk-aversive thinking which you developed in Exercise 1.17.

3. Implement each of the behavioral elements in your plan. For example, you *do* all the preliminary research if it's applying for a new job, and then *submit* your application!

4. Continue to refute and reframe your risk-aversive thinking (Exercise 1.17), even after you act on your goal. This is important because risk-aversive people often second guess and torment themselves with doubt even after they translate their goal into action.

5. Provide your reflections below about your experience in implementing your plan of action:

6. This is an incredible milestone, so congratulate yourself!

Working on Your Other Goals

In Exercise 1.2, you described at least two and as many as five goals that you would like to fulfill but have been blocked by risk-aversive *can't*stipation. Now that you have worked through your first, short-term goal, you can continue working to fulfill the other goals you described, or you can even add new goals.

The process is the same, and you have already gone through it in addressing your short-term goal. You have also already formulated the risk-aversive reasoning chains blocking you from attaining these other goals and have also refuted Premise 1 and Conclusions 3 and 4 of each of them. So, you are already well on your way to accomplishing these other goals and strengthening your guiding virtues. Here is a summary of the process:

1. Formulate your risk-aversive thinking (Exercise 1.4).
2. Refute Premise 1 and Conclusions 3 and 4 of this thinking (Exercise 1.5).
3. Embrace your guiding virtues (Exercises 1.6 through 1.9).
4. Get empowering wisdom from the sages on pursuing the virtues (Exercises 1.10 through 1.14).
5. Use this counsel to construct a cognitive-behavioral plan (Exercise 1.15).
6. Work on your cognitive-behavioral plan (Exercises 1.16 through 1.20).

Having worked through the exercises in this chapter, you are now in an excellent position to take impressive strides toward greater and greater freedom and fulfillment in life as you detach yourself more and more from your risk-aversive *can't*stipation. Clearly, building your guiding virtues of Courage, Foresightedness, and Decisiveness takes continual practice. Using the exercise sets in this chapter as the framework, you can do this work by regularly going through the above six steps.

Keep working at it!

NOTE

1 Some people who are risk-aversive about flying may also have a phobia about flying. Phobias are covered in this *Workbook* in Chapter 4.

REFERENCES

Chisholm, R.M. (1957). *Perceiving: A philosophical study.* Cornell University Press.

Emerson, R.W. (1904). Courage. In *The complete works of Ralph Waldo Emerson.* Houghton, Mifflin & Co, Vol. VII. Retrieved from www.bartleby.com/90/0710.html

James, W. (1912). The will to believe and other essays in popular philosophy. Longman, Green, and Co. Retrieved from The Project Gutenberg E-text of *The Will to Believe*, by William James.

Mill, J.S. (1882). *A system of logic: Ratiocinative and inductive.* 8th ed. Harper & Brothers, Publishers. Retrieved from www.gutenberg.org/files/27942/27942-h/27942-h.html

Nietzsche, F. (1913). *The genealogy of morals.* T.N. Foulis. Retrieved from www.gutenberg.org/files/52319/52319-h/52319-h.htm

Popper, K. (2001). *All life is problem solving,* Routledge.

Russell, B. (2013). *The problems of philosophy.* Gutenberg ebook. Retrieved from www.gutenberg.org/files/5827/5827-h/5827-h.htm#link2HCH0012

Sartre, J.P. (2007). *Existentialism is a humanism,* Carol Macomber (Trans.). Yale University Press.

2

Overcoming Low Frustration Tolerance

As you have seen in the Introduction to this *Workbook*, low frustration tolerance (LFT) is a behavioral type of *can't*stipation that creates and sustains low frustration tolerance. That is, you feel like you are incapable of "standing" or "tolerating" the frustration of succeeding at goals you imagine to be too difficult, challenging, or otherwise unpleasant to you. Unfortunately, this can prevent you from developing your talents, advancing your career goals, cultivating interpersonal relationships, or other enriching activities that take considerable time and effort to accomplish.

1. GOALS OF THE CHAPTER

Accordingly, the goals of this chapter are to:

1. Increase awareness of your LFT thinking and the language you are using to create and sustain your LFT.
2. Refute this thinking.
3. Identify guiding virtues that counteract your LFT.
4. Identify empowering wisdom from great sages on how to seek these virtues.
5. Use this learned counsel to construct a cognitive-behavioral plan for increasing your virtues.
6. Work on your plan, including accomplishing some goals that are difficult, challenging, or otherwise unpleasant to you.

2. THE NATURE OF LFT THINKING

People with LFT feel like they "can't stand" or "tolerate" things such as:

- rigorous work schedules or routines;
- goal-directed activities that require lengthy courses of study or training such as law and medicine;
- domestic chores that are not "fun";
- activities that require regular practice such as learning a musical instrument;

DOI: 10.4324/9781003035282-3

- activities that might not "come easy," or which seem challenging or difficult, for example, mathematics;
- encounters or associations with people they "can't stand";
- exams or assignments that require careful preparation or research;
- relationships with significant others that become problematic (for example, illness or financial challenges);
- attempting to correct or improve things at which they have made mistakes or failed.

So, instead of persisting in these activities, you tell yourself you can't. For example, consider the reasoning by which people with LFT keep themselves from making constructive change:

- If I take that job, I will have to work on Saturdays, which is my fun day.
  So, it would *destroy my life*.
  So, I can't do it!
- If I go in for law, I will need to be in school for another three years if I go full-time.
  So, I couldn't do anything else for all that time except study law, which would *drive me crazy*.
  So, I just can't go to law school.
- If I agree to clean up the house all weekend, I won't be able to hang out with my friends or do anything fun.
  So, it would be *sooooo boring*.
  So, I just couldn't stand it.
- If I take guitar lessons it would be cool, but I would have to practice every day.
  So, it would always be a *serious pain in the ass*.
  So, I just can't make this commitment.
- If I major in something hard like math or bio, then I would really have to work hard.
  So, it would make my life *a nightmare*.
  So, I just can't major in anything that's hard!
- If I agree to visit my mother-in-law, I'll have to listen to her complaining about things the whole time.
  So, I would have a *miserable time*.
  So, I just couldn't take it!
- If I agree to help you, something might go wrong and take a lot of work to fix it.
  So, it would be an *awful mistake* to agree to do it.
  So, unfortunately, I really can't help you.

In cases like these you imagine yourself being challenged; inconvenienced; having to work hard for an extended period; putting up with something or someone you don't like; or otherwise doing something that is not pleasurable, which *feels* frustrating to you. So, you express this frustration, using strong emotional language, which only increases your frustration; making you feel disempowered; which you, in turn, express by proclaiming, "I can't!"

Now, look carefully at some of this disempowering language:

- "destroy my life"
- "drive me crazy"
- "soooo boring"
- "a serious pain in the ass"
- "a nightmare"
- "miserable time"
- "awful mistake."

When you utter these strong negative words, they affirm, and even amplify the frustration you are already feeling by making it official that the activity in question is unbearable; giving you this unsettling feeling that you just can't do it.

Notice that this language is unforgivingly absolutistic (no exceptions, please!); 100% negative; making you feel like there is no virtue in engaging in the activity in question; fueling a sense of deprivation of happiness, peace, or pleasure; which is beyond your power to "stand" or "tolerate." As a result, you give up potential long-term happiness or pleasure, by not pursuing the activities in question, for the sake of a short-term reprieve from immediate dissatisfaction or frustration.

Your Demand for Immediate Gratification

Implicit in each of the above examples of LFT thinking is a very self-defeating assumption. This is an absolutistic, uncompromising *demand for immediate gratification*, that you *must* get what you want, when you want it, without having to suffer any significant frustration. Unfortunately, this assumption is unrealistic because most things in life that bring lasting satisfaction do not come easy without hard work and perseverance. So, maybe you don't want to work on Saturday because it's your "fun day." However, it is the inflexibility of this *demand* that generates the deep frustration that folks feel who suffer from LFT.

When you demand to yourself that you *must* have immediate gratification, you also realize that what you really want (maybe a promising career, a developed talent or skill, or a long and prosperous relationship with a loved one) is not likely to happen without putting off immediate gratification. So now there is a *conflict* going on inside you between your demand for immediate gratification and achieving your life goal. For the person with LFT, this conflict is resolved by giving up the life goal in favor of immediate gratification or avoidance of frustration. This leaves you constantly looking for an immediate happiness fix to fill the void of long-term happiness.

Let's look at your LFT thinking that keeps you in this sorry state. With your demand for immediate gratification added, your chain of LFT thinking looks something like this:

1. I *must* get what I want immediately (or very fast).
2. But it's not possible for me to get what I really want immediately, such as a career in law. It would take years!
3. Therefore, for me, it would be a long, drawn-out nightmare!
4. Therefore, I *can't* get a law degree.

In Premise 1 you demand immediate gratification, and in Premise 2 you perceive that what you really want does not satisfy your demand. This leaves you in a state of conflict, which feels very frustrating, which, unfortunately, you embellish with self-defeating language like "It would be a long, drawn-out nightmare!" You therefore give up your life goal to resolve the conflict, declaring that "I can't get a law degree' (or whatever desired, long-term life goal you may have). So, you substitute short-term pleasures (for example, food, sex, and partying) for more long-term satisfaction such as a career doing something intrinsically rewarding, building a serious relationship, developing a special talent, or taking on meaningful projects.

As for the "must" in Premise 1, it is based on a *felt need for immediate gratification* (a feeling deep inside you). Such a feeling stems from past negative experiences. For example, you may have experienced deprivation of affection such as parental love or support, leaving you feeling very frustrated and powerless. A representation of this feeling itself (not just the event of being deprived of affection) is then stored in your brain's memory circuits (more specifically, in somatosensory structures in the forebrain) and this feeling is, in turn, associated with the felt need for immediate gratification. So, when you imagine not having your demand for immediate gratification fulfilled, the feeling of frustration and attendant sense of powerlessness you have stored up plays out in your imagination, which feels like you *need* to have gratification now!

Exercise 2.1 is an icebreaker to help you get more in touch with the feelings going on inside you when you tell yourself you can't do things that involve postponement of immediate gratification.

EXERCISE 2.1

Write down your answers to the following questions in the space provided. Use separate pieces of paper if necessary:

1. When you think about doing something that may be especially challenging, take a long time, or unpleasant, what goes through your mind? What feelings do you experience?

```



```

2. Think of something you recently wanted to do but decided against because you thought it would be too hard, take too much time, or would otherwise be too unpleasant. Rerun in your mind how you *felt* when you had these negative thoughts.

3. Now, place a check next to any of the following words that describe how you feel when having these negative thoughts about things you want to do. You are also free to add some of your own ideas to this list that might capture how you feel.

- Conflicted ____
- Frustrated ____
- Anxious ____
- Powerless ____
- Afraid ____
- Unfulfilled ____
- Discouraged____
- Empty ____
- Depressed ____
- Angry _____

a.   When you have such negative feelings about doing something, how do you usually resolve them?

```



```

b.   Are you satisfied with the way you usually resolve them? Explain.

```



```

The Self-Defeating Nature of Your LFT Thinking

Because we are human, all of us experience frustration when we try to do things that are not working out the way we would like, or which take more time than we would prefer. Unfortunately, your LFT thinking can manufacture intense frustration, which you resolve by concluding, "I can't." The self-defeating result of this syndrome is that you keep yourself ensconced in a vicious cycle of superficial, unfulfilling activities that offer short spurts of pleasure, leaving a void soon to be filled by your next short-lived pleasure fix.

3. EXAMINING *YOUR* LFT THINKING

In this section you will have the opportunity to examine the nature of your own LFT thinking. So, what does *your* LFT thinking look like? Exercises 2.2 through 2.4 will help you to answer this question.

EXERCISE 2.2

Let's start by briefly describing at least two and as many as five things you would like to do or that could be beneficial to do but you are telling yourself you can't do because they are too challenging, take too long, or are otherwise too unpleasant for you. *At least one of these things should be something you could do short term*, such as taking a course in a challenging subject; taking music lessons; visiting your mother-in-law to please your partner; trying to repair something that's hard to fix; or whatever other activity you could do in the short term but is likely to place a strain on your frustration tolerance.

1.

2.

3.

4.

5.

EXERCISE 2.3

Now, make a list of the disempowering, catastrophic language you are using to convince yourself that you can't do the activities involved in each of the cases you listed in Exercise 2.2. For example, maybe you are telling yourself that it would "kill you" if you had to spend all those hours taking that online course to get your certificate; or maybe you are telling yourself that it would "drive you crazy" to try to stay even one more day at a job you don't like, even though you don't have another job and you need the money to pay your expenses.

Your Catastrophic/Disempowering Language List

With the above filled in, you have a list of at least some of the disempowering words or phrases you tend to use to draw regrettable inferences about what you think you can't do. Feel free to add to this list later if you think of other words or phrases. These are terms you will need to retire from your vocabulary!

EXERCISE 2.4

Next, for each of the cases you listed in Exercise 2.2, write down your LFT thinking (chain of thinking leading you to say you can't) using the language you identified in Exercise 2.3. To formulate each of your cases, please follow the below form:

1. I *must* get what I want without having to endure any (or much) frustration.
2. But [insert here what you want] would involve [insert here a certain type of frustration you are not prepared to endure].
3. So, this would [insert a catastrophic/disempowering term].
4. So, I *can't* do it.

In premise 2, where it says "insert here what you want" some examples are:

- a certain professional degree or certificate
- a certain type of job
- a certain skill or competence (such as getting good at playing an instrument, sport, or professional activity)
- a certain honor or recognition (for example, get an award for acting or for academic achievement)
- making some constructive change in your life such as going back to school; cleaning up the mess in your garage, etc.
- something else not on this list that you are considering as a possible goal.

Also, in premise 2, some common types of frustration you might insert include:

- having to wait a certain amount of time you are not prepared to wait (for example, six months);
- working "too hard" such as having to work some weekends also;
- being overly challenged or burdened in a certain way (for example, not being able to figure things out right away);
- dealing with too much frustration or unpleasantness such as things going wrong, having to fix things, correct mistakes, etc.;
- any type of frustration of yours not on this list that concerns you about the possible goal just mentioned in premise 2.

In premise 3, where it says, "insert a catastrophic/disempowering term," insert a term from your Catastrophic/Disempowering Language List which you created in Exercise 2.3.

For example, suppose you once told yourself you couldn't *get good grades* because you would have to *do homework every day*, which would *be boring as hell*. Then your thinking would look like this:

1. I *must* get what I want without having to endure much frustration.
2. But <u>trying to get good grades</u> would involve <u>doing homework every day.</u>
3. So, this would <u>be boring as hell.</u>
4. So, I *can't* do it.

Now it's your turn to formulate *your* LFT thinking:

Case	Your LFT Thinking
1	1. 2. 3. 4.
2	1. 2. 3. 4.
3	1. 2. 3. 4.
4	1. 2. 3. 4.
5	1. 2. 3. 4.

Refuting Your LFT Thinking

Now that you have formulated your LFT thinking, it's time to look at it carefully to prove to yourself that it's irrational. Providing such a proof in cognitive-behavior therapy is known as *refutation*.

To illustrate, suppose this is how you are thinking:

1. I *must* get what I want without having to endure much frustration.
2. But majoring in premed would involve taking difficult courses like organic chemistry.
3. So, this would be *too much* for me.
4. So, I *can't* do it.

Using the above reasoning as an example, Table 2.1 provides examples of some rational questions you can ask yourself in refuting the irrational parts of your LFT thinking. These irrational parts are Premise 1 and Conclusions 3 and 4.

TABLE 2.1
Example of refutation of Premises 1 and 3, and Conclusion 4 of LFT thinking

Part of LFT Thinking to Be Refuted	Ask Yourself This Question to Refute the Given Part of Your LFT Thinking
1. I *must* get what I want without having to endure much frustration.	*Where is it written that I must get what I want without enduring much frustration?*
	Answer: Nowhere except in my head!
Premise 1 again	*Do other people always get what they want? If not, then why are you special?*
	Answer: Just because you want something doesn't mean you *must* get it!
Premise 1 again	*Am I even being consistent when I demand that I get what I want without much frustration?*
	Answer: There are many occasions where I have endured a lot of frustration to get what I want. I got accepted into college because I took college prep courses and struggled with some of them yet managed to pass them.
3. So, this would be *too much* for me.	*What is "too much" for me anyway? Don't I decide that myself?*
	Answer: This is my subjective value judgment about how much effort you are prepared to make. So, if it's "too much" only if I say so, then it's not too much if I *don't* say so!
Conclusion 3 again	*What's the practical outcome of not majoring in premed?*
	Answer: I won't get into med school and won't become a physician. And, if becoming a physician is what I want, then I simply won't get what I want!
4. So, I *can't* do it.	*Is it really true that I can't be a premed major or is it rather that I am just telling myself I can't?*
	Answer: I may *feel* like I can't be a premed major because I'm demanding that I not do anything challenging; but feeling like I can't does not mean I *really* can't. I can prove to myself I can by actually doing it!

It's now time for you to refute your own LFT thinking.

EXERCISE 2.5

Asking yourself the questions provided in Table 2.1 (as relevant), refute Premise 1 and Conclusions 3 and 4 of each of the LFT thinking chains you have constructed in Exercise 2.4. Write down the irrational premise or conclusion and your respective refutation of it in the respective columns in Table 2.1A.

TABLE 2.1A
Refutations of my LFT thinking

My LFT Thinking	My Refutation
Chain 1:	
Premise 1:	Refutation of Premise 1:
Conclusion 3:	Refutation of Conclusion 3:
Conclusion 4:	Refutation of Conclusion 4:

TABLE 2.1A
Continued

My LFT Thinking	My Refutation
Chain 2:	
Premise 1:	Refutation of Premise 1:
Conclusion 3:	Refutation of Conclusion 3:
Conclusion 4:	Refutation of Conclusion 4:
Chain 3:	
Premise 1:	Refutation of Premise 1:
Conclusion 3:	Refutation of Conclusion 3:
Conclusion 4:	Refutation of Conclusion 4:
Chain 4:	
Premise 1:	Refutation of Premise 1:
Conclusion 3:	Refutation of Conclusion 3:
Conclusion 4:	Refutation of Conclusion 4:
Chain 5:	
Premise 1:	Refutation of Premise 1:
Conclusion 3:	Refutation of Conclusion 3:
Conclusion 4:	Refutation of Conclusion 4:

4. EMBRACING YOUR GUIDING VIRTUES

The guiding virtues introduced in this section will help you to overcome your LFT and set you free to attain more permanent satisfactions in your life. These virtues are *Prudence*, *Perseverance*, and *Patience*. Embracing these virtues will counteract your tendencies to demand immediate gratification, avoiding the inevitable frustrations of working toward constructive change; and to allow this low frustration boiling point and its disempowering language to thwart your sense of autonomy and self-efficacy. *These virtues will replace your disempowering language with the language of rational decision-making and long-term satisfaction instead of a spurious desire for immediate or short-term gratification; and promote positive feelings about your capacity to engage in challenging and exciting life pursuits.*

Before proceeding, please carefully review the definitions of these virtues in Table 2.2.

TABLE 2.2
Definitions of your guiding virtues

Guiding Virtue	Description
1. *Prudence*	A grasp of what is in your power and what is not, including an appreciation of what things in your power are worth attaining; along with the skill to figure out the means to attaining them.
2. *Perseverance*	Tenacious persistence, within rational limits, in striving for reasonable goals with keen awareness that such persistence can be key to accomplishing such goals.
3. *Patience*	Willpower to sacrifice short-term, fleeting pleasures for more long-term, lasting ones, with appreciation that good things often involve hard work and overcoming obstacles.

These virtues set exciting goals for you in overcoming your LFT! Because they are ideals, and, because you are human, which means imperfect by nature, you will never attain them 100%. So, you can continue to get better and better at them, which is actually exciting! Even an accomplished musician has no limits to how good she can get. So, like a fine virtuoso, you can continue, over a lifetime to get better and better!

Prudence

Notice the definition of Prudence involves three things:

1. Knowing what's in your power and what's not.
2. Knowing what things in your power are worth attaining.
3. Knowing how to attain these things.

So, prudent people are realistic about what they can do. For example, they don't expect to always succeed at whatever they attempt. Nor do they sell themselves short, however. For example, they don't tell themselves they can't control the desire for immediate gratification, or its frustration, when long-term satisfactions are put in jeopardy. Likewise, such individuals know that the latter is more important to pursue than the former; that seeking short-term pleasure or relieving short-term discomfort, at the expense of long-term satisfaction (indulging fleeting and momentary desires when there is important work to be done), is not worth the expense.

Finally, such individuals tend to keep their eye on the ball and make their decisions through the exercise of reason rather than allowing the desire for short-term gain to distract them from achieving their long-term goals. As all humans, such people are imperfect and sometimes get distracted, and sometimes mess up. But they are also perseverant and work diligently to rationally reassess their situation.

So how prudent are you? Exercise 2.6 will help you to reflect on this question.

EXERCISE 2.6

1. When experiencing strong desires for short-term gain (gratification or reduction of short-term displeasure), while desirable, long-term goals hang in the balance, how do you usually resolve the conflict? Do you end up caving in to the short-term desires? If so, give some examples and describe some of the things you tell yourself that may be undermining some of

the meaningful life goals you would like to achieve. Write down your thoughts in the space provided below:

2. Being rational, what would you tell yourself now about your capacity or power to manage your short-term frustrations for the sake of attaining your long-term goals? Is this consistent with what you actually tell yourself when you resolve conflicts between these things? Are you being prudent? Explain.

3. How do you distinguish between goals that are worthy and ones that are not? Are you prudent in choosing your long-term goals? Are you prudent in the way you go about trying to attain these goals? Explain.

Perseverance

Prudent individuals also possess the virtue of Perseverance because they do not allow frustration with failure to keep them from getting back on track. Often the key lies in rational adjustment in the plan of attack. As a prudent person, the perseverant person does not persist in the same thing that consistently leads to failure, but instead reassesses the situation, and makes suitable changes in the plan of attack. "Okay, I only studied the textbook but the exam was also on the class notes; so next time I'll study the notes too."

This does not mean that there are no points at which a perseverant person will decide to give up on a particular goal. Indeed, there are rational limits in which a person can keep trying to do something without success. "I've taken the same course several times; tried several different approaches, and still don't seem to get it. Maybe I should consider a different major." What the persistent person does *not* do is to allow the frustration of failure to blind her to future long-term satisfactions and to instead inhabit a subjective universe of fleeting immediate gratification and flight from the inevitable frustrations of achieving worthwhile goals.

How perseverant are you? Exercise 2.7 can help you reflect on this question.

EXERCISE 2.7

1. Briefly describe how you tend to deal with failure.

2. What changes do you think are needed for you to become more perseverant?

Patience

To persevere, you will also need Patience. Willpower is not something that you are simply born with. It takes practice. The more you are used to caving in to desires for short-term fixes, the more you will tend to do the same in the future. On the other hand, the more you practice *resisting* this tendency, the better you will get at it. So, you will need to work at it.

This is just how the brain works. There is a part of your brain called the striatum, which controls getting into habits arising from goal-directed behavior. When you achieve your goal, certain dopamine neurons in this part of the brain fire, which feels good; and which helps to reinforce the habit. So, it can actually be extremely rewarding for you to achieve your goals!

It most definitely lies in your power to overcome the inertia that you have built up over the years by demanding short-term pleasure or relief from short-term frustration. Yes, you *can* do it, by practicing Patience!

So how patient are you? Exercise 2.8 can help you reflect on this question.

EXERCISE 2.8

1. Discuss briefly how you usually deal with goals that take a relatively long time to accomplish.

2. What about short-term goals? How do you manage them if you start to feel frustrated about things not going well?

3. What do you think you can do differently to increase your Patience when you begin to feel frustrated?

As you can see, the virtues of Prudence, Perseverance, and Patience "hang together" so that in working on one of them, you are also working on the others. So, to have Prudence you would need to have Perseverance, and to have Perseverance you would need to have Patience. Let's do some further preliminary self-reflections about these three virtues with Exercise 2.9.

EXERCISE 2.9

1. How do you think embracing these virtues could change your life?

[blank box]

2. Do you know anyone who embraces these virtues? How does this impact their lives and the lives of those around them?

[blank box]

3. Would you like to be more like these people? Why, or why not?

[blank box]

5. EMPOWERING WISDOM FROM THE SAGES ON PURSUING THE VIRTUES

Following is some empowering counsel from some of the most prominent thinkers in the history of thought on how to develop Prudence, Perseverance, and Patience. These gems of condensed wisdom can help you form a worldview that can help you overcome your LFT!

Prudence

Empowering Wisdom from Epicurus:

• *Do everything with discretion, gentleness and moderation of sober reasoning—and enjoy long-lasting absence of pain in the body and of trouble in the soul.*

You might have heard mention of the ancient Greek philosopher, Epicurus, in connection with "Epicurean delights" such as an ice cream sundae that has everything in it but the kitchen sink. This idea that Epicurus favored living as a "hedonist pig" who eats and drinks himself into oblivion is a myth. Truly, this sober sage was very modest and believed that the simple sauce could be just as enjoyable as the fancy one. He declared that moderation in pleasure-seeking was what was most pleasing *in the long run*. "Where it is practically necessary for you to pursue or avoid anything," he admonished, "do even this with *discretion* and *gentleness* and *moderation*" (Epicurus, n.d. ch. 2, emphasis added).

This is the core meaning of Prudence for Epicurus: knowing when enough is enough and having the willpower to stop. For him, Prudence, so defined, is the mother of all virtues; it is, he said, "precious," because without it, you could not even hope to live a pleasant life, which he thought was the point of living.

According to this sage, pleasure is "the absence of pain in the body and of trouble in the soul" (Epicurus, n.d.). Unfortunately, folks who demand immediate gratification easily get frustrated when they don't get it, defeat their own purposes, and end up with more pain than pleasure in the end. So, you need the "sober reasoning" of Prudence to stand guard against going down the road of demanding immediate gratification. Take some counsel from Epicurus and give up this demand, which will only continue to cause "trouble in your soul" and defeat your quest for a pleasant life!

Empowering Wisdom from Jeremy Bentham:

- *Before pursuing a potentially pleasant activity, ask:*
  1. *Is it "pure"—chance it won't produce more pain than pleasure in the long run?*
  2. What is its "fecundity"—chance of producing other pleasures rather than pains in the long run?

According to the great British thinker, Jeremy Bentham, the best way to get the most pleasure out of life is to calculate what will bring you the greatest balance of pleasure over pain in deciding what to do. So, he came up with a set of standards to use to make such calculations.

If you really want to make a rational decision about going after pleasure, he said, you need to consider how intense the pleasure is, how long it will last, how long you need to wait to get it, and what the likelihood is that you will get it. But this is not the end of the story. Since pleasures can also lead to further pleasures or further pains, you also need to consider the chance that the pleasure will cause more pleasures, which he calls the "fecundity" or "fruitfulness" of the pleasure; and the chance it will *not* cause pain, which he calls "purity" (Bentham, 1907).

Unfortunately, when you demand immediate gratification, you do not think about whether this will produce more pleasure or lead to pain. You only think about the immediate pleasure. The same is true about frustration. So, you might quickly get frustrated and give up, say on a tedious work project, not thinking about how giving up will only lead to more frustration (reprimand from the boss) and less pleasure in the long run (he gives you a pink slip).

Mr. Bentham therefore admonishes you to do the math! "If I give up on things that I really want out of my life and go after immediate pleasures or relief from frustration, will that produce the greatest balance of pleasure over pain in the long run? If not, then it would not be prudent for me to go down that road. Better to forego immediate gratification for the sake of maximizing my balance of pleasure in the long run!"

Empowering Wisdom from Shantideva:

- *No sufferings belong to anyone.*

It is an old Buddhist insight that when you become too fixated on your own pleasures, you may paradoxically sabotage your own peace of mind. So, you demand pleasure and freedom from suffering and make yourself miserable when you don't get it.

According to the 8th-century Indian Buddhist monk, Shantideva (1995),

> Without exception, no sufferings belong to anyone. They are to be warded off simply because they are suffering. Why is any limitation put on this?

So, here's a prudent antidote to being overconcerned about yourself. Human suffering is a shared problem, and your *self* has no special claim when it comes to caring about human suffering. So instead of focusing on yourself, focus on compassionately trying to help others feel better too!

Exercise 2.10 can help you reflect on the implications of the aforementioned wisdom for your own life.

EXERCISE 2.10

Discuss briefly your approach, and how you might use the empowering wisdom offered by Epicurus, Bentham, and Shantideva to be more prudent about seeking pleasure and avoiding pain.

Perseverance

More Empowering Wisdom from Shantideva:

- *Face frustration with zestful vigor for being constructive.*
- *Nothing shall triumph over you with a positive outlook.*
- *Fulfillment comes through strong intention, steadfastness, delight, letting go, and readily accepting and taking control.*

The Venerable Shantideva has also provided you with several uplifting tips to guide you in working toward greater Perseverance. I have italicized the positive, uplifting language he uses because this language feels good and can inspire you to do bigger and better things (Shantideva, 2005):

- I shall strive for "Joyful Perseverance," which is "zestful" (enthusiastic) "vigor" (excitement) "for being constructive." This is the antidote to lack of enthusiasm, "clinging to" negative or unimportant things, and underestimating my own capacity.
- Getting discouraged and giving up won't liberate me from your feelings of frustration and powerlessness. "But *by strengthening my effort through having my pride [positive outlook], even huge [negative] things will have difficulty triumphing (over me).*"
- "*I shall triumph over everything and nothing shall triumph over me! …*"
- "*the supporting forces for fulfilling the aims of [human] beings are strong intention, steadfastness, delight, and letting go.*" Strong intention is developed by reframing dread of suffering as something that can have positive benefits (for example, I can learn from my experience).
- Overcoming my lack of enthusiasm, "clinging to" negative or unimportant things, and underestimating my own capacity, I shall strive to further my enthusiastic excitement for being constructive "*with the forces of strong intention, having pride [a positive outlook], delight, and letting go, also readily accepting and taking control.*"

Shantideva's connection of Perseverance with joyfulness ("joyful perseverance") is clearly calculated to arouse positive emotions as means to overcoming the inertia of negative emotions ("clinging to what's negative"); lack of energy or enthusiasm ("lethargy"); and underestimating your own capacity ("disparaging oneself"). To the contrary, in having a positive outlook ("pride"), you can triumph over "even huge things." With this positive, life affirming outlook, you can enthusiastically declare, "[I] triumph over everything and nothing shall triumph over me!"

Shantideva uses the words, "strong intention," "steadfastness," "delight," "pride," and "letting go" to show you what it means to have Perseverance. The idea of "letting go" is a central idea in Buddhist philosophy. To "let go" means to let go of your demand for immediate gratification, and so to accept reality as it *is*, not as you *demand* it to be. This means that you no longer feel the need for things to go *your* way so you cease to catastrophize when they don't.

In this way, you can "take control" and experience an incredible sense of freedom and release from the self-generated stresses of demanding that you get what you want when you want it. Instead of being in conflict with the world as it is, you approach it with zest, vigor, and excitement, welcoming the challenges of life as they happen!

Empowering Wisdom from John Dewey:

- *Your mistakes are a stimulus and guide to the trained thinker!*

Folks with LFT generally see making mistakes or errors as a sign that it's time to give up. Even the thought of messing up or failing may feel frustrating, so you may be inclined to give up even before you actually mess up or fail. But this can be a big mistake, says 20th-century philosopher of education, John Dewey. According to this esteemed philosopher,

> Nothing shows the *trained thinker* better than the use he makes of his errors and mistakes. What merely annoys and discourages a person not accustomed to thinking, or what starts him out on a new course of aimless attack by mere cut-and-try methods, is a *stimulus and a guide* to the trained inquirer.
>
> (Dewey, 1986, p. 206, emphasis added)

Suppose you are not sure how to repair that leaky kitchen drainpipe and in an attempt to stop the leak tighten it too much only to crack it. Well, for the person not accustomed to thinking that can be a source of great frustration, especially after he looks inside the pipe only to see a corroded washer! But for the trained thinker (and novice plumber) it can be a profoundly useful experience that enables her to repair the leak by replacing the pipe along with a new washer. And it can feel so good to have learned something that really helped to solve your problem. *Vive l'erreur!*

Empowering Wisdom from Aristotle:

- *The activity itself, not its results is most pleasant and most lovable.*

Now, what makes life so interesting is that there *are* challenges, without which life would be humdrum and boring. According to the ancient Greek genius, Aristotle,

> What is pleasant is the activity of the present, the hope of the future, the memory of the past; but *most pleasant* is that which depends on activity, and similarly this is *most lovable*.
>
> (Aristotle, 1941, bk. 9, ch. 7, p. 1085, emphasis added)

If you are focused on avoiding frustration or getting your pleasure fix right away, you are bound not to realize that you are taking yourself out of the game. For, indeed, the greatest source of pleasure lies in the joy you can get by *doing* things. It is not the product of your action that is a lot of fun; it is the doing itself. So, a novice athlete may focus so much on winning that she stresses herself out only to lose. On the other hand, the true pro enjoys playing the game, and this often, in turn, leads to victory. But even if it does not, most of the excitement lies in playing the game, not in winning it. So, Aristotle admonishes you to be a life pro and enjoy the ride as you go through life!

So how do you look at life and its outlets for enjoyment? Exercise 2.11 can help you reflect on this question.

EXERCISE 2.11

Discuss briefly your approach, and how you might use the counsel offered by Shantideva, Dewey, and Aristotle to become more perseverant in confronting life challenges.

Patience

Empowering Wisdom from Epictetus:

- *You have free, unrestricted, and unhindered power over your own affairs.*
- *Accept what is not in your power to control—the affairs of others.*

Did you ever hear the expression, "being stoic"? Well, this means exercising self-control over the things that are in your power to control and accepting what is not in your control. The Stoics were an ancient group of Greek and Roman philosophers who emphasized making this distinction as a way to live in peace and tranquility. According to one highly regarded representative of this group, Epictetus,

> There are things which are within our power, and there are things which are beyond our power. Within our power are opinion, aim, desire, aversion, and, in one word, whatever affairs are our own. Beyond our power are body, property, reputation, office, and, in one word, whatever are not properly our own affairs.
>
> (Epictetus, 1948, ch. 1)

Epictetus (1948) adds, "the things within our power are by nature free, unrestricted, unhindered; but those beyond our power are weak, dependent, restricted, alien" (ch. 1). For instance, even though you may *feel* like you can't stand the frustration of having to put off immediate gratification (say, sticking with that challenging math course), this does not mean that you really can't.

First, we humans often do things we don't feel like doing; but we still do them! Second, your frustration arises in the first place only because you are telling yourself that you *must* control what is not yours to control—the time things take, their level of difficulty, etc. Unfortunately, people with LFT tend to confuse what is in their power with what is not by denying that their own thoughts, feelings, and actions are under their control.

So, take an important counsel from Epictetus and his tranquil band of Stoics. Increase your level of Patience by affirming your "free, unrestricted, unhindered" power over *your own* affairs, and accept what is not in your power to control—namely, the affairs of others. In so doing, he assures, you will live contentedly, free of needless, self-imposed frustration; and you will also no longer stress yourself out and feel anxiety about what others think, feel, or do, since such needless stress arises only when you attempt to control the affairs of others rather than your own.

Empowering Wisdom from Lao-Tzu:

- *Wait and let the mud settle on its own and the water will then be clear.*
- *Everything will pass on its own as long as you don't hold on to it.*

In the famous text, *Tao Te Ching*, ancient Chinese philosopher Lao-Tzu (n.d.) admonished,

> Do you have the patience to wait
> till your mud settles and the water is clear?
> Can you remain unmoving
> till the right action arises by itself?
>
> (ch. 15)

The point is that sometimes the only thing you really need to solve your problem is Patience. To illustrate this point contemporary Buddhists (Bodhipaksa, n.d.) tell a story about Buddha, who, while traveling, asked an impatient student of his to bring him some water to drink. So, the student went to a lake where some oxen were crossing it, which stirred up the dirt at the bottom, making the water muddy and undrinkable. The student returned from the lake to inform Buddha that the water was too dirty to drink. Buddha waited about a half an hour, and again asked his student to go to the lake for drinking water. Again, the student returned without the water, informing Buddha that it was muddy. Buddha did not respond to the student, who by now was very frustrated, and again soon asked the disciple to fetch the water. The student was now furious but out of respect complied with the request. Surprise! Now the water was suitable to drink, so the student returned with some. "What have you done to clean the water?" asked Buddha. "What do you mean?" asked the now perplexed student. Buddha responded,

> You waited and let it be. Therefore, the mud settled on its own and now the water is clear. Your mind is like that too! When it's muddy, you have to let it be. Give it some time. Don't be impatient. On the contrary, be patient. It'll reach a balance on its own. You don't have to make any effort to calm it down. Everything will pass on its own as long as you don't hold on to it.
>
> (Soulful Arogya, 2016)

No doubt you have already gleaned the moral of the story. Patience is a prophylactic for frustration! Let the frustration go. Let the mind settle. You don't have to look elsewhere for immediate gratification. You just need to have patience, keep at your task, and you will eventually succeed!

Exercise 2.12 now gives you an opportunity to do some preliminary reflection on the counsel offered by Epictetus and Lao-Tzu.

EXERCISE 2.12

Discuss briefly your own approach to dealing with frustration, and how you could use the counsel offered by Epictetus and Lao-Tzu to become more Patient.

Do you have a favorite sage of your own who you think gives constructive advice on how to be more prudent, perseverant, or patient? Add them to your list by completing Exercise 2.13!

EXERCISE 2.13

1. If you have a favorite sage of your own who offers empowering wisdom on how to be more prudent, perseverant, or patient, then formulate this counsel below in the space indicated. (Even if you don't know the name of the person from whom the counsel comes, that's still okay.)

Additional Empowering Wisdom for Prudence

Additional Empowering Wisdom for Perseverance

Additional Empowering Wisdom for Patience

Compiling a Master List of Empowering Wisdom

Epicurus, Bentham, and Shantideva have given you language to formulate their learned counsel that can go on a list of empowering wisdom to inspire Prudence. For instance, for each of the formulations in the Prudence column of Table 2.3, focus, one at a time, on the

TABLE 2.3
Empowering wisdom regarding Prudence, Perseverance, and Patience

Prudence	Perseverance	Patience
Epicurus:	**Shantideva:**	**Epictetus:**
Do everything with discretion, gentleness and moderation of sober reasoning—and enjoy long-lasting absence of pain in the body and of trouble in the soul.	Face Frustration with Zestful Vigor for being constructive. __Nothing shall triumph over you with a positive outlook.	You have free, unrestricted, and unhindered power over your own affairs. __Accept what is not in your power to control—the affairs of others.
Bentham:	__Fulfillment comes through strong intention, steadfastness, delight, letting go, and readily accepting and taking control.	**Lao-Tzu:**
Before pursuing a potentially pleasant activity, ask:	**Dewey:**	Wait and let the mud settle on its own and the water will then be clear.
1. Is it "pure"—chance it won't produce more pain than pleasure in the long run?	Your mistakes are a stimulus and guide to the trained thinker!	__Everything will pass on its own as long as you don't hold on to it.
2. What is its "fecundity"—chance of producing other pleasures rather than pains in the long run?	**Aristotle:**	
Shantideva:	The activity itself, not its results is most pleasant and most lovable.	
No sufferings belong to anyone.		

formulation with your mind's eye, and key into how it *feels. Does it make you want to be more prudent in taking risks*!? If yes, keep it on your list of empowering wisdom; if not, take it off or change the language!

Similarly, for each of the formulations in the Perseverance column of Table 2.3, focus, one at a time, on the formulation with your mind's eye, and key into how it *feels. Does it make you feel more empowered to persevere?* If yes, keep it on your list of empowering wisdom; if not, take it off or change the language!

Finally, for each of the formulations in the Patience column of Table 2.3, focus, one at a time, on the formulation with your mind's eye, and key into how it *feels. Does it make you feel more empowered to exercise patience?* If yes, keep it on your list of empowering wisdom; if not, take it off or change the language!

Have you found the formulations of the sage's counsel in Table 2.3 to have a positive feeling of empowerment or uplift? Language use is an important part of why the tips of the philosophers seem to help us to feel more inspired to take risks.

Exercise 2.14 gives you the opportunity to tailor the language and content included in Table 2.3 to especially suit you.

EXERCISE 2.14

This exercise will help you to modify Table 2.3 to provide a **master list of wisdom that is especially empowering for you**.

Please modify Table 2.3 in responding to the following instructions:

1. For each of the three guiding virtues, place a checkmark in front of each learned counsel you intend to use. Your selections should resonate with you, that is, feel uplifting, consoling, or otherwise empowering to you.

2. If you are not satisfied with the formulation of any of the counsels in Table 2.3, on a separate piece of paper, please rewrite it using language that resonates with you. For example, when I think of Shantideva's counsel about Perseverance, I think of "enthusiastic excitement," "positive outlook," and "taking control." And when I think of Epictetus' counsel, I think of being "master of your own affairs." You are free to reformulate or tweak the sages' counsel using any language that is empowering to you!

3. Please also add any empowering insights to Table 2.3 that you may have formulated in Exercise 2.12. Again, it is important that the language you use is empowering *for you*.

4. Now, congratulate yourself! You now have a master list of wisdom that is empowering for you!

---

6. CREATING A COGNITIVE-BEHAVIORAL PLAN

Are you ready to harness the wisdom of the sages to build a plan of action for overcoming your LFT? This is an exciting venture because it will open new avenues of freedom for you!

Suppose you have told yourself that you can't learn to play guitar, even though you would love to be able to play, because you just don't have the patience to take lessons and practice all the time, which would be a royal pain the ass.

Now let's say you realize that this has been a serious problem of yours since you have tended to make the same excuse for most long-term commitments in your life, leaving you pretty much in the same unfilled situation in many respects. So, you resolve to be more *prudent* in the future by following the following plan:

- Doing some *sober reasoning* about how to fit guitar lessons into your schedule, you plan to watch an hour less TV each day, and to practice instead; therefore taking a *moderate* approach, as Epicurus would recommend.
- As you tend to get discouraged very quickly when you don't get something right away, you propose to remind yourself to seek pleasures that are fruitful and pure, realizing that giving up may relieve some immediate frustration but would thwart your desire to learn the instrument. You realize the latter would be a much purer pleasure, creating further avenues for obtaining pleasure such as playing at social events, or as a respite from work and other pressures.
- Think of learning to play the guitar as a way to benefit others by bringing music into their lives; so not just for yourself, as Shantideva would counsel.

To exercise *Perseverance*, you decide to

- Reframe your frustration in terms of "zestful vigor for being constructive," therefore, "letting go" your self-defeating demand for immediate gratification, so that "nothing will triumph over you!"
- Reframe mistakes you make in learning to play as a *guide* to what you need to work on, rather than as a sign to give up.
- Enjoy the aesthetic experience of playing guitar, itself, as Aristotle would counsel, instead of learning to play *just* to look cool or as a social outlet.

To be more *patient*, you plan to

- Take a page from Epictetus' playbill and focus your attention on practicing and learning rather than on what others may think of your playing, whether they like it or not.
- "Let the mud settle," as Lau Tzu would counsel, by waiting for your fingers to adjust to new positions when you have difficulties executing passages or forming chords.

Now, it's your turn to build a plan of action based on the learned counsel you have received. Exercise 2.15 can help with this!

EXERCISE 2.15

1. Choose a relatively short-term goal from one of the ones you described in Exercise 2.2, which you are now willing to try to achieve. Recall you were asked to include at least one short-term goal. Restate this goal in the space provided below:

2. Now, restate the LFT thinking you formulated in Exercise 2.4 that has blocked you from attempting to achieve this goal.

```
1.

2.

3.

4.
```

Using your empowering wisdom, the remainder of this exercise will help you to construct the elements of a cognitive-behavioral plan to overcome Conclusion 4 of the above LFT thinking!

3. Using the counsel offered by Epicurus, Bentham, and Shantideva or any empowering wisdom you may have added in Exercise 2.13 for becoming *more prudent*, what cognitive-behavioral changes would you make to overcome your LFT thinking? For example, what changes would the Venerable Shantideva tell you to make in the way you may be focusing exclusively on your *own* frustration when you encounter obstacles? What would Bentham tell you to do differently based on his standards of pleasure seeking? Are you following Epicurus' counsel on seeking modest pleasures, for example, setting your sights on an exotic vacation beyond your means instead of a more modest one that could be just as enjoyable? List at least three cognitive-behavioral changes you plan to make:

```
1.

2.

3.

4.

5.
```

4. Using counsel offered by Shantideva, Dewey, and Aristotle or any other empowering wisdom you may have added in Exercise 2.13 for becoming *more perseverant*, what cognitive-behavioral changes would you make to overcome your LFT thinking? List at least three:

```
1.

2.

3.

4.

5.
```

5. Using counsel offered by Epictetus and Lao-Tzu, or any other empowering wisdom you may have added in Exercise 2.13 for becoming *more decisive*, what cognitive-behavioral changes would you make to overcome your LFT thinking? List at least two:

1.

2.

3.

4.

5.

6. Now, congratulate yourself! You have just constructed a cognitive-behavioral plan!!

---

7. WORKING ON YOUR COGNITIVE-BEHAVIORAL PLAN

You will now have an opportunity to begin to build your habits of Prudence, Perseverance, and Patience instead of defaulting to your self-defeating habit of LFT thinking.

Cognitive–Affective Imagery

As you know, when folks with LFT think about blocks to immediate gratification such as having to wait extended periods or not getting things right the first time, they tend to *feel* threatened by the conflict with their demand for immediate gratification, which leads them to catastrophize about it, and then they tell themselves they can't. "It would drive me crazy to wait that long! No can do!" Imagery exercises can help you change such negative feelings to positive, uplifting, empowering ones! Exercise 2.16 will help you to set up and practice cognitive–affective imagery.

EXERCISE 2.16

1. Choose a formulation from the Prudence column of your master list of empowering wisdom (see Exercise 2.14) that is especially empowering or uplifting for you. Keep it in the back of your mind at this point.

2. Refer to the LFT thinking you identified in Exercise 2.15, which is blocking a *short-term goal* you also identified in Exercise 2.15.

3. Now here are instructions for doing cognitive–affective imagery. If you are working with a therapist, the therapist can provide guidance until you get the hang of it and can do it on your own. If you are not being assisted by a therapist, then please read these directions carefully now, memorize them (three steps), and then follow the three-step sequence laid out for you below:

Step 1: Focus your mind exclusively on your LFT thinking (as identified in Exercise 2.15). Keep going over it in your mind like you did when you first decided you couldn't accomplish your goal. Keep it up until you feel that negative visceral threatening feeling, the clashing of your felt need for immediate gratification with the realization that you won't get it in pursuing the goal you are now considering. Let yourself resonate with the feeling of powerlessness that emerges, and that "No way! I can't do this!" feeling.

Step 2: At the peak of feeling this intense negative feeling, shift your focus of mind exclusively to the positive language that you have selected for feeling empowered to become prudent. Let yourself *feel* the uplift, the empowerment to confront the frustration; letting yourself feel the freedom to take control.

Step 3: Once you have fully brought yourself to resonate with the positivity of the experience, gently shift your attention to reflecting on your experience and what you have learned or discovered from it.

4. Try to reserve a time each day to practice your guided imagery exercise. Next time, however, choose a word or phrase from the *Perseverance* column of your master list of empowering wisdom that is especially empowering or uplifting for you.

5. Similarly, the subsequent day, repeat the exercise except this time choose a word or phrase from the *Patience* column of your master list of empowering wisdom.

6. Practice regularly shifting between your empowering wisdom to support *each of the three* guiding virtues.

7. What have you learned or discovered about yourself from your experience practicing your cognitive–affective imagery? Write down your reflections below:

My Reflections about My Experience:

Great work!!

Refuting and Reframing

By inspecting your LFT thinking, premise by premise, it is possible to refute and reframe your self-defeating thinking. As discussed in the Introduction to this book, reframing involves placing your negative thinking in a more positive light. For example, to reframe your demand for immediate gratification, which is obstructing your goal to learn guitar, you might reframe this in terms of Shantideva's counsel to focus on compassion for others, seeing this as an opportunity to bring music into the lives of others. To reframe your catastrophizing that lessons would be a "pain in the ass," you can take a counsel from Bentham and think about how learning the guitar can produce pure pleasures that keep on giving. And to reframe your conclusion that you can't do it, you can key into Lao-Tzu's metaphor of "letting the mud settle" by not prejudging your capacity to learn to play the instrument.

Accordingly, Exercise 2.17 will give you some practice refuting and reframing your LFT thinking!

EXERCISE 2.17

1. Refer again to the LFT thinking you identified in Exercise 2.15, which is preventing you from dealing rationally with the situation you also identified in Exercise 2.15. Look carefully at Premise 1 in your LFT thinking, the one that *demands that you must get what you want without having to endure any (or much) frustration*. In Exercise 2.5, you have already refuted this premise so you can see how irrational it truly is. Think about this refutation until it resonates with you, that is, you get the "I get it" feeling that this premise is truly irrational. If this doesn't happen, then go back to Exercise 2.5 and find a refutation that *does* resonate with you. Write down your refutation in Table 2.4 in the refutation column for Premise 1.

Now, select empowering wisdom from one or more of your sages (it could even be counsel you added in Exercise 2.13), and use it to reframe your demand not to endure frustration. In Table 2.4, write down this empowering wisdom in the reframing column for Premise 1.

2. Just as you have done for the Premise 1, refute and reframe Conclusions 3 and 4 of the LFT thinking you identified in Exercise 2.15. Use Table 2.4 to write down your refutation and reframing for each of these respective conclusions of your LAC thinking.

TABLE 2.4
Refuting and reframing your LFT thinking

Part	Refutation	Reframing
Premise 1		
Conclusion 3		
Conclusion 4		

Mindfulness Meditation

This type of meditation can be useful because it can help you to stop focusing on yourself, which is the source of your LFT thinking. If you stop focusing on your own *self*, and instead on something else such as your breathing, you can then take your attention away from *self*-gratification, which can, in turn, dismantle your demand for self-gratification. This allows you to detach from your self-absorbed, gratification-demanding self, to become, instead, a non-judgmental, impartial observer!

I recommend beginning now with a recognized program of mindfulness meditation. The Palouse Mindfulness program can be quite helpful (Palouse Mindfulness, n.d.). You start with filling out the "Getting Started" worksheet, which will allow you to set up a schedule of when it will be convenient for you to practice 30 minutes of mindfulness six days a week. I recommend working through the entire eight-week program. If you have a therapist, then your therapist may suggest an alternative program or approach to helping you develop this valuable skill. Exercise 2.18 keys into just one session from the Palouse Mindfulness program.

EXERCISE 2.18

1. Refer to the Palouse Mindfulness program (palousemindfulness.com). On the left-hand margin under "Practices," you will find a practice session called "Sitting Meditation." Listen to this guided audio presentation and follow the directions.

2. Now, refer again to the LFT thinking you identified in Exercise 2.15, which was blocking the short-term goal you also identified in Exercise 2.15. First, *carefully read through* each step of the below three directions:
   - Step 1: Focus your attention on your short-term goal and while you are doing so, try detaching yourself from it, as though you were an objective observer, much as you did when you were focusing on your breathing in your "Sitting Meditation," only now focusing your attention on your goal.
   - Step 2: Taking this nonjudgmental perspective, let go of any negative thoughts you have about it, should they enter your mind, gently pushing them away.
   - Step 3: While you are taking this non-judgmental perspective, imagine yourself acting on this goal of yours. Allow yourself a minute or two to imagine this.

3. Now, this time, *actually go through these three steps*. Immediately after completing the three steps, when it's fresh in your mind, describe your experience using the space below to write down your observations:

```


```

4. Continue working through the Palouse Mindfulness program and practice the three steps of Exercise 2.18 each time you have completed the next weekly practice session, and as many times as you can between sessions. Use extra paper to record your observations and compare them with previous runs of this exercise. As you improve your mindfulness skills, you may begin to notice greater ease in which you nonjudgmentally focus on imagining yourself acting on your goal without having negative thoughts.

Compassion-Based ("Loving-Kindness") Meditation

This type of meditation can be helpful for overcoming LFT especially when it comes to relating to other people. Suppose you tend to get very frustrated with others when they misunderstand what you are telling them, or you have to repeatedly explain things to them before they finally comprehend your meaning. "No! That's not what I'm saying. Why don't you get it? Do you have wax in your ears!?"

By emphasizing your interconnectedness with others instead of focusing on your separateness and *self*-gratification, you can reframe your relationship, sending others, as well as yourself, wishes for "solidarity," "unity," "harmony," "love," "peace," "health," "happiness," and "kindness" so that the boundaries between you and the other evaporate and you see yourself in the other and the other in you. This very uplifting sense of unity and bondedness is what compassion-based mediation seeks to build, which can help to move you past your own self-absorption, seeing yourself as part of the greater interconnected universe. In this way, your own *demand* for self-gratification begins to fade in relation to the grand totality of beings to which you are seamlessly bonded in "loving kindness." Exercise 2.19 can help to build this uplifting feeling of interconnectedness and thereby help you to overcome your LFT.

EXERCISE 2.19

Please listen to the guided meditation audio recording called "Loving Kindness Meditation" presented by Dr. Kristin Neff. This audio recording is (at the time of this writing) freely accessible from the following link: https://self-compassion.org/guided-self-compassion-meditations-mp3-2/. When you have finished following the audio tape, respond to the below questions.

1. Reflect on your demand for self-gratification. How does this *demand* feel within the grander scope of your loving kindness wishes and feelings for the totality of all living beings?

2. When you reflect on your LFT thinking that has blocked your short-term goal (as described in Exercise 2.15), how does this thinking now feel in relation to the grander scope of your connectedness with all living beings?

3. Please feel free to repeat this exercise as often as you like, especially when you are beginning to feel frustrated by your everyday encounters.

Acting on Your Goal

This is the final stage of your process of working on your cognitive-behavioral plan. It involves doing all the things you listed in your cognitive-behavioral plan, which you developed in Exercise 2.15. This also includes *acting* on your goal itself. For example, if your goal is to learn the guitar, to exercise Prudence, you will create a functional practice schedule; reframe your narrow-self-absorbed thinking in the wider context of bringing joy to others as well as yourself through music; perceive any short-term frustration arising from your new project in the broader context of obtaining long-term, prolific pleasure. And so forth for your other guiding virtues.

This is the point where you have honed your skills through the practical exercises you have done, from refuting and reframing to meditating. As such, you have primed your pump and are ready to take the plunge, for instance, signing up for guitar lessons and starting them! So exciting! But, this is not the end of your working to overcome your LFT thinking but rather the beginning. Continuing to practice the cognitive-behavior skills you have learned in this chapter is of the utmost importance to counter the old feelings that will inevitably arise as you encounter obstacles in seeing your goals to completion. This means practicing refuting and reframing your LFT thinking using the empowering wisdom from your sages to attain your guiding virtues; it means practicing your cognitive–affective imagery, your mindfulness, and loving kindness meditations.

Exercise 2.20 can guide you through this process.

EXERCISE 2.20

1. Review the cognitive-behavioral items on your behavioral plan created in Exercise 2.15.

2. Review the refutation and reframing of Premise 1 and Conclusions 3 and 4 of your LFT thinking which you developed in Exercise 2.17.

3. Implement each of the *behavioral* elements in your plan. For example, sign up for guitar lessons, start taking your lessons, and follow through with your practice schedule!

4. Continue to refute and reframe your LFT thinking (Exercise 2.17), while, and even after you act on your goal. Also continue to practice your cognitive–affective imagery (Exercise 2.16), and your meditations (Exercise 2.18; 2.19). This is important because folks with LFT can get easily frustrated at first even after they have gotten over the initial hurdle of acting on their goals. Indeed, honing your skills is a lifelong project since there is no limit to how honed you can get, and always the possibility of getting rusty if you stop practicing them and attempt to rest on your laurels!

5. Provide your reflections in the space below about your experience of acting on your goal:

6. This is an incredible milestone, so congratulate yourself!

Working on Your Other Goals

In Exercise 2.2, you described at least two goals that you would like to fulfill but have been blocked by LFT. Now you can continue working to fulfill the other goal/s you described, or you can even add new goals.

The process is the same, and you have already gone through it in addressing your short-term goal. You have also already formulated the risk-avoidant reasoning chains blocking you from attaining these other goals and have also refuted Premise 1 and Conclusions 3 and 4 of each of them. So, you are already well on your way to accomplishing these other goals and strengthening your guiding virtues. Here is a summary of the process:

1. Formulate your LFT thinking (Exercise 2.4).
2. Refute Premise 1 and Conclusions 3 and 4 of this thinking (Exercise 2.5).
3. Embrace your guiding virtues (Exercises 2.6 through 2.9).
4. Get empowering wisdom from the sages on pursuing the virtues (Exercises 2.10 through 2.14).
5. Use this learned counsel to construct a cognitive-behavioral plan (Exercise 2.15).
6. Work on your cognitive-behavioral plan (Exercises 2.16 through 2.20).

Having worked through the exercises in this chapter, you are now in an excellent position to take impressive strides toward greater and greater freedom and fulfillment in life as you detach yourself more and more from your LFT. Clearly, building your guiding virtues of Prudence, Perseverance, and Patience takes continual practice. Using the exercise sets in this chapter as the framework, you can do this work by regularly going through the above six steps.

Keep working at it!

REFERENCES

Aristotle. (1941). *Nicomachean ethics*. In McKeon, R. (Ed.). *The Basic Works of Aristotle*. Random House.

Bentham, J. (1907). *An introduction to the principles of morals and legislation*. Retrieved from www.self.gutenberg. org/wplbn0001162153-an-introduction-to-the-principles-of-morals-and-legislation-by-bentham-jeremy. aspx?Epicurus

Bodhipaksa (n.d.). Fake Buddha quotes. Retrieved from "If you let cloudy water settle it will become clear. If you let your upset mind settle, your course will also become clear"—Fake Buddha Quotes.

Dewey, J. (1986). How we think: a restatement of the relation of reflective thinking to the educative process. In Boydston, J.A. (Ed.), *The later works, 1925–1953*, Vol. 8. Southern Illinois University Press.

Epictetus. (1948). *The Enchiridion*. Higgins, T.W. (Trans.). Liberal Arts Press. Retrieved from the www.gutenberg.org/files/ 45109/45109-h/45109-h.htm

Epicurus. (n.d.). Letter to Menoeceus, trans. Hicks, R.D. Retrieved from http://classics.mit.edu/Epicurus/menoec.html

Lao-Tzu. (n.d.). *Tao te ching*. Mitchell, S. (Trans.). Retrieved from www.organism.earth/library/document/tao-te-ching

Palouse Mindfulness. (n.d.). Online Mindfulness-Based Stress Reduction (MBSR). Online MBSR/Mindfulness (Free) (palousemindfulness.com)

Shantideva. (1995). Bodhicaryāvatāra. Crosby, K. & Skilton, A. (Trans.). Oxford University Press.

Shantideva. (2005). *Engaging in Bodhisattva behavior*. Berzin, A. (Trans.). Retrieved from https://studybuddhism.com/en/ tibetan-buddhism/original-texts/sutra-texts/engaging-in-bodhisattva-behavior/perseverance

Soulful Arogya. (June 5, 2016). A story about buddha you probably haven't heard before. Retrieved from https://medium. com/@soulfularogya/a-story-about-buddha-you-probably-havent-heard-before-fada7e3f9589

3

Overcoming Low Anger Control

As you have seen in the Introduction to this Workbook, low anger control (LAC) is an emotional type of *can'tstipation* that sustains and intensifies anger. It results from *blaming another for treating you unfairly*, which, in turn, keeps you in a constant state of anger directed toward the person you perceive to have treated you unfairly. As such you deny your capacity to control how you feel. "You *made me angry* by treating me like that. It's your fault! So, I *can't help* feeling angry." In this way, you absolve yourself of any responsibility for your feelings by blaming them on somebody else. Unfortunately, folks with LAC often behave in self-defeating ways they later come to regret. So, over a lifetime, this constant source of self-imposed, needless stress can take an unhealthy toll on your happiness!

1. GOALS OF THE CHAPTER

Accordingly, the goals of this chapter are to:

1. Increase awareness of the thinking and language you are using that sustains your anger.
2. Refute this thinking.
3. Identify guiding virtues that counteract your anger thinking.
4. Identify empowering wisdom from great sages on how to seek these virtues.
5. Use this learned counsel to construct a cognitive-behavioral plan for increasing your virtues.
6. Work on your plan to help you relate to others without the anger subverting your relationships.

2. THE NATURE OF ANGER THINKING

Folks with LAC tend to hold grudges toward others rather than to move on. They may also be easily agitated by others because they feel unable to control how they feel in response to the treatment of others. So, while it may be relatively easy for many people to overlook or let go a small offense, say a sarcastic remark, folks with LAC catastrophize about it and turn it into a major transgression that continues to play out in their minds. This does not mean that anger is always out of place or that there is no rational anger. The problem instead lies with maintaining control over the anger rather than permitting it to maintain control over you.

DOI: 10.4324/9781003035282-4

Consider some examples of the thinking by which people with LAC keep themselves in a self-defeating state of anger:

- You falsely accused me of lying to you.
  So, what you did to me was *so horrible*.
  So, you're a *rotten person*.
  So, I can't help being angry at you.
- You lied to me.
  So, the way you treated me was *so unkind*.
  So, you are a *two-faced bastard*.
  So, I can't stop being angry at you.
- You acknowledged everyone else but me after I helped you get that award.
  So, this was *inexcusable*.
  So, you *deserve to rot in hell*.
  So, I can't help being so pissed off by you.
- Your joke was at my expense.
  So, that was *really shitty of you*.
  So, you are a *son-of-a-bitch*.
  So, I can't help being so angry at you.
- You promised to be there on time, but you let me down when I was counting on you.
  So you treated me *like I was a nothing*.
  So, you are a *real dirtball*.
  So, I can't stop being pissed at you.

Now, when people get angry, they imagine themselves being treated by someone else in some way that *feels wrong* or *unfair*, which they direct toward a *person* they feel wronged by, or toward an *action* the person did. Folks with LAC usually blame the *person* for causing their anger. "How could you do something like this to me, you rotten SOB!" In so doing, you build a narrative in your mind about how this "horrible person" has done something "so awful" to "piss you off."

However, be careful! Just because you are angry *at someone* does not mean this person *caused* your anger. Another way of putting this is that the object of your anger, the external thing you are consciously focused on (whether the person or his action) is not the cause of your anger. So, who or what *is* the cause?

Please look at the language I have italicized in the above examples of low anger control (LAC) thinking:

- "so horrible"
- "rotten person"
- "two-faced bastard"
- "so unkind"
- "two-faced bastard"
- "inexcusable"
- "deserve to rot in hell"
- "really shitty of you"
- "son-of-a-bitch"
- "like I was a nothing"
- "real dirtball."

These are fighting words! So, when you express your feeling of being wronged in such catastrophic and damning language, you add fuel to the fire, whereby you work yourself up into a state of intense anger (even rage), leaving you to feel disempowered over your anger; which, in turn, you express by proclaiming, "I can't help feeling like this!"

As such, you yourself have a big hand in *making yourself angry*, even though you tell yourself that it is others that make you angry. But there is more to the thinking you use to make and keep yourself angry.

Your Demand Never to Be Treated Unfairly

Implicit in each of the above examples of LAC thinking is a very self-defeating assumption. This is a perfectionistic *demand never to be treated unfairly*: that others *should* never treat you unfairly. Unfortunately, this assumption is unrealistic because others will inevitably treat you in ways you will take to be unfair. So, it is futile to live in such a never-never-land.

When you make such a demand to yourself it invariably *conflicts* with reality. So, someone does not treat you fairly, as you *should* be treated; and this violation of "should" feels so wrong, which is the origin of your anger in the first place! You see, it is you all along calling the shots by making such an unrealistic demand!

When you add this unrealistic demand for fair treatment to your chain of LAC thinking, this thinking looks something like this:

1. Others should never treat me unfairly.
2. But you falsely accused me of lying to you.
3. So, the way you treated me was *so horrible*.
4. So, you are a *rotten person*.
5. So, I can't help being so angry at you.

In Premise 1 you demand fairness, and in Premise 2 you see that the way you were treated does not align with your demand. This leaves you in a state of conflict, which feels wrong, which, unfortunately, you amplify in Conclusion 3 with self-defeating language like "so horrible." Then, in Conclusion 4, you *blame* the person who treated you "so horribly" by calling him a "rotten person." In calling him a rotten person, you have found a fall guy for your anger. It is not you; instead it is this rotten person. So, there you are, minding your own business, and this "rotten person" *makes* you angry. Consequently, because you are just this passive vessel that was so horribly treated by this rotten person, you feel out of control, which you then express as "I can't help being so angry at you."

As for the "should" in Premise 1, it is based on a *felt wrongness* (a feeling deep inside you). Such a feeling stems from past negative experiences of having been treated unfairly. For example, as a child you may have been excluded from social events by other children, ostracized, or bullied, leaving you with a strong feeling of wrongness about treatment you have labeled as "unfair." A representation of this feeling (not just the event of being treated unfairly) is then stored in your brain's memory circuits (in somatosensory structures in the forebrain) and this feeling is, in turn, associated with a *felt should never*, a deep, all pervasive bodily feeling that this should never happen. Exercise 3.1 is an icebreaker to help you get more in touch with your own feelings.

EXERCISE 3.1

Write down your answers to the following questions in the space provided. Use separate pieces of paper if necessary:

1. When you think about being treated unfairly, what goes through your mind? What feelings do you experience?

```
┌─────────────────────────────────────────────────────────────────────┐
│                                                                       │
│                                                                       │
│                                                                       │
│                                                                       │
│                                                                       │
└─────────────────────────────────────────────────────────────────────┘
```

2. Think about the last time you were treated unfairly and felt like you couldn't help getting so angry. Imagine you are now in this situation and get yourself to feel just like you felt when you were actually treated unfairly.

3. Now, place a check next to any of the following words that describe how you are feeling. You are also free to add some of your own ideas to this list that might capture how you are feeling.

```
┌─────────────────────────────────────────────────────────────────────┐
│                                                                       │
│   •   Conflicted ____                                                 │
│   •   Wronged ____                                                    │
│   •   Powerless (over your feeling) ____                              │
│   •   Angry _____                                                     │
│   •   Anxious _____                                                   │
│   •   Vindictive _____                                                │
│   •   Hateful _____                                                   │
│   •   Enraged _____                                                   │
│   •   Explosive _____                                                 │
│                                                                       │
│                                                                       │
└─────────────────────────────────────────────────────────────────────┘
```

    a.   When you have such negative feelings about doing something, how do you usually resolve them?

    b.   Are you satisfied with the way you usually resolve them? Explain.

```
┌─────────────────────────────────────────────────────────────────────┐
│                                                                       │
│   a.                                                                  │
│                                                                       │
│                                                                       │
│   b.                                                                  │
│                                                                       │
└─────────────────────────────────────────────────────────────────────┘
```

The Self-Defeating Nature of Your LAC thinking

Because we are human, all of us experience angry feelings when we think we are or have been mistreated. Unfortunately, your LAC thinking can manufacture intense anger, which you deny capacity to control by proclaiming, "I can't." The self-defeating result of this proclamation is that you make yourself a slave to your anger and allow yourself to be carried off by it to say and do things you subsequently regret.

3. EXAMINING *YOUR* LAC THINKING

In this section you will have the opportunity to examine the nature of your own LAC thinking. So, what does *your* LAC thinking look like? Exercises 3.2 through 3.4 will help you answer this question.

EXERCISE 3.2

Please briefly describe at least three and as many as five types of situations in which you tend to experience intense anger that feels out of control, so that you tell yourself you can't control your anger. For example, perhaps you tend to get intensely angry when others insult you, laugh at you, talk behind your back, or exclude you from a social event.

At least one of these situations in which you experience intense anger should be one you could easily intentionally arrange in the near future. For example, you may know someone who inevitably manages to unfairly criticize you (such as a critical parent, in-law, sibling, colleague, or supervisor). So, if you were at any time to call this person on the phone, attend a regularly scheduled meeting with, or otherwise directly encounter this person, it is very likely, based on past experience, he or she would unfairly or wrongfully criticize you.

1.
2.
3.
4.
5.

EXERCISE 3.3

1. Please make a list of the catastrophic language you have used to make yourself feel angrier in each of the cases you listed in Exercise 3.2. For example, maybe you tell yourself the way you were treated was "despicable" or "disgusting."

Your Catastrophic Language List

Your Catastrophic Language List

You now have a list of at least some of the catastrophic words or phrases you tend to use to *make yourself* angry. Feel free to add to this list later if you think of other words or phrases. These are terms you will need to retire from your vocabulary!

2. Now make a second list of *damning* things you sometimes say (or think) about the person who you believe treated you unfairly such as calling the person a "rotten piece of garbage" (or worse!). Damning language like this can add further fuel to your low anger control.

Your Damning Others Language List

You now have a list of at least some of the disempowering words or phrases you tend to use *to damn others*. Feel free to add to this list later if you think of other words or phrases. These are terms you will also need to retire from your vocabulary!

EXERCISE 3.4

Next, for each of the cases you listed in Exercise 3.2, write down your LAC thinking (chain of thinking leading you to say you can't) using the language you identified in Exercise 3.3. To formulate each of your cases, please follow the below form:

1. Others should never treat me unfairly.
2. But [enter person] [enter unfair treatment].
3. So, the way [enter person again] treated me was [enter catastrophic term].
4. So, [enter person again] is/are [enter damning term].
5. So, I can't help being so angry at [enter person again].

In Premise 2, where it says, "enter person," enter the person you think treated you unfairly. And where it says, "enter unfair treatment" describe the treatment itself, for example, "lied to me" or "ignored me."

In Conclusion 3, where it says, "enter person again," enter the same person again; and where it says, "insert a catastrophic disempowering term" insert a term from your Catastrophic Language List which you created in Exercise 3.3(1), for example, your Conclusion 3 might read, "So, the way John treated me was so awful."

In Conclusion 4, where it says, "enter person again," enter the same person again; and where it says, "enter damning term," enter one of the terms from your damning language list you created in Exercise 3.3(2), for example, "So, John is a piece of crap."

Finally, in Conclusion 5, where it says, "enter person again," simply enter the same person again.

So, suppose you have told yourself how *horrible* it was that *your boss ranked you out in front of your coworkers*, and how he was *such a worthless slimeball* for treating you like this, so that you could not help getting so angry at him. Then your thinking would look like this:

1. Others should never treat me unfairly.
2. But my boss ranked me out in front of my co-workers.
3. So, the way my boss treated me was horrible.
4. So, my boss is such a worthless slimeball.
5. So, I can't help being so angry at my boss.

Now it's your turn to formulate *your* LAC thinking:

Case	Your LAC Thinking
1.	1. 2. 3. 4. 5.
2.	1. 2. 3. 4. 5.
3.	1. 2. 3. 4. 5.

Case	Your LAC Thinking
4.	1.
	2.
	3.
	4.
	5.
5.	1.
	2.
	3.
	4.
	5.

Refuting Your LAC thinking

Now that you have formulated your LAC thinking, it's time to look at it carefully to prove to yourself that it's irrational. Providing such a proof in cognitive-behavior therapy is known as *refutation*.

To illustrate (using the example from Exercise 3.4), suppose you are thinking:

1. Others should never treat me unfairly.
2. But my boss ranked me out in front of my co-workers.
3. So, the way my boss treated me was horrible.
4. So, my boss is such a worthless slimeball.
5. So, I can't help being so angry at my boss.

Given the above reasoning as an example, Table 3.1 provides examples of some rational questions you can ask yourself in refuting the irrational parts of your own LAC thinking. These irrational parts are Premise 1 and Conclusions 3, 4, and 5:

TABLE 3.1

Example of refutation of Premises 1 and Conclusions 3, 4, and 5 of LAC thinking

Part of Your LAC thinking to Be Refuted	Ask Yourself This Question to Refute Given Part of Your LAC Thinking
1. Others should never treat me unfairly.	*Where is it written that others should never treat me unfairly?*
	Answer: Nowhere except in my head!
Premise 1 again	*Have you ever treated anyone else unfairly?*
	Answer: If so then you have a double standard!
3. So, the way my boss treated me was horrible.	*Is it really "horrible"?*
	Answer: If this is truly "horrible" then how would you comparatively rank tsunamis, earthquakes, and being boiled alive on a slow boil in olive oil?
Conclusion 3 again	*What is truly "horrible" anyway? Don't I decide that myself?*
	Answer: This is my subjective value judgment. So, if it's "horrible" only if I say so, then it's not horrible if I *don't* say so!

TABLE 3.1
Continued

Part of Your LAC thinking to Be Refuted	Ask Yourself This Question to Refute Given Part of Your LAC Thinking
4. So, my boss is such a worthless slimeball.	*Is there anyone, including myself, who has never treated anyone else unfairly?*
	Answer: If not, then that would mean we are all worthless slimeballs, which would be absurd!
Conclusion 4 again	*Has your boss ever done anything worthy?*
	Answer: If so, then how can he be *worthless*!
5. So, I can't help being so angry at my boss.	*Is it really true that I can't or that I am just telling myself I can't?*
	Answer: I may *feel* like I can't help my anger because I'm demanding that others not treat me the way my boss treated me; but feeling like I can't does not mean I *really* can't!

It's now time for you to refute your own LAC thinking in Exercise 3.5.

EXERCISE 3.5

Asking yourself the questions provided in Table 3.1 (as relevant), refute Premise 1 and Conclusions 3, 4, and 5 of each of the LAC thinking chains you have constructed in Exercise 3.4. Write down the irrational premise or conclusion and your respective refutation of it in the respective columns in Table 3.1A.

TABLE 3.1A
Refutations of my LAC thinking

My LAC Thinking	My Refutation
Chain 1:	
Premise 1:	Refutation of Premise 1:
Conclusion 3:	Refutation of Conclusion 3:
Conclusion 4:	Refutation of Conclusion 4:
Conclusion 5:	Refutation of Conclusion 5:
Chain 2:	
Premise 1:	Refutation of Premise 1:
Conclusion 3:	Refutation of Conclusion 3:
Conclusion 4:	Refutation of Conclusion 4:
Conclusion 5:	Refutation of Conclusion 5:

TABLE 3.1A
Continued

My LAC Thinking	My Refutation
Chain 3:	
Premise 1:	Refutation of Premise 1:
Conclusion 3:	Refutation of Conclusion 3:
Conclusion 4:	Refutation of Conclusion 4:
Conclusion 5:	Refutation of Conclusion 5:
Chain 4:	
Premise 1:	Refutation of Premise 1:
Conclusion 3:	Refutation of Conclusion 3:
Conclusion 4:	Refutation of Conclusion 4:
Conclusion 5:	Refutation of Conclusion 5:
Chain 5:	
Premise 1:	Refutation of Premise 1:
Conclusion 3:	Refutation of Conclusion 3:
Conclusion 4:	Refutation of Conclusion 4:
Conclusion 5:	Refutation of Conclusion 5:

4. EMBRACING YOUR GUIDING VIRTUES

The guiding virtues introduced in this section will help you to overcome your LAC and set you free to attain greater anger control. These virtues are *Courage, Respect for Others*, and *Temperance*. Embracing these virtues will counteract your tendencies to demand that you not ever be treated unfairly by others; and to allow this demand to draw you into a sense of powerlessness over self-defeating anger amplified by disempowering language. These virtues will replace your disempowering language with the language of rational assessment of the gravity of the misdeed, rather than damning the doer. They will promote an awareness of your own contribution to your anger, rather than blaming it entirely on someone else; and they will promote feelings of empowerment to control your emotional response to the perceived unfairness.

Before proceeding, please carefully review the definitions of these virtues in Table 3.2.

These virtues set exciting goals for you in overcoming your LAC! They are ideals and therefore not 100% attainable, which means you can continue to get better and better at

TABLE 3.2
Definitions of your guiding virtues

Guiding Virtue	Description
1. Courage	Confronting adversity without under- or overestimating the danger. It means fearing things to the extent that it is reasonable to fear them and, in the face of danger, acting according to the merits of the situation.
2. Respect for Others	Unconditional respect for the worth and dignity of other human beings.
3. Temperance	Taking responsibility for, and exercising control over one's emotions without making excuses, and without first having to overcome irrational emotional tendencies.

them. As imperfect creatures we human beings always have ahead of us the task of self-improvement. This is what makes life interesting. If you were already perfect there would be nothing to strive for and life would be boring!

Courage

In the context of anger control, Courage means rationally confronting the threat others pose to you without over- or under-inflating it. A sarcastic joke "at your expense" is not a kind gesture but it is also not a homicidal assault on your life. Putting the perceived offense into perspective does indeed draw on rational constraint in assessing the severity of the misdeed. It means addressing and seeking redress for the misdeed in a reasonable manner, for instance, by rational discussion or legal means rather than by violence or other unlawful means; and then being willing to move on with your life instead of being consumed by hatred or animosity towards the other.

So how courageous are you? Exercise 3.6 can help you to reflect on this question.

EXERCISE 3.6

1. Briefly describe how you tend to deal with perceived wrongdoings by others, and what you might do differently to exercise Courage.

Respect for Others

In the context of anger control, having respect for others means avoiding name-calling and personal attacks. It also means sticking to assessing the deed instead of the doer. So, what another person did may be misguided, unfair, unethical, inconsiderate, a violation of your rights, unlawful, or degrading; but this does not mean the person performing this action is a rotten SOB, a moron, a piece of poop, or a stupid jackass. While the former assessment of deeds may lead to actions aimed at remediating the wrongdoing, the latter helps to generate and sustain self-defeating anger. So, you may end up regretting the verbal assault (or physical confrontation that might be precipitated by it).

This does not mean that getting angry at someone else's mistreatment of you is irrational. Indeed, you can be (and feel) angry within rational limits. This means that you do not work yourself up by catastrophizing and globally damning others. It means that you do not thereby disempower yourself and then deny your capacity to let go of your anger and move on with your life. For, the person who respects others realizes that human beings (including oneself) are imperfect creatures who do not always treat others fairly, and that, therefore, it is unrealistic to demand otherwise.

How respectful of others are you? Exercise 3.7 can help you reflect on this question.

EXERCISE 3.7

1. Briefly describe how you tend to deal with the unfairness or wrongdoings of others.

```
┌─────────────────────────────────────────────────┐
│                                                 │
│                                                 │
│                                                 │
│                                                 │
│                                                 │
└─────────────────────────────────────────────────┘
```

2. What changes do you think are needed for you to become more respectful of others?

```
┌─────────────────────────────────────────────────┐
│                                                 │
│                                                 │
│                                                 │
│                                                 │
│                                                 │
└─────────────────────────────────────────────────┘
```

Temperance

In the context of anger control, Temperance means not overreacting emotionally to mistreatment by others. It is thus also a condition of Courage since the latter requires keeping a rational perspective on mistreatment by others. Of course, even people who tend to be temperate may lose their tempers at times. So, it is important not to demand perfection in emotional control. As a human, you are a work in process and always in a state of becoming. You are not born with such willpower, indeed, quite the opposite. Consider the temper tantrums young children tend to display, and this fact should be apparent; so, it takes practice.

Temperance also involves taking responsibility for irrational outbursts of anger. Clearly, without such accountability one is not likely to make progress toward becoming more temperate. For people with LAC, taking responsibility entails avoiding rationalizations proclaiming lack of ability to control one's anger, and instead accepting one's capacity to make constructive change through practice.

"Easier said than done" is a common rejoinder by many who have LAC; and this is a reasonable response, because making constructive change involves more than simply saying you can. The latter is an important condition, but you must also back this up by putting in the effort. This means persistent practice along the lines described later in this chapter (section on "Creating a Cognitive-Behavioral Plan").

Building guiding virtues such as Temperance begin with awareness of how you may presently be approaching situations that call for controlling your anger. Exercise 3.8 gives you an opportunity to reflect on this question.

So how temperate are you? Exercise 3.8 can help you reflect on this question.

EXERCISE 3.8

1. Discuss briefly how you usually deal with situations that call for emotional control. Illustrate your response using an example or two.

```
┌─────────────────────────────────────────────────────────────────────┐
│                                                                       │
│                                                                       │
│                                                                       │
│                                                                       │
│                                                                       │
│                                                                       │
└─────────────────────────────────────────────────────────────────────┘
```

2. Does this way of dealing with such situations help to build Temperance? Why or why not?

```
┌─────────────────────────────────────────────────────────────────────┐
│                                                                       │
│                                                                       │
│                                                                       │
│                                                                       │
│                                                                       │
│                                                                       │
└─────────────────────────────────────────────────────────────────────┘
```

3. What do you think you could do differently to increase Temperance when you confront situations that call for emotional control?

```
┌─────────────────────────────────────────────────────────────────────┐
│                                                                       │
│                                                                       │
│                                                                       │
│                                                                       │
│                                                                       │
└─────────────────────────────────────────────────────────────────────┘
```

As you can see, the virtues of Courage, Respect for Others, and Temperance "hang together" so that in working on one of them, you are also working on the others. So, to have Courage you would need to have Temperance, and to have Temperance you would need to have Respect for Others (since thinking that fosters lack of Respect for Others such as damnation of others fuels irrational anger).

Let's now do some further preliminary self-reflections about these three virtues with Exercise 3.9.

EXERCISE 3.9

1. How do you think embracing these virtues could change your life?

2. Do you know anyone who embraces these virtues? How does this impact their lives and the lives of those around them?

Would you like to be more like these people? Why, or why not?

---

5. EMPOWERING WISDOM FROM THE SAGES
ON PURSUING THE VIRTUES

Below is some empowering wisdom from some of the world's most revered thinkers on how to develop Courage, Respect for Others, and Temperance. These counsels can help you form a worldview that can help overcome your LAC!

Courage

Empowering Wisdom from Epictetus:

- *Imagine much worse, comparatively, and you will no longer think the worst of your actual situation.*

When you put things into perspective by doing a comparative analysis, you can get a clearer idea of just how distorted your negative assessment actually is. So, you tell yourself that your boss' passing you up for that promotion was really a terrible thing. How terrible? "Well about a 9 or 10 on the bad scale!" where 10 is the absolute worst thing possible.

Indeed, it may *feel* like a 9 or 10 when you imagine your boss deliberately passing over you for someone who has less experience. And that angry feeling boiling up inside of you, really does feel super intense. However, if you imagine your boss going on a rampage, murdering all his employees, including yourself, then, comparatively speaking, it becomes clear that his not promoting you was not a 9 or 10 on the bad scale. For, if not promoting you were the worst or near-worst thing possible, then where would you rank the murderous rampage on the bad scale? Accordingly, ancient Roman philosopher Epictetus (1758) admonishes,

> Keep before your eyes day by day death and exile, and everything that seems terrible, but most of all death; and then you will never have any abject thought, nor will you ever yearn for anything beyond measure.

In other words, in keeping in mind how much worse things could have been, you will feel better, and stop wishing things were not so "terrible"! This broader, more realistic perspective can, in turn, help you to build Courage in confronting the apparent misdeeds of others.

Empowering Wisdom from Friedrich Nietzsche:

- *Let everything wicked in others inspire you to become the opposite.*
- *Allow your inventive faculty and spirit to develop into subtlety and daring under oppression and compulsion, and your Will to Life to become the unconditioned Will to Power.*

The famous 19th-century German philosopher, Friedrich Nietzsche tells you to think of misfortune and mistreatment as opportunities to make yourself stronger. Instead of feeling sorry for yourself because you were mistreated, Nietzsche (1954) in his work entitled, *Beyond Good and Evil*, tells you that it is a fallacy to think that you will thrive in a world in which things come easy for you and everyone treats you just as you want to be treated. No, he says, it is just the opposite! He states,

> [W]e believe that severity, violence, slavery, danger in the street and in the heart, secrecy, stoicism, tempter's art and devilry of every kind—that everything wicked, terrible, tyrannical, predatory, and serpentine in man, serves as well for the elevation of the human species as its opposite.
>
> (Sec. 44, p. 429)

Thus, the black man who has suffered racial oppression becomes a civil rights activist to advance important legislative changes. The woman who has been a victim of physical and/or sexual assault becomes a motivational speaker for domestic violence victims. The hourly worker who is unjustly laid off goes back to school to become an attorney who defends workers against unfair labor practices. Compare these cases to the person who flies into a rage and winds up in jail; turns to drugs or alcohol; or blames others for her lack of ambition. While the former builds Courage, the latter keeps you in a perpetual state of *self*-oppression.

The person who is courageous, explains Nietzsche (1909), allows "his inventive faculty and dissembling power [spirit] ... to develop into subtlety and daring under long oppression and compulsion, and his Will to Life ... increased to the unconditioned Will to Power" (Sec. 44, p. 59). Shifting your attention away from the negative polarity of language like "terrible," "tyrannical," "predatory," and "serpentine," toward positive language such as "inventive faculty," "spirit," "Will to Life," and "unconditional Will to Power" can be incredibly powerful in counteracting this negative-mindedness and inspiring Courage!

Empowering Wisdom from Martin Luther King:

• *Forgive your enemy, and let the evil act no longer remain a barrier to a fresh start and new beginning.*

The idea of forgiveness is entrenched in both Eastern and Western traditions. Both Buddhists and Christians see anger and hatred as barriers to love. Building love requires their surrender, which requires forgiveness. Without forgiveness, we remain in a state of persistent antagonism. Peace requires forgiveness. Martin Luther King (2012) eloquently expressed this idea:

> He who is devoid of the power to forgive is devoid of the power to love. ... Forgiveness does not mean ignoring what has been done or putting a false label on an evil act. It means, rather, that the evil act no longer remains as a barrier to the relationship. Forgiveness is a catalyst creating the atmosphere necessary for a fresh start and a new beginning. It is the lifting of a burden or the cancelling of a debt ... Forgiveness means reconciliation, a coming together again. Without this, no man can love his enemies. The degree to which we are able to forgive determines the degree to which we are able to love our enemies.
>
> (ch. 5)

Once there is forgiveness in the sense of reconciliation and a coming together again, the Christian Biblical prescription to "love your enemy" loses its paradoxical aura; for in forgiveness there is letting go of the ill will entailed by calling someone your enemy. In letting go the ill will, there emerges the possibility of building a respectful and even a loving relationship.

King was an exemplar of forgiveness. His goal was to use love, and hence forgiveness to disarm racism and its oppressive institutions. Indeed, violence begets violence, but love and forgiveness are stopgaps to violence and war. According to King, the former is "an absolute necessity for our survival" and "the key to the solution of the problems of our world."

Indeed, it takes Courage to forgive someone who has done you wrong. But in the end, it can be self-defeating to hold a grudge, or keep yourself mired in agitation and fruitless conflict when, through forgiveness and establishing a "new beginning," there is potential for mutual cooperation, respect, and even love.

Exercise 3.10 can help you reflect on the implications of the counsel offered by Nietzsche, the Dalai Lama, and King for managing your anger.

EXERCISE 3.10

Discuss briefly how you might use the counsel offered by Epictetus, Nietzsche, and King to be more courageous in managing your anger. Give at least two examples.

Respect for Others

Empowering Wisdom from Immanuel Kant:

• *Treat other people (as well as yourself) as ends in themselves, that is, as beings who must not be used merely as a means, and who are, therefore, worthy of your respect.*

German philosopher, Immanuel Kant (1785), is well known for having said that we should treat others as well as ourselves as "ends in themselves" and not as "mere means." He explains,

> Rational beings ... are called persons, because their very nature points them out as ends in themselves, that is as something which must not be used merely as means ... and is an object of respect.

What he means here is that people are not objects, whose worth and dignity depend on a particular use, such that if they cease to serve this use, they lose their value. For example, when your pen runs out of ink you throw it away. However, people are not like pens, which are disposable when they cease to serve a certain purpose. Instead, people are "ends in themselves," not "mere means" or instruments to be used for this or that purpose. That is, they have *unconditional worth and dignity*. It does not matter whether they mess up, do bad things, or are just not helpful.

According to Kant, this value exists because people are very special. Unlike the object, people have *dignity* because they *have autonomy*; that is, they can think and make decisions. They can act rationally and think for themselves, even if they don't always do so. This marks them out as subjects that have dignity and are proper objects of respect. If you are religious you might even see this value as arising as a result of being children of the same God. In any event, this value is unconditional.

So if someone does something wrong to you, you make a fundamental error by assuming that it is permissible to denounce this person as a "worthless piece of garbage" (or the like) and then proceed to treat them as such. Instead, because persons are capable of rational thinking and self-determination, it behooves you to treat them as such. Taking a wrongdoer to court is okay because it respects their rational dignity. They are held accountable. Explaining to them what they did wrong is also okay for the same reason. Severing a (business, professional, or personal) relationship with others who abuse the relationship is okay because it also holds the parties accountable and therefore respects their rational dignity. However, manipulating them physically or emotionally or otherwise treating them like objects is not okay, according to Kant.

Empowering Wisdom from Martin Buber:

- *Say the primary word "I–Thou" to someone, and He is not He or She, bounded from every other He and She, … he is Thou and fills the heavens.*

Existential philosopher Martin Buber puts an Eastern twist on Kant's distinction between "ends in themselves" (persons) and "mere means" (objects). He distinguishes between "I–It" and "I–Thou" relationships. In the I–It relationship, you look upon either other people or material objects as something to be used for this or that purpose. You regard the subject as having value only because it serves a purpose, not because it has value in itself. For example, you might see a tree as useful to shade you from the damaging rays of the sun. You might also see another person as an "It" whose value lies in a service performed, for example, someone to pick up your trash or mow your lawn.

On the other hand, when you bear an I–Thou relation to someone or something, you look upon the subject *as a whole*, not in terms of a service performed or other function. Further, you see yourself as bound up intimately with this subject so that there is no separation between you and this other being. Even further, you experience a union with all else in the world, so that there are no partitions between you and all else that is. Think about a walk in nature where you see an animal in its natural habitat; you see the surrounding vista of trees, sky, water, and feel a sense of bondedness with all of it. This is in contrast to walking through a forest with fear of being attacked by a wild animal. In this case, you see the animal and nature itself as an "It" and experience yourself as separate from it.

Now you can also experience another person as a "Thou" rather than an "It." Here is how Buber (1937) expresses this idea:

> If I face a human being as my Thou, and say the primary word I–Thou to him, he is not a thing among things, and does not consist of things. This human being is not He or She, bounded from every other He and She, a specific point in space and time within the net of the world ; nor is he a nature able to be experienced and described, a loose bundle of named qualities. But with no neighbour, and whole in himself, he is Thou and fills the heavens. This does not mean that nothing exists except himself. But all else lives in his light.
>
> (p. 8)

In entering into such a relationship with other people, you can get past your low LAC because you are no longer demanding that this person treat you fairly. You are not looking at him as a something that acts this or that way. You are not analyzing him; you are seeing him holistically and everything else in the universe coalescing with him—and you. So there is no You there and Me here. We are intimately integrated in one unified whole. So there is no room for critique, catastrophizing, and damning. This is the language of I–It relationships according to Buber, not that of I–Thou.

Calling someone "Thou" can be accomplished through compassion-based meditation, which you will have an opportunity to practice in the section in this chapter on "Working on Your Cognitive-Behavior Plan."

So how do *you* view the status and worth of other people? Exercise 3.11 can help you reflect on this question.

EXERCISE 3.11

Discuss briefly your own approach to dealing with others who you think have treated you unfairly, and how you might use the counsel offered by Kant and Buber to become more other respecting. Give at least two examples.

Temperance

Empowering Wisdom from Marcus Aurelius and Epictetus:

- *No wrongful act of another brings shame on you (Aurelius).*
- *You are disturbed, not by the events in your life, but by your judgments about them (Epictetus).*

According to Epictetus (1758), people disturb themselves by the judgments they make about the events in the world or about others. "Men are disturbed," he says, "not by things, but by the principles and notions which they form concerning things" (sec. 5). So, blaming others for your anger is irrational. After all, it is you who tells yourself how *awful* it is that this *rotten person* did such a *horrible thing* to you (such as making an off-color joke about you). With this judgment expressed using negatively charged language, you place the blame on others rather than on yourself. However, the other person did not put these negative words in your head. *You* did that, and as a result you succeed in amplifying and sustaining your anger.

Give up the catastrophic and damning language, admonishes Epictetus, and your anger will fade away. You have the power! Ancient Roman thinker, Marcus Aurelius (1862), backs this point up. "Take away these opinions," he says, "and resolve to dismiss thy judgement about an act as if it were something grievous, and thy anger is gone." And Aurelius asks, "How then shall I take away these opinions?" And he answers: "By reflecting that no wrongful act of another brings shame on thee." In other words, when others treat you badly, they bring shame on themselves, not on you. So why on earth should *you* get angry? Shame on them, not on you!

However, in damning the other and losing your temper, this *does* reflect badly on your exercise of self-control. On the other hand, in keeping your cool, you can work on building Temperance, which is a positive gain. "There I go again, blaming this person for my anger when I don't have to *demand* that I be treated fairly in the first place, and then *damn the person* for not doing so. Here's my chance to build character by remaining calm!"

Empowering Wisdom from the Dalai Lama:

- *Without enemies you could not fully engage in the practice of patience—tolerance and forbearance, so an enemy is the greatest teacher of altruism, and for that reason, instead of hating, we must respect him.*

Instead of catastrophizing about those who treat us unfairly, the Dalai Lama (2006) tells us to be appreciative of them for what they can teach us! The Venerable one states,

> The worst consequence of not being mindful of the unintended kindness of others comes into view when we consider our enemies. Without enemies you could not fully engage in the practice of patience—tolerance and forbearance. We need enemies, and should be grateful to them. From the viewpoint of training in altruism, an enemy is really your guru, your teacher; only an enemy can teach you tolerance. An enemy is the greatest teacher of altruism, and for that reason, instead of hating, we must respect him.

Indeed, it takes Temperance to say, "I do not approve of what this person has done to me, but at the same time, it has afforded me an opportunity to build Tolerance, Temperance, and Respect for Others." Much easier to go into a fit of rage and to end up regretting it later. Facing iniquity does not mean permitting it to persist. However, in addressing the harm, there is little sense in flying into a rage. The harm has been done and cannot be undone, but how one reacts is still in your power.

Exercise 3.12 now gives you an opportunity to do some preliminary reflection on the counsel offered by Aurelius, Epictetus, and the Dalai Lama.

EXERCISE 3.12

Discuss briefly how you could use the counsel offered by Epictetus, Aurelius, and the Dalai Lama to become more temperate in dealing with others. Give at least two examples.

```
┌─────────────────────────────────────────────────────────────────────┐
│                                                                       │
│                                                                       │
│                                                                       │
│                                                                       │
│                                                                       │
│                                                                       │
│                                                                       │
└─────────────────────────────────────────────────────────────────────┘
```

Do you have a favorite sage of your own who you think gives constructive advice on how to be more prudent, perseverant, or patient? Add them to your list by completing Exercise 3.13!

EXERCISE 3.13

1. If you have a favorite sage of your own who offers empowering wisdom on how to be more courageous, respectful of others, or temperate then formulate this counsel below in the space indicated. (Even if you don't know the name of the person from whom the advice comes, that's still okay.)

Additional Empowering Wisdom for Courage

Additional Empowering Wisdom Respect for Others

Additional Empowering Wisdom for Temperance

Compiling a Master List of Empowering Wisdom

Nietzsche, Epictetus, and King have given you language to formulate their learned counsel that can go on a list of empowering wisdom to inspire Courage. For instance, for each of the formulations in the Courage column of Table 3.3, focus, one at a time, on the formulation

TABLE 3.3
Empowering wisdom regarding Courage, Respect for Others, and Temperance

Courage	*Respect for Others*	*Temperance*
Epictetus:	**Kant:**	**Aurelius:**
Imagine much worse, comparatively, and you will no longer think the worst of your actual situation.	Treat other people (as well as yourself) as ends in themselves, that is, as beings who must not be used merely as a means, and who are, therefore, worthy of your respect.	No wrongful act of another brings shame on you.
Nietzsche:		**Epictetus:**
Let everything wicked in others inspire you to become the opposite.		You are disturbed, not by the events in your life, but by your judgments about them.
__Allow your inventive faculty and spirit to develop into subtlety and daring under oppression and compulsion, and your Will to Life to become the unconditioned Will to Power.	**Buber:**	**Dalai Lama:**
King:	Say the primary word "I–Thou" to someone, and He is not He or She, bounded from every other He and She, ... he is Thou and fills the heavens.	Without enemies you could not fully engage in the practice of patience—tolerance and forbearance, so an enemy is the greatest teacher of altruism, and for that reason, instead of hating, we must respect him.
Forgive your enemy, and let the evil act no longer remain a barrier to a fresh start and new beginning.		

with your mind's eye, and key into how it *feels*. *Does it make you want to be more courageous in taking risks*!? If yes, keep it on your list of empowering wisdom; if not, take it off or change the language!

Similarly, for each of the formulations in the Respect for Others column of Table 3.3, focus, one at a time, on the formulation with your mind's eye, and key into how it *feels*. *Does it make you feel more empowered to unconditionally respect others?* If yes, keep it on your list of empowering wisdom; if not, take it off or change the language!

Finally, for each of the formulations in the Temperance column of Table 3.3, focus, one at a time, on the formulation with your mind's eye, and key into how it *feels*. *Does it make you feel more in control of your anger?* If yes, keep it on your list of empowering wisdom; if not, take it off or change the language!

Have you found the language in Table 3.3 to have a positive feeling of empowerment or consolation? Language use is an important part of why the wisdom of the sages seems to help us to feel more inspired to take risks.

Exercise 3.14 gives you the opportunity to expand or adjust the language and/or content of your lists to resonate especially with you.

EXERCISE 3.14

This exercise will help you to develop a *master list of wisdom that is especially empowering for you*.

Please modify Table 3.3 in responding to the following instructions:

1. For each of the three guiding virtues, place a checkmark in front of each learned counsel you intend to use. Your selections should resonate with you, that is, feel uplifting, consoling, or otherwise empowering to you.

2. If you are not satisfied with the formulation of any of the counsels in Table 3.3, on a separate piece of paper, please rewrite it using language that resonates with you. For example, when I think of Epictetus' counsel about Temperance, I think of "power," "freedom," and "taking control." You are encouraged to reformulate or tweak the sages' counsel using any language that is more empowering for you!

3. Please also add any empowering insights to Table 3.3 that you may have formulated in Exercise 3.12. Again, it is important that the language you use is empowering *for you*.

4. Now, congratulate yourself! You now have a master list of wisdom that is empowering for you!

---

6. CREATING A COGNITIVE-BEHAVIORAL PLAN

Are you ready to harness the wisdom of the sages to build a plan of action for overcoming your LAC? This will open new avenues of freedom for you!

Suppose you have told yourself that you can't control your anger when anyone talks trash to you. As soon as anyone "gives you lip," you feel this anger swelling up inside of you and you "unload" on the "smartass who started up with you." Occasionally, it has gotten physical, and you have sometimes been arrested.

Now let's say you realize that this has been a serious problem of yours since it has adversely affected your personal and business life. So, you resolve to be more *courageous* in the future, in dealing with people who treat you unfairly, by following the following plan:

- Try to put the misdeeds of others in perspective by realizing that relative to some really bad things like death, the things you get enraged about are not all that bad.
- Reframe the misdeeds of others as an opportunity to build your character by doing the opposite of what others who mistreat you are doing.
- Take advantage of such opportunities by acting on them. For example, taking rational actions to rectify the situation, if necessary, without overreacting.

To exercise *Respect for Others*, you decide to

- Eliminate words like "smartass" and other damning names from your vocabulary, instead evaluating the merit of the deed, not the doer.
- Hold others accountable in a way that treats them like persons, not objects. So you don't threaten them, use physical force, or otherwise attempt to manipulate or cajole them.

To build *Temperance* you plan to

- Stop blaming others for your anger and instead focus on the negative judgements you are making (your demand for fair treatment; your catastrophizing when you don't get it; and your damning of others) to *upset yourself*.
- Take a page from the playbill of Marcus Aurelius by reframing the misdeeds of others as not reflecting negatively on you.

Now, it's your turn to build a plan of action based on the learned counsel you have received. Exercise 3.15 will help with this!

EXERCISE 3.15

1. From the five situations in which you have anger control issues, which you described in Exercise 3.2, choose one of them that you can easily place yourself in. (Recall you were asked to include at least one situation that you could arrange to be in with relative ease, in the short term). Restate the description of this situation in the space provided below:

2. Now, restate the LAC thinking you formulated in Exercise 3.4 that has blocked you from attempting to deal rationally with this situation.

1.

2.

3.

4.

5.

Using your empowering wisdom, the remainder of this exercise will help you to construct the elements of a cognitive-behavioral plan to overcome Conclusion 5 of the above LAC thinking!

3. Accordingly, using the counsel offered by Nietzsche, and Epictetus, or any empowering wisdom you may have added in Exercise 3.13 for becoming *more courageous*, what cognitive-behavioral changes would you make to overcome your LAC thinking? For example, what changes would Nietzsche tell you to make to overcome your lack of emotional control in the situation in question? What would Epictetus tell you to do differently based on his counsel about calling things "terrible"? List at least three cognitive-behavioral changes you plan to make:

1.

2.

3.

4.

5.

4. Using the counsel offered by Kant and Buber or any other empowering wisdom you may have added in Exercise 3.13 for becoming *more respectful of others*, what cognitive-behavioral changes would you make to overcome your LAC thinking? List at least three:

1.

2.

3.

4.

5.

5. Using the counsel offered by Epictetus, Aurelius, and the Dalai Lama, or any other empowering wisdom you may have added in Exercise 3.13 for becoming *more decisive*, what cognitive-behavioral changes would you make to overcome your LAC thinking? List at least two:

1.

2.

3.

4.

5.

6. Now, congratulate yourself! You have just constructed a cognitive-behavioral plan!!

7. WORKING ON YOUR COGNITIVE-BEHAVIORAL PLAN

You will now have an opportunity to begin to build your habits of Courage, Respect for Others, and Temperance instead of defaulting to your self-defeating habit of LAC thinking.

Cognitive–Affective Imagery

As you know, when folks with LAC think about being treated unfairly, they tend to *feel* threatened by the conflict with their demand for fair treatment, which leads them to catastrophize about it, damn the perpetrator, and then tell themselves they can't control their anger. "How could that SOB have the gall to treat me so awful. I can't help feeling like knocking his lights out!" Imagery exercises can help you neutralize such negative feelings. Exercise 3.16 will help you to set up and practice cognitive–affective imagery.

EXERCISE 3.16

1. Choose a formulation from the Courage column of your master list of empowering wisdom (see Exercise 3.14) that is especially empowering, consoling, or uplifting for you. Keep it in the back of your mind at this point.

2. Refer to the LAC thinking you identified in Exercise 3.15, which is fueling your low anger control in the situation you also identified in Exercise 3.15.

3. Now here are instructions for doing cognitive–affective imagery. If you are working with a therapist, the therapist can provide guidance until you get the hang of it and can do it on your own. If you are not being assisted by a therapist, then please read these directions carefully now, memorize them (three steps), and then follow the three-step sequence laid out for you below:

- Step 1: Focus your mind exclusively on your LAC thinking (as identified in Exercise 3.15). Keep going over it in your mind like you did when you first told yourself you couldn't stop being so angry. Keep it up until you feel that negative visceral threatening feeling, the clashing of your *felt need* not to be treated unfairly with the realization that you *were*, nevertheless, treated unfairly. Let yourself resonate with the feeling of powerlessness that emerges, and that "No way I can assuage this anger!" feeling.
- Step 2: At the peak of feeling this intense negative feeling, shift your focus of mind exclusively to the empowering wisdom you have selected for feeling empowered to become courageous. Let yourself *feel* the uplift, the empowerment to confront the frustration; letting yourself feel the freedom to take control.
- Step 3: Once you have fully brought yourself to resonate with the positivity of the experience, gently shift your attention to reflecting on your experience and what you have learned or discovered from it.

4. Try to reserve a time each day to practice your guided imagery exercise. Next time, however, choose a formulation from the *Respect for Others* column of your master list of empowering wisdom (see Exercise 3.14) that is especially empowering or uplifting for you.

5. Similarly, the subsequent day, repeat the exercise except this time choose wisdom from the *Temperance* column of your master list of empowering wisdom.

6. Practice regularly, shifting between your empowering wisdom to support each of the *three* guiding virtues.

7. What have you learned or discovered about yourself from your experience practicing your cognitive–affective imagery? Write down your reflections below:

My Reflections about My Experience:

```
┌─────────────────────────────────────────────────────────────────┐
│                                                                   │
│                                                                   │
│                                                                   │
│                                                                   │
│                                                                   │
│                                                                   │
│                                                                   │
└─────────────────────────────────────────────────────────────────┘
```

Great work!!

Refuting and Reframing

By inspecting your LAC thinking, premise by premise, it is possible to refute and reframe your self-defeating thinking. As discussed in the Introduction to this book, reframing involves placing your negative thinking in a more positive light. For example, to reframe your demand never to be treated unfairly (which is preventing you from managing your anger about others whom you perceive to be rude), you might take counsel from Nietzsche to see being treated unfairly as an opportunity to build Courage by dealing civilly with the person who has mistreated you. To reframe your catastrophizing about what this person has done, you can take counsel from Epictetus and think about the act in question in relation to much worse things. And to reframe your conclusion that you can't control your anger, you can key into Marcus Aurelius' idea that this person has shamed not you but himself.

Accordingly, Exercise 3.17 gives you some practice refuting and reframing your LAC thinking!

EXERCISE 3.17

1. Refer again to the LAC thinking you identified in Exercise 3.15, which is preventing you from dealing rationally with the situation you also identified in Exercise 3.15. Look carefully at Premise 1 of your LAC thinking, the premise that *demands that you not be treated unfairly.* In Exercise 3.5, you have already refuted this premise so you can see how irrational it truly is. Think about this refutation until it resonates with you, that is, you get the "I get it" feeling that this premise is truly irrational. If this doesn't happen, then go back to Exercise 3.5 and find a refutation that *does* resonate with you. In Table 3.4, write down your refutation in the refutation column for Premise 1.

Now, select empowering wisdom from one or more of your sages (it could even be wisdom you added in Exercise 3.13), and use it to reframe your demand never to be treated unfairly. In Table 3.4, write down this empowering wisdom in the reframing column for Premise 1.

2. Just as you have done for Premise 1, refute and reframe Conclusions 3, 4, and 5 of the LAC thinking you identified in Exercise 3.15. Use Table 3.4 to write down your refutation and reframing for each of these respective conclusions of your LAC thinking.

TABLE 3.4
Refuting and reframing my LAC thinking

Part	Refutation	Reframing
Premise 1		
Conclusion 3		
Conclusion 4		
Conclusion 5		

Compassion-Based Meditation

This type of meditation can be useful because it can relieve your sense of alienation from others by increasing your compassion for others, even people who did things you don't like. The idea is to break down walls so that you feel an interconnectedness with all living beings, very much the sense of unity of the "I–Thou" relationship that Buber recommends. You can do this by sending messages of "loving kindness" to others, beginning first with those with whom you already feel a bond, and then expanding your circle of beings to others outside this inner circle until it encompasses *all living beings*. Exercise 3.18 can help you to build this uplifting feeling of interconnectedness and thereby overcome your LAC.

EXERCISE 3.18

1. Please listen to the guided meditation audio recording called "Loving Kindness Meditation" presented by Dr. Kristin Neff. This audio recording is (at the time of this writing) freely accessible from the following link: https://self-compassion.org/guided-self-compassion-meditations-mp3-2/. (If unavailable, find an alternative guided loving kindness meditation, on the Internet.) When you have finished following the audio tape, respond to the below questions.

2. Reflect on your *demand* that others never treat you unfairly. How does this demand *feel* when you think of your loving kindness wishes and feelings for the totality of all living beings, keeping in mind how seamlessly interconnected you are with all others in this grand totality of life?

3. How do the things that previously aroused your anger now feel in the light of your boundless interconnection with all life?

4. When you reflect on your LAC thinking (as formulated in Exercise 3.15), how does this thinking now feel in relation to the grander scope of your connectedness with all living beings?

5. Please feel free to repeat this exercise as often as you like, especially when you are beginning to feel frustrated by your everyday encounters.

Acting on Your Goal

This is the final stage of your process of working on your cognitive-behavioral plan. It involves doing all the things you listed in your cognitive-behavioral plan, which you developed in Exercise 3.15. This also includes *making behavioral changes*. For example, instead of acting aggressively to others who have mistreated you, you speak sternly but respectfully to them about their misdeeds, take legal action (if reasonable), or cease personal contact if the misdeed warrants it.

Indeed, it is only through continuously practicing the cognitive-behavioral skills you have learned in this chapter that you can continue to develop your guiding virtues of Courage, Respect for Others, and Temperance. This means practicing refuting and reframing your LAC thinking using the counsel from your sages to attain your guiding virtues; it means practicing your cognitive–affective imagery, and loving kindness meditations; and making behavioral changes consistent with these cognitive changes.

Exercise 3.19 will guide you through this process.

EXERCISE 3.19

1. Review the cognitive-behavioral items on your behavioral plan created in Exercise 3.15.

2. Review the refutation and reframing of Premise 1 and Conclusions 3, 4, and 5 of your LFT thinking which you developed in Exercise 3.17.

3. Implement each of the *behavioral* elements in your plan. This means changing the way you relate behaviorally to others you think have mistreated you.

4. Continue to refute and reframe your LAC thinking (Exercise 3.17), while, and even after you make behavioral changes. Also continue to practice your cognitive–affective imagery (Exercise 3.16). Keep in mind that you are not expected to be perfect. Losing your temper does not mean that you have failed at making constructive change. It means that you are a fallible human who needs to continue to work at it. It is important not to become discouraged.

5. Provide your reflections in the below space about your experience in acting on your goal:

6. This is an incredible milestone, so congratulate yourself!

Working on Your Other Low Anger Control Situations

In Exercise 3.2, you described at least three situations in which you tend to experience intense anger, which you would like to overcome. Now you are in a position to continue to work on low anger control in these other contexts.

The process is the same, and you have already gone through it. You have also already formulated the LAC thinking chains blocking you from dealing with the other situations you described in Exercise 3.2 and have also refuted Premise 1 and Conclusions 3, 4, and 5 of each of them. So, you are already well on your way to addressing these other situations and strengthening your guiding virtues. Here is a summary of the process:

1. Formulate your LAC thinking (Exercise 3.4).
2. Refute Premise 1 and Conclusions 3, 4, and 5 of this thinking (Exercise 3.5).
3. Embrace your guiding virtues (Exercises 3.6 through 3.9).
4. Get empowering wisdom from the sages on pursuing the virtues (Exercises 3.10 through 3.14).
5. Use this learned counsel to construct a cognitive-behavioral plan (Exercise 3.15).
6. Work on your cognitive-behavioral plan (Exercises 3.16 through 3.19).

Using the exercise sets in this chapter as the framework, you can continue to build and strengthen your guiding virtues of Courage, Respect for Others, and Temperance by regularly going through the above six steps.

Congratulations and keep up the excellent work!

REFERENCES

Aurelius, M. (1862). Meditations. Trans. Long, G. John Wiley & Sons. Retrieved from http://classics.mit.edu//Antoninus/meditations.html

Buber, M. (1937). *I and Thou*. Trans. Smith, R.G., T.&T. Clark. Retrieved from https://archive.org/details/IAndThou_572/mode/2up

Dalai Lama (2006). *How to expand love: Widening the circle of loving relationships*. Atria.

Epictetus. (1758). *Enchiridion*. Trans. Carter, E. Retrieved from http://classics.mit.edu/Epictetus/epicench.html

Kant, I. (1785) Fundamental Principles of the Metaphysics of Morals Trans. Thomas Kingsmill Abbott. Gutenberg ebook. Retrieved from www.gutenberg.org/files/5682/5682-h/5682-h.htm

King, M.L. (2012). A gift of love: Sermons from "Strength to Love" and other preachings (King Legacy). Beacon. Retrieved from www.penguinrandomhouse.ca/books/212014/a-gift-of-love-by-martin-luther-king-jr/9780807000632/excerpt

Nietzsche, F. (1954). *Beyond good and evil*. Trans. Helen Zimmern. In *The philosophy of Nietzsche*. Random House.

4

Overcoming Phobias

As you have seen in the introduction to this book, phobic *can't*stipation is an impulsive type of *can't*stipation that sustains intense fear. Phobias always involve an intense, irrational fear of something, and refusal to accept freedom and responsibility to control this fear. They are sustained by *distorting the danger of the thing in question and then catastrophizing about it*, which, in turn, keeps you in a constant state of anxiety. Because the thing in question *feels* so threatening to you, you deny your capacity to control the fear, which can adversely affect your sense of wellbeing. Often, folks with phobias feel like their very lives are being threatened, even though the probability of dying is non-existent or remote.

The objects of phobias may be *specific* such as spiders, dogs, blood, certain foods, and needles; *situations* such as flying, being alone, being in crowed spaces, being in the dark, riding in a car, being away from home, dying, and being touched. The situations may also be *social* such as speaking to strangers or being observed by others. As a result of your phobia, you may restrict your range of activities and potential for happiness. For example, if you have a phobia of flying, you may turn down a job with great career prospects if it requires air travel. You may force your family to sit long hours in a car or on a train to reach your vacation destination due to your flying phobia.

1. GOALS OF THE CHAPTER

Accordingly, the goals of this chapter are to:

1. Increase awareness of the thinking and language you are using that sustains your phobia.
2. Refute this thinking.
3. Identify guiding virtues that counteract your phobic thinking.
4. Identify empowering wisdom from great sages on how to seek these virtues.
5. Use this learned counsel to construct a cognitive-behavioral plan for building your virtues.
6. Work on your plan to help you overcome your phobia and increase your range of freedom.

2. THE NATURE OF PHOBIC THINKING

Here are some examples of phobic thinking:

- If I fly, then sooner or later the plane will crash, and I'll be dead.
  So, if I fly, it will be *like a nightmare for me*.
  So, I can't fly.

DOI: 10.4324/9781003035282-5

- If I'm in a crowded place, I will probably have a panic attack.
  So, if I am in crowded places, it's *horrible* for me.
  So, I can't be in a crowded place.
- If a dog comes near me, it will probably attack and bite me.
  So, if a dog comes near me, it's *awful*.
  So, I can't have a dog come near me.
- If I go in an elevator, it will (probably) get stuck between floors, and I will suffocate to death.
  So, if I go in an elevator, it will be *a slow torturous death*.
  So, I can't go in an elevator.
- If I am in the pitch dark, then I won't be able to see.
  If that happens, it's *like being buried alive*.
  So, I can't be in the pitch dark.
- If am in a high place (such as the top story of a skyscraper), I will fall to my death.
  So, it is *terrifying* for me to be in high places.
  So, I can't be in high places.
- If I see blood, it makes me sick to my stomach and I feel like fainting.
  So, if I see blood, it's *just too disgusting* for me.
  So, I can't see blood.
- If it rains when I'm driving, I will probably get into an accident and die.
  So, if it rains when I'm driving, it's *the worst thing that can happen to me*.
  So, I can't have it rain when I'm driving.
- If I leave the house, I might get sick and no one would be there to help me.
  So, it would be *crazy* for me to leave the house.
  So, I can't leave the house.

In each of these cases, you imagine the object in question and associate it with a negative event (the plane crashing and killing you, having a panic attack, a dog attacking and biting you, the elevator getting stuck with you in it, being in the dark unable to see) and then use catastrophic terms to rate the event in question. Notice the terms in italics:

- nightmare
- horrible
- awful
- slow, torturous death
- like being buried alive
- terrifying
- just too disgusting
- the worst thing that can happen to me
- crazy.

These words express the dread you feel inside when you think of the object of your phobia, and they also add fuel to the fire, that is, help to amplify the dread. It is the old "one two" where first you exaggerate the probable adverse effects on you of the object in question, and then you rate it using such catastrophic terms. In some cases, you paint a macabre picture in your mind, such as "slow torturous death" or "like being buried alive."

So how did you come to associate such negative events with the object or situation in question in the first place? In at least some cases, there may be a genetic tendency to fear the object or situation such as fear of heights (Tucker, 2013). However, most often there is a negative experience you may have had associated with the object or situation (Healthline, n.d.).

For example, you may have had a dog attack you; or you may have been caught in an elevator when you were a child. The feelings you had when you had these experiences are saved in your brain's emotional memory circuits (in the amygdala and hippocampus) and they replay in your mind when you think of a similar object or situation to the one that initiated the fear, for example, you think of going into an elevator.

However, you are not a merely passive recipient of your phobic response. Instead, *you* sustain the fear by thinking that the negative effect will *probably* happen. You then rate the object or situation by using catastrophic language like the ones mentioned above.

Exercise 4.1 will help break the ice about your phobia.

EXERCISE 4.1

Write down your answers to the following questions in the space provided. Use separate pieces of paper if necessary:

1. Please briefly describe your phobia. What are you intensely afraid of?

```
┌──────────────────────────────────────────────────────┐
│                                                        │
│                                                        │
│                                                        │
│                                                        │
│                                                        │
└──────────────────────────────────────────────────────┘
```

2. When you think about this object or situation you fear, what negative event do you think about?

```
┌──────────────────────────────────────────────────────┐
│                                                        │
│                                                        │
│                                                        │
│                                                        │
│                                                        │
│                                                        │
└──────────────────────────────────────────────────────┘
```

3. How do you *feel* when you think about this event happening? Place a check next to any of the following words that describe how you are feeling. You are also free to add some of your own ideas to this list that might capture how you are feeling.

```
┌──────────────────────────────────────────────────────┐
│  • Anxious ___                                         │
│  • Powerless (over your feeling) ___                   │
│  • Afraid ___                                          │
│  • Frustrated ___                                      │
│  • Faint ___                                           │
│  • Fluttering or racing heartbeat ___                  │
│  • Nauseated ___                                       │
│  • Light-headed ___                                    │
│                                                        │
│                                                        │
└──────────────────────────────────────────────────────┘
```

4. When you have such negative feelings, how do you usually deal with them?

5. Do you ever find yourself avoiding certain activities you would otherwise like to engage in? Explain.

6. Are you satisfied with the way you deal with your phobia? Explain.

The Self-Defeating Nature of Your Phobic Thinking

Because we humans are like other animals, we experience fear when we think our lives are in danger. Unfortunately, your phobic thinking manufactures the danger and casts it in catastrophic terms, which leads you to proclaim, "I can't." The self-defeating result of this proclamation is that you needlessly stress yourself out and restrict your activities.

3. EXAMINING *YOUR* PHOBIC THINKING

In this section you will have the opportunity to examine the nature of your own phobic thinking. So, what does *your* phobic thinking look like? Exercises 4.2 through 4.4 will help you answer this question.

EXERCISE 4.2

Please briefly describe at least two situations and as many as five in which your phobia restricts your range of activities. For example, perhaps you have a dog phobia which leads you to avoid going for walks in your neighborhood, going to the park, or visiting friends who own dogs. Or perhaps you have a phobia of going into crowded places, which leads you to avoid going mall shopping with your friends or going to social events.

At least one of these situations in which you experience intense fear should be one you could easily intentionally arrange in the near future, and which you would especially like to work on. For example, you could arrange to go mall shopping with a friend or visit a park where there are likely to be dogs.

1.

2.

3.

4.

5.

EXERCISE 4.3

1. Please make a list of the catastrophic language you have used when experiencing anxiety about each of the cases you listed in Exercise 4.2. For example, maybe you tell yourself how *horrible* it would be if you were caught in the dark without a flashlight.

Your Catastrophic Language List

Your Catastrophic Language List

You now have a list of at least some of the catastrophic words or phrases you tend to use to *sustain* your phobia. Feel free to add to this list later if you think of other words or phrases. These are terms you will need to retire from your vocabulary!

EXERCISE 4.4

Next, for each of the cases you listed in Exercise 4.2, write down your phobic thinking (chain of thinking leading you to say you can't) using the language you identified in Exercise 4.3.

To formulate each of your cases, please follow the below form:

1. If [enter the object or situation feared], then [enter the negative event you associate with it].
2. So, if [enter again the object/situation feared] then it is/will/would be [enter the catastrophic terms you use to rate the object/situation].
3. So, I can't [enter again the object/situation feared].

In Premise 1, where it says, "enter the object or situation feared," enter what you have a phobia of, for example, flying. And where it says, "enter the negative event you associate with it" describe the danger you think this object or event presents to you, for example, the plane will crash and kill you.

In Conclusion 2, where it says, "enter again the object/situation feared," enter again what you have a phobia of; and where it says "enter the catastrophic terms you use to rate the object/ situation" insert a term from your Catastrophic Language List you created in Exercise 4.3(1), for example, "awful."

Finally, In Conclusion 3, where it says, "enter again the object/situation feared," simply enter the same object/situation again.

So, suppose you have come to associate thunderstorms with being struck dead by lightning, and therefore, rate being in a thunderstorm as *horrifying to you*, so that you can't be in thunderstorms. Then your thinking would look like this:

1. If <u>I get caught in a thunderstorm</u>, then <u>I am going to be struck dead by lightning</u>.
2. So, if <u>I am in a thunderstorm</u>, then it would be <u>horrifying to me</u>.
3. So, I can't <u>get caught in a thunderstorm</u>.

Now it's your turn to formulate *your* phobic thinking:

Case	Your Phobic Thinking
1	1. 2. 3.
2	1. 2. 3.
3	1. 2. 3.
4	1. 2. 3.
5	1. 2. 3.

Refuting Your Phobic Thinking

Now that you have formulated your phobic thinking, it's time to *refute* it, that is, look at it carefully to prove to yourself that it's irrational.

To illustrate (using the example from Exercise 4.4), suppose you are thinking:

1. If I get caught in a thunderstorm, then I am going to be struck dead by lightning.
2. So, if I get caught in a thunderstorm, then it would be horrifying to me.
3. So, I can't get caught in a thunderstorm.

Given the above reasoning as an example, Table 4.1 provides examples of some rational questions you can ask yourself in refuting the irrational parts of your own phobic thinking. These irrational parts are Premise 1 and Conclusions 2 and 3:

TABLE 4.1
Example of refutation of parts 1 through 3 of phobic thinking

Part of Your Phobic Thinking to Be Refuted	Ask Yourself This Question to Refute this Part of Your Thinking
1. If I get caught in a thunderstorm, then I am going to be struck dead by lightening.	*How often have you been through thunderstorms without being struck?* Answer: Numerous times, so you are just exaggerating this possibility.
2. So, if I get caught in a thunderstorm, then it would be horrifying to me.	*Is being in a thunderstorm "horrifying to you" when you see that you will probably not be struck by lightning?*

TABLE 4.1
Continued

Part of Your Phobic Thinking to Be Refuted	Ask Yourself This Question to Refute this Part of Your Thinking
	Answer: No, I am basing my catastrophizing on a false assumption. And even if there were a good chance I would be struck by lightning, what use would it serve to stress myself out by catastrophizing over it since that would change nothing!
3. So, I can't be in a thunderstorm.	Is it really true that I can't or that I am just telling myself I can't?
	Answer: I may *feel* like I can't because I have disempowered myself by exaggerating the danger; but feeling like I can't does not mean I *really* can't!

It's now time for you to refute your own phobic thinking in Exercise 4.5.

EXERCISE 4.5

Asking yourself the questions provided in Table 4.1 (as relevant), refute Premise 1 and Conclusions 2 and 3 of each of the phobic thinking chains you have constructed in Exercise 4.4. Write down the irrational premise or conclusion and your respective refutation of it in the columns provided in Table 4.1A.

TABLE 4.1A
Refutations of my phobic thinking

My Phobic Thinking	My Refutation
Chain 1:	
Premise 1:	Refutation of Premise 1:
Conclusion 2:	Refutation of Conclusion 2:
Conclusion 3:	Refutation of Conclusion 3:
Chain 2:	
Premise 1:	Refutation of Premise 1:
Conclusion 2:	Refutation of Conclusion 2:
Conclusion 3:	Refutation of Conclusion 3:
Chain 3:	
Premise 1:	Refutation of Premise 1:
Conclusion 2:	Refutation of Conclusion 2:
Conclusion 3:	Refutation of Conclusion 3:

TABLE 4.1A
Continued

My Phobic Thinking	My Refutation
Chain 4:	
Premise 1:	Refutation of Premise 1:
Conclusion 2:	Refutation of Conclusion 2:
Conclusion 3:	Refutation of Conclusion 3:
Chain 5:	
Premise 1:	Refutation of Premise 1:
Conclusion 2:	Refutation of Conclusion 2:
Conclusion 3:	Refutation of Conclusion 3:

4. EMBRACING YOUR GUIDING VIRTUES

The guiding virtues introduced in this section will help you to overcome your phobic thinking and set you free to attain greater control of your fear. These virtues are *Courage*, *Foresightedness*, and *Continence*. Embracing these virtues will counteract your tendency to disempower yourself and restrict your range of fulfilling activities. These virtues will replace your disempowering language with the language of rational risk assessment, rather than catastrophizing about over-inflated risks. Accordingly, they will help you confront the object or situation in question without self-defeating fear, anxiety, and restriction of freedom.

Before proceeding, please carefully review the definitions of these virtues in Table 4.2. Please keep in mind that these virtues are ideals which are therefore never 100% attainable this side of heaven! So, you can continue to get better and better at them, which makes life an exciting adventure!

Courage

In the context of overcoming a phobia, Courage means rationally putting danger into perspective without over- or under-inflating it. The chance of a plane crash is not a pleasant

TABLE 4.2
Definitions of your guiding virtues

Guiding Virtue	Description
1. Courage	Confronting adversity without under- or overestimating the danger. It means fearing things to the extent that it is reasonable to fear them and, in the face of danger, acting according to the merits of the situation.
2. Foresightedness	Making generalizations and predictions that are probable relative to available evidence.
3. Countenance	Willpower to constrain physical desires or aversions, neither over- nor under-doing them.

thought, but it is also not something to keep you from boarding a flight offered by an airline with a strong safety record. While planes do occasionally crash, elevators in rare cases do get stuck, and lightning does sometimes strike people, such events are extraordinary. It is only by exaggerating the danger of such untoward things happening that you can drive yourself into a state of fear or anxiety. Being courageous thus means not allowing your freedom to be curtailed by such remote possibilities. This means boarding the plane, stepping into the elevator, or weathering the thunderstorm.

Exercise 4.6 can help you to think further about exercising Courage in the face of your fear.

EXERCISE 4.6

1. Describe how you presently tend to deal with your fear.

```
┌─────────────────────────────────────────────────────────────┐
│                                                               │
│                                                               │
│                                                               │
│                                                               │
│                                                               │
│                                                               │
│                                                               │
└─────────────────────────────────────────────────────────────┘
```

2. What might you do differently to exercise Courage?

```
┌─────────────────────────────────────────────────────────────┐
│                                                               │
│                                                               │
│                                                               │
│                                                               │
│                                                               │
│                                                               │
└─────────────────────────────────────────────────────────────┘
```

Foresightedness

Courage also requires Foresightedness to rationally assess danger. In the context of overcoming a phobia, this means basing your predictions of danger on evidence. "This airline operates hundreds of flights per day and no crashes have been reported in many years; nor do I have any evidence of technology problems with the plane I am about to board." It also means exercising caution in the use of the language of risk. "What evidence do I have to keep telling myself the plane will *probably* crash? I shall reserve the word "probably" for cases where I actually have evidence!"

Exercise 4.7 can help you think further about exercising foresight in assessing probabilities.

EXERCISE 4.7

1. In areas of your life other than your phobia, how do you go about determining risk or probability of danger?

2. Do you follow the same approach in determining risk or probability of danger when it comes to your phobia? Explain.

3. What changes do you think are needed for you to become more foresighted in dealing with your phobia?

Continence

In the context of overcoming a phobia, Continence means exercising willpower over your fear so that it does not disrupt your life. So, while you may *feel* like you *can't* do the thing you fear, being continent means exercise of willpower to do so despite this feeling.

Such willpower takes practice, but the good news is that it gets easier the more practiced you get! Helping you to build such willpower through practice will be a focus of the section in this chapter on "Working on Your Cognitive-Behavioral Plan."

Like Foresightedness, Continence is also a condition of Courage. If you do not exercise the willpower to control your fear, you will also not act courageously!

Exercise 4.8 can help you to think more critically about your phobia and how you can exercise greater willpower to overcome it.

EXERCISE 4.8

1. Discuss briefly how you usually deal with situations in which you feel like you can't do the thing you fear. Illustrate your response using an example or two.

2. Does this way of dealing with such situations help to build Continence? Why or why not?

3. What do you think you could do differently to increase Continence in confronting your fear?

As you can see, the virtues of Courage, Foresightedness, and Continence "hang together" since to exercise Courage you would need also to exercise Foresightedness as well as Continence. Let's now do some further preliminary self-reflections about these three virtues with Exercise 4.9.

EXERCISE 4.9

1. How do you think embracing these virtues could change your life?

2. Do you know anyone who embraces these virtues? How does this impact their lives and the lives of those around them?

3. Would you like to be more like these people? Why, or why not?

---

5. EMPOWERING WISDOM FROM THE SAGES ON PURSUING THE VIRTUES

Below is some empowering wisdom from some of the world's most revered thinkers on how to develop Courage, Foresightedness, and Continence. These counsels can help you form a worldview that can help you overcome your phobia!

Courage

Empowering Wisdom from Epicurus:

- *Death is nothing to the living.*
- *When we are, death is not, and, when death is, we are not.*

Phobias typically feel so threatening because people with phobias often fear for their lives. But this assumes that death is itself something to be feared. However, one great ancient Greek philosopher named Epicurus, casts some rational doubt on this quite common assumption.

He tells you to practice believing that death is "nothing to the living," neither good nor bad, because when you are dead you are no longer aware of things, so nothing will seem good or bad to you. And, once you give up this false assumption that somehow death is a terrible thing, you will release yourself to enjoy your life!

He further tells you that, even though you think death is "the most awful of evils" it is really, instead, "nothing to us, seeing that, when we are, death is not, and, when death is, we are not. It is nothing, then, either to the living or to the dead" (Epicurus, n.d.). Hard to question this logic, right? No matter how you look at it, you never experience death!

Empowering Wisdom from Epictetus:

- *The terror consists in our notion of death, that it is terrible not in death itself.*
- *So it is you, not death, that disturbs you.*

Another Greek sage, Epictetus (1948) drives home the same point by pointing out that *you* are the one catastrophizing about death, by calling it "awful," "horrible," or "terrible." He tells you that you *disturb yourself* about death by telling yourself that it is a terrible thing. "[T]he terror consists in our notion of death, that it is terrible" (ch. 5). So, once you stop catastrophizing about death, the "terror" of death disappears. It is just in your mind, not in reality!

Exercise 2.10 can help you reflect on the implications of the aforementioned wisdom for your own life.

EXERCISE 4.10

Discuss briefly how you can use the counsel offered by Epicurus and Epictetus to be more courageous in managing your phobia. Give at least two examples.

Foresightedness

Empowering Wisdom from William James:

True ideas:

- *make a practical difference in actual life.*
- *have cash-value in experiential terms.*
- *help us to deal with reality.*

- *do not entangle our progress in frustrations.*
- *FIT, in fact, and adapt our life to reality.*

One useful way of working toward Foresightedness in overcoming phobias is to think of truth in terms of what it means practically to believe what's true versus what's false. This view was famously introduced by the American pragmatist, William James. To find out whether your belief is true or false, James tells you to ask yourself this question: "[W]hat concrete difference will its being true make in any one's actual life? … What, in short, is the truth's cash-value in experiential terms?" And he answers:

> Any idea that helps us to deal, whether practically or intellectually, with either the reality or its belongings, that doesn't entangle our progress in frustrations, that FITS, in fact, and adapts our life to the reality's whole setting, will agree sufficiently to meet the requirement. It will be true of that reality.
>
> (James, 2013)

So, what concrete difference will believing that you will perish if you board the plane make? Clearly, you will not get to go where you want to go while the plane will likely arrive without you! The elevator will go to the fourth floor while you watch the lights as they signal movement from one floor to the next, but you will remain on ground floor. Life will go on pretty much as it did before, only you will deprive yourself of the opportunity to satisfy your goals. That's how you will know whether your belief is true or false. If false, it will frustrate rather than satisfy your goals or expectations. Phobias almost invariably lead to such frustration!

Empowering Wisdom from W.K. Clifford:

- *You have a duty to question all that you believe and to believe only on sufficient evidence.*
- *True beliefs are ones which have stood in the fierce light of free and fearless questioning.*
- *Belief, that sacred faculty is ours, not for ourselves but for humanity.*

English mathematician, W.K. Clifford (1886), also keys into the practical value of true belief and drives home the importance of believing things on the basis of evidence in order to attain the truth. In fact, he proclaims, all human beings have a *duty to question all that they believe and to believe only on sufficient evidence.* He warns, "every time we let ourselves believe for unworthy reasons, we weaken our powers of self-control, of doubting, of judicially and fairly weighing evidence" (p. 4); which, in turn, contributes to a self-defeating habit of believing falsely. Not only are such habits of believing on insufficient evidence bad for you; they are also bad for others with whom you relate. "Habitual want of care about what I believe leads to habitual want of care in others about the truth of what is told to me" (p. 5).

In other words, such bad habits are contagious. "Men speak the truth to one another," he admonishes, "when each reveres the truth in his own mind and in the other's mind; but how shall my friend revere the truth in my mind when I myself am careless about it" (p. 5). So we all have the same duty to believe on sufficient evidence:

> Belief, that sacred faculty which prompts the decisions of our will, and knits into harmonious working all the compacted energies of our being, is ours not for ourselves, but for humanity. It is rightly used on truths which have been established by long experience and waiting toil, and which have stood in the fierce light of free and fearless questioning.
>
> (Clifford, 1986, p. 3)

So, are you prepared to place your phobia-sustaining beliefs "in the fierce light of free and fearless questioning"? Are you to claim that there is sufficient evidence to believe you will *probably* perish if you board a plane or travel during a storm? Clifford reminds you of your duty to question such groundless assumptions and to give them up.

Exercise 4.11 now asks you to reflect on such wisdom in relation to your phobia.

EXERCISE 4.11

Discuss briefly how you can use the counsel offered by James and Clifford to become more foresighted in dealing with your phobia. Give at least two examples.

Continence

Empowering Wisdom from Patanjali:

- *The causes of suffering are not seeing things as they are as when you get carried away by 'I', attachment, aversion, and clinging to life.*
- *When you become unattached to these things, the seeds of suffering wither, and pure awareness illuminates your mind.*

According to the ancient Yoga sage, Patanjali (2011), your phobia is a result of becoming preoccupied with causes and effects in the material world. Thus you may be preoccupied with the possibility that the plane might malfunction and crash; or that being in a crowded place could make it hard for you to breathe. You may be preoccupied with the possibility that you might fall out of a high building and be killed on impact with the ground; or that a lightning bolt might strike you and stop your heart; or that a snake might bite you and inject you with lethal venom. As such, your preoccupation with fear hinders you from living peacefully. "The causes of suffering," says Patanjali, "are not seeing things as they are, the sense of 'I', attachment, aversion, and clinging to life" (sutra 2.3). So, according to Patanjali, your fear is "illusory," not even real! By learning to simply observe the sensory world, without reacting to it ("This is horrible!") you can attain to "pure awareness" where you are no longer dragged along by the illusions of your material senses. "When one is unattached ... the seeds of suffering wither, and pure awareness knows it stands alone" (sutra 3.51).

The good news is that you can attain this level of "pure awareness" through a mindful mediative process, unhindered by your fear or other material desires and aversions. To accomplish this, you need to focus your attention on an *inner feeling* such as your breathing. It is important not to interpret or evaluate the feeling, but instead to *nonjudgmentally observe it*.

The goal again is attaining "pure awareness" of the feeling, not its interpretation or evaluation. It is the interpretation or evaluation of your fear that leads you to catastrophize about it and think you are going to die. By nonjudgmentally observing your feeling you can liberate yourself from this self-imposed painful consciousness. Patanjali uses the metaphor of a "luminous mind" to capture this state of nonjudgmental awareness. This conjures up the image of a bright light illuminating your mind to grasp the true nature of reality (Chapple, 2008), free from the turbulent, painful illusions of fear and anxiety. As discussed later in setting up your cognitive-behavioral plan, to develop this skill, you will need to practice. In practicing this uplifting Yoga philosophy of "liberation," "pure awareness," and a "luminous mind," you can indeed take important steps to strengthen your willpower over your phobia!

Empowering Wisdom from Jean-Paul Sartre:

- *Saying "I can't help my feeling" is to live in bad faith.*
- *You are condemned to be free.*
- *Your fear is not a devastating torrent that inevitably compels you to commit certain acts, and which, therefore, is an excuse. You are responsible for your own passion.*

According to the famous French existentialist philosopher, Jean-Paul Sartre (2007), you are responsible for your fear, and therefore can choose, or not choose to do something about it. So you are living in "bad faith" (lying to yourself) when you try to claim that you can't help being afraid. The main point is that your "I can't" is really a choice, not the result of the laws of causality acting on you as though you were an object without free will or responsibility for how you act. Existentialists, he explains, "will never regard a great passion as a devastating torrent that inevitably compels man to commit certain acts and which, therefore, is an excuse. They think that man is responsible for his own passion" (p. 29).

The feeling of powerlessness you experience when you say you can't help being afraid is just that, *a feeling*, which you can freely choose to regard or disregard (pp. 47–48). No matter what you decide, you must decide, so Sartre admonishes that you are "condemned to be free." This is your wakeup call from Sartre to (choose to) overcome your feeling of powerlessness (p. 29)!

Exercise 1.12 now gives you an opportunity to do some preliminary reflection on the learned counsel offered by Patanjali and Sartre.

EXERCISE 4.12

Discuss briefly how you can use the counsel offered by Patanjali and Sartre to become more continent in controlling your phobia. Give at least two examples.

Do you have a favorite sage of your own who you think gives constructive advice on how to be more courageous, foresighted, or continent? Add them to your list by completing Exercise 4.13!

EXERCISE 4.13

1. If you have a favorite sage of your own who offers some empowering wisdom on how to be more courageous, foresighted, or continent then formulate this wisdom below in the space indicated. (Even if you don't know the name of the person from whom the counsel comes, that's still okay).

Additional Empowering Wisdom for Courage

Additional Empowering Wisdom for Foresightedness

Additional Empowering Wisdom for Continence

Compiling a Master List of Empowering Wisdom

Epicurus and Epictetus have given you language to formulate their learned counsel that can go on a list of empowering wisdom to inspire Courage. For instance, for each of the formulations in the Courage column of Table 4.3, focus, one at a time, on the formulation with your mind's eye, and key into how it *feels*. *Does it make you want to be more courageous in taking risks*!? If yes, keep it on your list of empowering wisdom; if not, take it off or change the language!

Similarly, for each of formulations in the Foresightedness column of Table 4.3, focus, one at a time, on the formulation with your mind's eye, and key into how it *feels*. *Does it empower you to work toward becoming more Foresighted in overcoming making catastrophic predictions of danger?* If yes, keep it on your list of empowering wisdom; if not, take it off or change the language!

Finally, for each of the formulations in the Continence column of Table 4.3, focus, one at a time, on the formulation with your mind's eye, and key into how it *feels*. *Does it make you feel more empowered to exercise your willpower over your feeling of powerlessness?* If yes, keep it on your list of empowering wisdom; if not, take it off or change the language!

Have you found the language in Table 4.3 to have a positive feeling of empowerment or uplift? This language can help you to feel more empowered about overcoming your phobia.

Exercise 4.14 gives you the opportunity to expand or adjust the language and/or content of your lists to resonate especially with you.

TABLE 4.3
Empowering wisdom regarding Courage, Foresightedness, and Continence

Courage	Foresightedness	Continence
Epicurus:	**James:**	**Patanjali:**
Death is nothing to the living.	True ideas:	The causes of suffering are not seeing
__When we are, death is not, and, when death is, we are not	__make a practical difference in actual life.	things as they are as when you get carried away by 'I', attachment,
Epictetus:	__have cash-value in experiential terms.	aversion, and clinging to life.
The terror consists in our notion of death, that it is terrible, not in death itself.	__help us to deal with reality.	__When you become unattached to these things, the seeds of suffering wither, and
	__do not entangle our progress in frustrations.	pure awareness illuminates your mind.
__So it is you, not death, that disturbs you.	__FIT, in fact, and adapt our life to reality.	**Sartre:**
	Clifford:	Saying "I can't help my feeling" is to live in bad faith.
	You have a duty to question all that you believe and to believe only on sufficient evidence.	__You are condemned to be free.
	__True beliefs are ones which have stood in the fierce light of free and fearless questioning.	__Your fear is not a devastating torrent that inevitably compels you to commit certain acts, and which,
	__Belief, that sacred faculty is ours, not for ourselves but for humanity.	therefore, is an excuse. You are responsible for your own passion.

EXERCISE 4.14

This exercise will help you to develop a *master list of wisdom that is especially empowering for you.*

Please feel free to modify Table 4.3 in responding to the following instructions:

1. For each of the three guiding virtues, place a checkmark in front of each learned counsel you intend to use. Your selections should resonate with you, that is, feel uplifting, consoling, or otherwise empowering to you.

2. If you are not satisfied with the formulation of any of the counsels in Table 4.3, on a separate piece of paper, please rewrite it using language that resonates with you. For example, when I think of James' counsel about developing Foresightedness, I think of "satisfaction," "freedom from frustration," and "The truth works (to accomplish your goals)." You are encouraged to reformulate or tweak the sages' counsel using any language that is more empowering for you!

3. Please also add any empowering insights to Table 4.3 that you may have formulated in Exercise 4.12. Again, it is important that the language you use is empowering *for you.*

4. Now, congratulate yourself! You now have a master list of wisdom that is empowering for you!

6. CREATING A COGNITIVE-BEHAVIORAL PLAN

Are you ready to put the wisdom of the sages to work in a plan of action for overcoming your phobia-sustaining *can't*stipation? This will open new avenues of freedom for you!

Suppose you have told yourself that you can't help being afraid to leave your house. In just thinking about it, you feel the anxiety brewing inside you. You take a few steps outside your door, start to feel like you can't breathe, start to think you are going to die, and quickly turn back, concluding, "No, I can't!" As a result of your phobia, you have lost your job and most of your friends have stopped calling you.

Now, you clearly see that this is a serious problem for you. So, you resolve to try to be more *courageous* in confronting your phobia by following the following plan:

- Reframe your idea of death as not terrible in the first place since it is a state of non-existence in which you do not suffer.
- Reframe your fear of death as something *you* are creating by telling yourself how terrible dying would be.

To exercise *Foresightedness*, you decide to

- Think of yourself as having a duty to believe only on sufficient evidence, and to challenge any of your beliefs that fail to meet up, especially your assessment of danger.
- Ask yourself regularly, what is the "cash value" of keeping yourself prisoner in your home, and whether this really serves any overriding useful purpose.

To build *Continence* you plan to

- Practice regular mindfulness meditation that allows you to nonjudgmentally observe your feelings instead of evaluating or interpreting them.
- Accept responsibility for your phobia by reframing it as a choice instead of living in "bad faith" about your incapacity to overcome your fear.
- Act on your freedom to choose by leaving your home.

Now, it's your turn to build a plan of action based on the empowering wisdom you have embraced. Exercise 4.15 can help with this!

EXERCISE 4.15

1. From the situations in which you experience your phobia, as described in Exercise 4.2, choose one of them that you can easily place yourself in, and which you want especially to work on. (Recall you were asked to include at least one such situation that you could arrange to be in with relative ease in the short term.) Restate the description of this situation in the space provided below:

```
┌─────────────────────────────────────────────────────────────────────┐
│                                                                       │
│                                                                       │
│                                                                       │
│                                                                       │
│                                                                       │
│                                                                       │
└─────────────────────────────────────────────────────────────────────┘
```

2. Now, restate the phobic thinking you formulated in Exercise 4.4 that has blocked you from attempting to deal rationally with this situation.

1.

2.

3.

The primary goal of your cognitive-behavioral plan will be to help you do precisely what the conclusion in your above phobic thinking says you *can't* do! The rest of this exercise will help you to formulate this plan using the wisdom of the sages!

3. Using the counsel offered by Epicurus and Epictetus, or any empowering wisdom you may have added in Exercise 4.13 for becoming *more courageous*, what cognitive-behavioral changes would you make to overcome your phobic thinking? What changes would Epicurus tell you to make to overcome your phobia in the situation in question? What would Epictetus tell you to do differently based on his counsel about calling things "terrible"? List at least two cognitive-behavioral changes you plan to make:

1.

2.

3.

4.

5.

---

4. Using the counsel offered by James and Clifford, or any other empowering wisdom you may have added in Exercise 4.13 for becoming *more foresighted*, what cognitive-behavioral changes would you make to overcome your phobic thinking? List at least two:

1.

2.

3.

4.

5.

5. Using the counsel offered by Patanjali and Sartre, or any other empowering wisdom you may have added in Exercise 4.13 for becoming *more continent*, what cognitive-behavioral changes would you make to overcome your phobic thinking? List at least three:

1.

2.

3.

4.

5.

6. Now, congratulate yourself! You have just constructed a cognitive-behavioral plan!!

7. WORKING ON YOUR COGNITIVE-BEHAVIORAL PLAN

You will now have an opportunity to begin to build your habits of Courage, Foresightedness, and Continence instead of defaulting to your self-defeating habit of phobic thinking.

Cognitive–Affective Imagery

As you know, when folks with phobias think about doing what they fear, they tend to *feel* threatened, which leads them to catastrophize about it, and then tell themselves they can't do it. Imagery exercises can help you neutralize such negative feelings. Exercise 4.16 will help you to set up and practice cognitive–affective imagery.

EXERCISE 4.16

1. Choose some empowering wisdom from the Courage column of your master list of empowering wisdom (see Exercise 4.14) that is especially empowering or uplifting for you. Keep it in the back of your mind at this point.

2. Refer to the phobic thinking you identified in Exercise 4.15, which is fueling your phobia in the situation you also identified in Exercise 4.15.

3. Now here are instructions for doing cognitive–affective imagery. If you are working with a therapist, the therapist can provide guidance until you get the hang of it and can do it on your own. If you are not being assisted by a therapist, then please read these directions carefully now, memorize them (three steps), and then follow the three-step sequence laid out for you below:

- Step 1: Focus your mind exclusively on your phobic thinking (as identified in Exercise 4.15). Keep going over it in your mind like you did when you first told yourself you can't do the thing you fear. Keep it up until you feel that negative visceral threatening feeling. Let yourself resonate with the feeling of powerlessness that emerges, and that "No way I can assuage this threatening feeling!" feeling.
- Step 2: At the peak of feeling this intense negative feeling, shift your focus of mind exclusively to the positive language that you have selected for feeling empowered to become more courageous. Let yourself *feel* the uplift, the empowerment to confront your fear; letting yourself feel the freedom to take control.
- Step 3: Once you have fully brought yourself to resonate with the positivity of the experience, gently shift your attention to reflecting on your experience and what you have learned or discovered from it.

4. Try to reserve a time each day to practice your guided imagery exercise. Next time, however, choose some empowering wisdom from the *Foresightedness* column of your master list of empowering wisdom that is especially empowering or uplifting for you.

5. Similarly, the subsequent day, repeat the exercise except this time choose some empowering wisdom from the *Continence* column of your master list of empowering wisdom.

6. Practice regularly shifting between your empowering wisdom to support each of the *three* guiding virtues.

7. What have you learned or discovered about yourself from your experience practicing your cognitive–affective imagery? Write down your reflections below:

My Reflections about My Experience:

Congratulations on implementing your cognitive-affective imagery routine!!

Refuting and Reframing

By inspecting your phobic thinking, premise by premise, it is possible to refute and reframe your self-defeating thinking. As discussed in the Introduction to this book, reframing involves placing your negative thinking in a more positive light. For example, to reframe your catastrophizing you could take counsel from Epictetus to build Courage. "I am creating the terror by calling this terrible, so I will stop telling myself this!" To reframe your prediction of death or serious injury, you can take a counsel from Clifford to subject your prediction to "the fierce light of free and fearless questioning" to see that it is false to fact. And to reframe your conclusion that you can't do the thing in question, you can use Sartre's idea that you are living in "bad faith."

Accordingly, Exercise 4.17 will give you some practice refuting and reframing your phobic thinking!

EXERCISE 4.17

1. Refer again to the phobic thinking you identified in Exercise 4.15, which is preventing you from dealing rationally with the situation you also identified in Exercise 4.15. Look carefully at Premise 1 in your phobic thinking, the one that *predicts grave danger*. In Exercise 4.5, you have already refuted this premise so you can see how irrational it truly is. Think about this refutation until it resonates with you, that is, you get the "I get it" feeling that this premise is truly irrational. If this doesn't happen, then go back to Exercise 2.5 and find a refutation that *does* resonate with you. In Table 4.4, write down your refutation in the refutation column for Premise 1.

Now, select empowering wisdom from one or more of your sages (it could even be wisdom you added in Exercise 4.13), and use it to reframe this premise. In Table 4.4, write down this empowering wisdom in the reframing column for Premise 1.

2. Just as you have done for Premise 1, refute and reframe Conclusions 2 and 3 of the phobic thinking you identified in Exercise 4.15. Use Table 4.4 below to write down your refutation and reframing for each of these respective conclusions of your phobic thinking.

TABLE 4.4
Refuting and reframing my phobia thinking

Part	Refutation	Reframing
Premise 1		
Conclusion 2		
Conclusion 3		

Yoga Meditation

This meditation is also a useful part of your phobia action plan because it can teach you how to tune out your catastrophizing. As you have seen in talking about Patanjali's Yoga philosophy, the goal is "pure awareness," nonjudgmentally observing your feeling, not interpreting or evaluating it.

Exercise 4.18 can help you to build this uplifting feeling of interconnectedness and thereby overcome your LAC.

EXERCISE 4.18

1. Please listen to the guided meditation audio recording called "Guided Meditation for Overcoming Fear & Shifting Reality" presented by Boho Beautiful Yoga. This audio recording is (at the time of this writing) freely accessible from the following link: https://www.youtube.com/watch?v=DZ3Vc_72TJE. (If unavailable, find an alternative guided Yoga meditation, on the Internet, for overcoming fear.) As soon as you have finished listening to the audio recording, follow the following directions.

2. How do you now feel?

```



```

3. Reflect on your phobic thinking (as described in Exercise 3.15). Observe the feelings it evokes in you without interpreting or evaluating them. Strive for "pure awareness" of it.

4. Please repeat this exercise daily until you feel a sense of tranquility even when reflecting on your phobic thinking.

5. In the space provided, describe your progress in striving for tranquility through Yoga meditation.

```



```

Systematic Exposure

You need to change your behavior to overcome your phobias. Systematic exposure involves taking small steps toward doing what you are afraid to do, until you actually do it. Suppose you have a phobia about going to crowded places like the mall. You might begin by watching a video of shoppers at a mall; then driving by the mall; parking in the parking lot; walking up to the mall entrance; going in the entrance and walking back out; gradually increasing the amount of time you spend in the mall.

While working up to it, you should also be practicing your refutation and framing exercises as well as your Yoga meditation, which can help the ease at which you build Courage, Foresightedness, and Continence as you move closer and closer toward your goal of overcoming your phobia.

Don't be discouraged if you backslide or experience fear as you proceed toward your goal. Keep in mind that you are human, which means you are imperfect. Persevere and you will succeed!

Exercise 4.19 will guide you through this process.

EXERCISE 4.19

1. Work toward gradually implementing each of the *behavioral* elements on your behavioral plan created in Exercise 4.15. This includes doing the very thing you are afraid to do. To accomplish this, in the space provided below, create a list of gradual steps you are prepared to take to move finally toward doing what you have a phobia of. For example, if you have a phobia of leaving your house and your behavioral plan includes leaving your house, you will devise a set of gradual steps to eventually leave your house for a specified amount of time. Your plan should also include a schedule of when you will implement each step. For example, "I will stand outside my house for five minutes on Saturday. On Sunday I will take a stroll halfway down the block and back."

```
 
```

2. Take the gradual steps you have listed. Don't get discouraged if you go off schedule or things otherwise don't go according to plan. You don't have to be perfect! Just pick up where you left off. Schedules are not carved in stone and can be modified.

3. Continue to refute and reframe your phobic thinking (Exercise 4.17), while, and even after you make each successive behavioral change. Also continue to practice your cognitive–affective imagery (Exercise 4.16).

4. In the space provided, provide your reflections about your experience in taking the steps you listed in Part 1 of this Exercise to overcome your phobia:

5. This is an incredible milestone, so congratulate yourself!

Working on Your Other Phobic Situations

In Exercise 4.2, you described at least two situations in which you experience intense anxiety, which you would like to overcome. So, for example, you may have now succeeded in getting out of the house, but a further situation you fear may be dining in a restaurant. Accordingly, you are now in a position to continue working on overcoming your phobia in such other situations.

The process is the same, and you have already gone through it. Here is a summary of the process:

1. Formulate your phobic thinking (Exercise 4.4).
2. Refute lines 1, 2, and 3 of this thinking (Exercise 4.5).
3. Embrace your guiding virtues (Exercises 4.6 through 4.9).
4. Get empowering wisdom from the sages on pursuing the virtues (Exercises 4.10 through 4.14).
5. Use this learned counsel to construct a cognitive-behavioral plan (Exercise 4.15).
6. Work on your cognitive-behavioral plan (Exercises 4.16 through 4.19).

Using the exercise sets in this chapter as the framework, you can continue to build and strengthen your guiding virtues of Courage, Foresightedness, and Continence by regularly going through the above six steps.

Keep working at it!

REFERENCES

Chapple, C.K. (2008). *Yoga and the luminous: Patañjali's spiritual path to freedom*. State University of New York Press.

Clifford, W.K. (1886). The ethics of belief. In Stephen, L. & Pollock, F. (Eds.), *Lectures and Essays*. Macmillan & Co. Retrieved from http://people.brandeis.edu/~teuber/Clifford_ethics.pdf

Epictetus. (1948). *The Enchiridion*. Higgins, T.W. (Trans.). Liberal Arts Press. Retrieved from www.gutenberg.org/files/45109/45109-h/45109-h.htm

Epicurus. (n.d.). Letter to Menoeceus, trans. Hicks, R.D. Retrieved from http://classics.mit.edu/Epicurus/menoec.html

Healthline (n.d.). What are phobias? Retrieved from www.healthline.com/health/phobia-simple-specific

James, W. (2013). The meaning of truth. Retrieved from *The meaning of truth*, by William James (gutenberg.org).

Patanjali. (2011). The yoga-sutra. In Hartranft, C. (Ed.), The yoga-sutra of Patanjali: A new translation with commentary. Shambhala. Retrieved from www.arlingtoncenter.org/Sanskrit-English.pdf

Sartre, J.P. (2007). *Existentialism is a humanism*. Macomber, C. (Trans.). Yale University Press.

Tucker, R. (Dec. 2, 2013). Afraid of heights? Blame your parents: New study suggests phobias may be genetic. *National Post*. Retrieved from https://nationalpost.com/health/afraid-of-heights-blame-your-parents-new-study-suggests-phobias-may-be-genetic

Overcoming Low Self-Reliance

As you have seen in the introduction to this chapter, low self-reliance (LSR) is a behavioral type of *can't*stipation that creates and sustains dependency on others. This can prevent you from exercising your own autonomy, thereby preventing you from *doing* things that can promote your personal and interpersonal happiness. Instead, you stay in a dependent relationship; not making your own decisions or managing your own life affairs; being told what to do by another; doing little or nothing to make constructive change in your life.

1. GOALS OF THE CHAPTER:

Accordingly, the goals of this chapter are to:

1. Increase awareness of your low self-reliance (LSR) thinking and the language you are using to create and sustain dependency on others.
2. Refute this thinking.
3. Identify guiding virtues that counteract your LSR thinking.
4. Identify empowering wisdom from great sages on how to seek these virtues.
5. Use this learned counsel to construct a cognitive-behavioral plan for increasing your virtues.
6. Work on your plan, including exercising your own autonomy to make decisions.

2. THE NATURE OF LSR THINKING

This type of *can't*stipation is associated with anxiety about making your own decisions. These people tell themselves they need the approval of others to be worthy and tend to put themselves down and feel badly about themselves when they don't get this approval or think they won't get it.

People with low self-reliance often seek out partners who are domineering who can "take care of them" and tell them what to do. These relationships therefore tend to be dysfunctional, involving unequal power structures where the stronger partner exercises excessive control over the weaker partner, and not uncommonly the latter may be subjected to emotional/verbal abuse or even in some cases physical or sexual abuse by the former.

DOI: 10.4324/9781003035282-6

The dependent person demands the approval (or reassurance) of others and may blindly conform to what others do or say just to get this approval. Unfortunately, this can lead to regrettable behavior such as taking harmful drugs or engaging in other dangerous and unwarranted risks (Yiğitoğlu & Keskin, 2019).

Here are some examples of LSR thinking:

- I must get the approval of my partner.
  But, if I make this decision on my own and screw up, he'll be mad at me.
  So, that would make me a *screw up*.
  So, I can't make this decision on my own.
- Everyone must like me.
  But if I refuse to go along with them, they will reject me.
  So, that would make me a *reject*.
  So, I can't refuse them.
- I must impress my boss.
  But if I don't laugh at his sexist jokes, he won't like me anymore.
  So, that would make me a *loser*.
  So, I can't not laugh at his jokes.
- I must satisfy my partner in bed.
  But if I refuse to have the type of sex she wants, I won't keep her satisfied.
  So, that would make me *a terrible partner*.
  So, I can't refuse to perform those sex acts she wants.
- I must please my partner.
  But if I dress and cut my hair the way I like, he won't find me attractive anymore.
  So, that would make me *undesirable*.
  So, I can't dress or wear my hair the way I like.
- I must have my parent's blessings.
  But if I marry outside my religion, they will never give me their blessings.
  So, that would make me a *horrible daughter*.
  So, I can't marry outside my religion.

In cases like these you demand the approval or favor of others, and when you imagine losing this favor, your worth as a person feels diminished, which leads you to use self-degrading language, which only amplifies your diminished feeling of self-worth. This, in turn, makes you feel disempowered, which leads you to conclude, "I can't do it."

Now, look at this disempowering language:

- "screwup"
- "reject"
- "loser"
- "terrible partner"
- "undesirable"
- "horrible daughter."

These words, all of them, arouse strong negative feelings. As a result of attaching them to yourself, *you make your self-worth a function of others' approval of you.* This leads you to feel disempowered to assert your own autonomy, to act and be the person you want to be. As such, you set yourself up to declare, "I can't …!"

Exercise 5.1 is an icebreaker to help you get more in touch with the feelings going on inside you when you tell yourself you can't take control of your own life or make your own decisions.

EXERCISE 5.1

Write down your answers to the following questions in the space provided. Use a separate piece of paper if necessary:

1. When you are about to do something that you think may not meet with the approval of a person(s) from whom you seek approval, what goes through your mind? What feelings do you experience?

2. Think of something you recently wanted to do, or wanted not to do, but decided against it just because you thought another person, from whom you demand approval, would disapprove of your action. Rerun in your mind how you felt when you decided against it. Try your best to describe this feeling that moved you to respond as you did.

3. Place a check next to any of the following words that describe the way you feel in such situations. Feel free to add some of your own words to this list that might help capture how you feel.

- Screwup ___
- Reject ___
- Loser ___
- Dumb ___
- Powerless ___
- Failure ___
- Trapped ___
- Weak ___
- Helpless ___

4. When faced with such situations, how do you usually resolve them?

```



```

5. Are you satisfied with the way you usually resolve them? Explain.

```



```

The Self-Defeating Nature of Your LSR Thinking

Unfortunately, your LSR thinking creates intense anxiety, which you may tend to resolve by concluding, "I can't." The self-defeating result of this thinking is that you keep yourself in a subservient position and destroy your prospects for becoming an independent, self-reliant person.

3. EXAMINING *YOUR* LSR THINKING

In this section you will have the opportunity to examine your own LSR thinking. So what does *your* LSR thinking look like? Exercises 5.2 through 5.4 will help you to answer this question.

EXERCISE 5.2

Please briefly describe at least three and as many as five things, you would like to do, or not do, but are telling yourself you can't do because you could lose the approval or acceptance of another. At least one of these things should be something you can do short term such as asserting yourself in some way, but have avoided, such as deciding an imminent issue that could meet with the disapproval of your partner.

```
1.


2.


3.
```

4.

5.

EXERCISE 5.3

Now, make a list of some of the self-damning language you tend to use to keep yourself from asserting yourself in each of the cases you listed in Exercise 5.2.

Your Disempowering, Self-Damning Language List

With the above filled in, you have a list of at least some of the self-damning terms you tend to use to disempower yourself. These are words that you will need to retire from your vocabulary!

EXERCISE 5.4

Next, for each of the cases you listed in Exercise 5.2, write down your LSR thinking (chain of reasoning leading you to say you can't) using the language you identified in Exercise 5.3. To formulate each of your cases, please follow the below form:

1. I must get the approval of [enter person(s) from who you seek approval].
2. But, if I [enter the action that might not get this approval], then [enter again person(s) from who you seek approval] will not approve of me.
3. So, that would make me [enter the damning term from your list].
4. So, I can't [enter again the act in question].

For example, suppose you tell yourself you can't come out as a gay person because others of your religious faith would reject you; which you think would make you a *reject*. So, you have spent your life pretending you are straight and therefore living a lie. Then your thinking would look like this:

1. I must have the approval of <u>others of my faith</u>.
2. But if I <u>come out as a gay person</u>, then <u>others of my faith</u> will not approve of me.
3. So, that would make me <u>a reject.</u>
4. So, I *can't* <u>come out as a gay person</u>.

Now it's your turn to formulate *your* LSR thinking:

Case	Your LSR Thinking
1.	1. 2. 3. 4.
2.	1. 2. 3. 4.
3.	1. 2. 3. 4.
4.	1. 2. 3. 4.
5.	1. 2. 3. 4.

Refuting Your LSR thinking

Now that you have formulated the thinking you are doing to *can't*stipate yourself, it's time to look at it carefully with an eye to showing just how irrational it truly is.

TABLE 5.1
Examples of refutation of Premise 1 and Conclusions 3 and 4 of LSR thinking

Part of Your LSR Thinking to be Refuted	Ask Yourself This Question to Refute Given Part of Your Thinking
1. I must have the approval of others of my faith.	*Where is it written that I must have the approval of others of my faith?*
	Answer: Nowhere except in my head!
Premise 1 again	*Are the strong preferences of others always satisfied? If not, then why do yours have to be?*
	Answer: No one's preferences *need* to be satisfied!
Premise 1 again	*Am I even being consistent when I demand that I must have the approval of others of my faith?*
	Answer: Did Copernicus and Galileo have the permission of others of their faith when they challenged church doctrine about the nature of the solar system? Did Jesus have the approval of members of the Jewish faith when he said he was the son of God? Answer: No, so why must I have such approval!
3. So, that would make me a reject.	*Does not being accepted by other members of your faith truly make you a reject?*
	Answer: No! This would mean that others who have not conformed to orthodox church doctrine were rejects. It would make Martin Luther and Joan of Arc rejects too!!
4 So, I can't come out as a gay person.	*Is it really that I can't come out or is it rather that I am choosing not to?*
	Answer: Unless I lack free will like some preprogrammed machine, I *can* come out!
Conclusion 4 again	*What are the practical consequences of not coming out?*
	Answer: I will live an inauthentic and unhappy life, and probably mess up the lives of future partners whom I deceive about my sexual identity.

This step is known as *refutation* in cognitive-behavior therapy. It can help you to appreciate exactly why your thinking is irrational!

To illustrate, consider again the previous example from Exercise 5.4:

1. I must have the approval of others of my faith.
2. But if I come out as a gay person, then others of my faith will not approve of me.
3. So, that would make me a reject.
4. So, I can't come out as a gay person.

Using the above reasoning as an example, Table 5.1 provides examples of some rational questions you can ask yourself in refuting the irrational parts of your own LSR thinking. These irrational parts are Premise 1, and Conclusions 3 and 4:

It's now time for you to refute your own LSR thinking with Exercise 5.5!

EXERCISE 5.5

Asking yourself the questions provided in Table 5.1 (as relevant), refute each of the LSR thinking chains you have constructed in Exercise 5.4. Write down the irrational premise or conclusion and your respective refutation in the columns provided in Table 5.1A.

TABLE 5.1A
Refutations of my LSR thinking

My LSR Thinking	My Refutation
Chain 1:	
Premise 1:	Refutation of Premise 1:
Conclusion 3:	Refutation of Conclusion 3:
Conclusion 4:	Refutation of Conclusion 4:
Chain 2:	
Premise 1:	Refutation of Premise 1:
Conclusion 3:	Refutation of Conclusion 3:
Conclusion 4:	Refutation of Conclusion 4:
Chain 3:	
Premise 1:	Refutation of Premise 1:
Conclusion 3:	Refutation of Conclusion 3:
Conclusion 4:	Refutation of Conclusion 4:
Chain 4:	
Premise 1:	Refutation of Premise 1:
Conclusion 3:	Refutation of Conclusion 3:
Conclusion 4:	Refutation of Conclusion 4:
Chain 5:	
Premise 1:	Refutation of Premise 1:
Conclusion 3:	Refutation of Conclusion 3:
Conclusion 4:	Refutation of Conclusion 4:

5. EMBRACING YOUR GUIDING VIRTUES

By working on building certain "virtues" you can overcome your low self-reliance, thereby taking an oppressive, self-imposed weight off your shoulders, allowing yourself to live more freely, to feel and do better!

The guiding virtues that support the abovementioned refutations include Decisiveness, Authenticity, and Self-Respect. Before proceeding, please carefully review the definitions of each of these virtues in Table 5.2.

TABLE 5.2
Definitions of your guiding virtues

Guiding Virtue	Description
1. *Decisiveness*	Realistic trust in your ability to accomplish the goals you set; and being prepared to take rational risks to accomplish these goals under less-than-ideal conditions.
3. *Authenticity*	Autonomously and freely living according to your own creative lights as opposed to losing yourself on a bandwagon of social conformity.
4. *Self-Respect*	Unconditional, self-acceptance based on a deep philosophical understanding of human worth and dignity.

Decisiveness can counteract your low self-reliance by helping you to act against your "I can't"; Authenticity counteracts your demand for approval by helping you to live by your own values instead of blindly conforming to the values of others in order to get their approval. Finally, Self-Respect can help you to stop damning yours when you don't get the approval of others, and hence to give up your disempowering, damning language.

These are the ideals to which you are strongly encouraged to aspire! Because they are ideals, they can never be realized perfectly, so they set goals to strive for over the course of a lifetime. So don't be discouraged if you should backslide or fall short of the progress you hoped for. This is all part of making progress in striving for excellence! Just keep at it and you will keep getting better and better!

Decisiveness

Notice the definition of Decisiveness speaks in terms of being realistic. It is indeed realistic to *act* to assert yourself rather than conforming to the expectations of others just to get their approval. You may *feel* disempowered to do this, but feeling like you can't does not mean you *really* can't.

Of course, this does not mean you should do things that could jeopardize your safety or health, just to say you asserted yourself. Again, there is a difference between reasonable exercises of autonomy and those that are unreasonable. Waiting for the ideal situation to assert yourself will only lead to inaction since no situation is going to be ideal or perfect. Moreover, deciding is not the same thing as acting because you can decide to do something and still not do it. Being decisive means that you also *act* on your decision.

How decisive are you? Exercise 5.6 can help to address this question.

EXERCISE 5.6

1. When faced with a decision that involves exercising your own judgment, how do you usually deal with the situation? Do you sometimes decide to do things but end up not doing them? If so, give some examples and describe some of the things you tell yourself to avoid acting. Write your responses in the space provided below:

2. Do you sometimes just not reach a decision in the first place? If so, discuss some of the things you tell yourself that leads you not to decide in the first place.

Authenticity

Being authentic means freeing yourself from the shackles of conforming to the expectations and demands of others. Clearly, there are social and legal rules within which rational authenticity operates. For example, it is not usually helpful to break the law to assert yourself since there can be serious consequences (fines, prison time, etc.). But even here, many great reformers have challenged the law to help make constructive change. Still, your everyday life decisions are not of this grand nature. In the end, a reasonable goal for everyday living is to exercise rational autonomy within the boundaries of law and social norms, as well as personal safety. However, this is a broad area in which to exercise your autonomy. You can indeed choose not to take on a work project if it flaunts your values (for example, doing something you think is unethical). You can refuse to do something that others are doing because it is not in your best interest even if it meets with disapproval from others. You can make your own choices about education, personal appearance and hygiene; recreation; medical decisions; friendships; career planning; foods; and other areas of everyday living. Being considerate of others is a relevant consideration; but be careful not to use this as a rationale simply to seek the approval of others!

Exercise 5.7 can help you become clearer about how authentic you are.

EXERCISE 5.7

1. When the expectations of others conflict with values (morality, self-interests, personal goals, or aspirations, etc.) that are important to you, how do you generally deal with such situations?

2. When you have an opportunity to make your own decisions rather to consult and defer to others' advice, how do you generally deal with such situations?

Self-Respect

As you can see by the definition of Self-Respect, this virtue involves *unconditional* self-acceptance. This does not mean that self-respecting people don't admit their mistakes or criticize their own actions when warranted. However, there is a difference between damning the deed versus damning the doer. While the former can be a constructive way to learn from your mistakes, the latter serves no useful purpose and leads to loss of self-efficacy. In other words, you tell yourself that you are incapable of making constructive change.

To the contrary, to *unconditionally* accept yourself means that you do not question your self-efficacy or worthiness. These are constants, never negated by your mistakes in judgment or what others may do or say about you. You remain a worthy person who has the capacity to act and do constructive things, and to continue to learn and grow from your experiences, whether positive or negative. You remain a self-determining agent of change, capable of guiding your own ship of life!

This also means that you do not berate yourself using damning language ("loser," "failure," etc.) when you make mistakes or receive criticism from others. Such language only serves to discourage positive change, intensify negative self-feelings, and has no useful purpose.

Exercise 5.8 can help you become clearer about how self-respecting you are.

EXERCISE 5.8

When others from whom you seek approval express disapproval of you, how do you feel about yourself? Briefly describe these feelings.

2. What sort of language do you use to express such feelings about yourself? Give a few examples.

```
```

3. When you receive criticism from others about your actions, how do you usually deal with the criticism? What do you tell yourself about it?

```
```

Now, let's get to work on your virtues (Decisiveness, Authenticity, and Self-Respect) in Exercise 5.9, starting with some preliminary self-reflections.

EXERCISE 5.9

1. How do you think embracing these virtues could change your life?

```
```

2. Do you know anyone who embraces these virtues? How does this impact their lives and the lives of those around them?

3. Would you like to be more like these people? Why, or why not?

5. EMPOWERING WISDOM FROM THE SAGES ON PURSUING THE VIRTUES

So how can you become more decisive, authentic, and self-respecting? Great minds throughout history have pondered this question. Below you will find some of this wisdom condensed into virtue-guiding insights. This can help you to form a worldview that can be quite powerful in overcoming your low self-reliance!

Decisiveness

Empowering Wisdom from Sartre:

- *You are nothing more than the sum of [your] actions and therefore responsible for what you are or become.*
- *You are condemned to be free because you are responsible for everything you do (or don't do).*

French existentialist, Jean-Paul Sartre (2007), makes Decisiveness the key to becoming a self-realized person in her own right. He famously states.

> Man is nothing other than his own project. He exists only to the extent that he realizes himself, therefore he is nothing more than the sum of his actions … In life, a man commits himself and draws his own portrait, outside of which there is nothing.

(p. 37)

> [Therefore] man is responsible for what he is.

(p. 23)

That is what I mean when I say that man is condemned to be free: condemned, because he did not create himself, yet nonetheless free, because once cast into the world, he is responsible for everything he does.

(p. 29)

So, saying you can't is tantamount to defining yourself negatively, as nothing whatsoever. The good news is that you are free to choose. Sartre expresses this with the phrase "condemned to be free," meaning that not choosing is still a choice. The only "can't" that makes sense here is the one in the popular saying, "You can run but you can't hide." So, your low self-reliance is really just a way to try to hide from your freedom and responsibility, which is still a choice. So, you might as well embrace your freedom (since you can't escape it) and define yourself positively by acting in ways that will advance your happiness!

Empowering Wisdom from Epictetus:

- *Act on your own judgment as though it were a law and disrespectful not to obey it, regardless of what anyone else may think of you.*
- *Think of yourself as worthy of living as an adult with your own mind.*

According to ancient stoic thinker, Epictetus, you can also help yourself to act decisively by reframing your own convictions as "inviolate laws" by which you are bound: "Whatever rules you have adopted," instructs Epictetus, "abide by them as laws, and as if you would be impious to transgress them; and do not regard what anyone says of you, for this, after all, is no concern of yours." Otherwise, he says, you will "add procrastination to procrastination, purpose to purpose, and fix day after day in which you will attend to yourself" and accomplish nothing on your own (Epictetus, 1948, sec. 50). So never mind what anyone else may think; never mind that it won't meet with their approval; it is a law unto you to act on your own convictions.

This is not about pleasing or satisfying someone else. It's about making your own judgments and acting on them. "[T]hink yourself worthy of living as a man grown up and a proficient", admonishes Epictetus (1948, sec. 50). Otherwise, you will live in fear and not give yourself an opportunity to grow intellectually and emotionally.

Empowering Wisdom from John Stuart and Harriet Taylor Mill:

- *Don't allow others to enslave your mind.*
- *Don't be a "willing slave"!*

Well ahead of his time, moral philosopher John Stuart Mill coauthored with his wife, Harriet Taylor Mill, an essay titled *The Subjection of Women*. Striking at the core of relationships based on unequal power structures, the Mills (1869) state,

Men do not want solely the obedience of women, they want their sentiments. All men, except the most brutish, desire to have, in the woman most nearly connected with them, not a forced slave but a willing one, not a slave merely, but a favourite. They have therefore put everything in practice to enslave their minds.

(pp. 26–27).

These words ring true in many quarters of society today as they did back in 1861 when they were first penned. *But they go beyond the oppression of women, and can be applied to anyone, male or female, gay or straight, who is involved in an oppressive relationship.* The key idea here is that the stronger partner wants the weaker partner to be a "*willing* slave," not a forced one, and, clearly, not a co-equal partner. What keeps these forms of dysfunctional relationships going is such cooperation by the weaker partner who demands approval from the stronger partner.

Realizing that you may be a "willing slave" can be an eyeopener. It may *feel* like you can't decide on your own; but this feeling is likely the result of past conditioning (you may have been told repeatedly that you are "stupid" or otherwise incapable of deciding on your own; you may have been brought up with the sexist notion that women are not as rational as men). But this is just a feeling, which you can overcome by acting contrary to it. This is in your power, and the Mills entreat you to give up being a "willing slave" and instead make and act on your own decisions.

More Empowering Wisdom from John Stuart Mill:

- *You have incredible, native powers to perceive, judge, and discriminate. Strengthen them by making your own choices, not merely following others.*

Not only was John Stuart Mill a champion of women's rights; he believed that *all* human beings should make and act on their *own* judgments instead of simply conforming to the will of others. Mill (1859) states,

> The human faculties of perception, judgment, discriminative feeling, mental activity, and even moral preference, are exercised only in making a choice. ... The mental and moral, like the muscular powers, are improved only by being used. The faculties are called into no exercise by doing a thing merely because others do it, no more than by believing a thing only because others believe it. If the grounds of an opinion are not conclusive to the person's own reason, his reason cannot be strengthened, but is likely to be weakened by his adopting it.
>
> (ch. 3)

So, your willpower is like a muscle. It gets stronger if you flex it, and wanes if you don't. If you simply rely on what others tell you to do, you will end up with a flabby willpower muscle. You have some very impressive capacities—the distinctly human powers to perceive, judge, and discriminate, which are to be used, not simply left to deteriorate as a result of doing what others do or tell you to do.

Exercise 5.10 now gives you an opportunity to apply such empowering wisdom to your own life!

EXERCISE 5.10

Discuss briefly your approach to making decisions and how you could use the counsel offered by Sartre, Epictetus, and the Mills to be more decisive.

Authenticity

Still More Empowering Wisdom from John Stuart Mill:

- *Since you are imperfect and learn by experience, try out different modes of living to develop your character as a distinct individual, short of injury to others.*
- *Otherwise, missing is one of the principal ingredients of human happiness, namely your individuality.*

Not only did John Stuart Mill think that you should exercise your own judgment, he also believed that you should be open to diverse ways of doing things, instead of getting into fixed habits of doing the same old thing. Mill (1859) states:

> As it is useful that while mankind are imperfect there should be different opinions, so is it that there should be different experiments of living; that free scope should be given to varieties of character, short of injury to others; and that the worth of different modes of life should be proved practically, when any one thinks fit to try them. It is desirable, in short, that in things which do not primarily concern others, individuality should assert itself. Where, not the person's own character, but the traditions or customs of other people are the rule of conduct, there is wanting one of the principal ingredients of human happiness, and quite the chief ingredient of individual and social progress.
>
> (ch. 3)

Face it, as human beings we have our own distinct characters and while one style of living may suit me, the same might not suit you. So you should be prepared to try out different ways of living to see which one is right for you. For example, while one person may find a life of an out-doorsman (lumberjack, fisherman, sailor …) to be quite compatible with her dispositions and talents, another may find the same to be incompatible with his character, preferring, for example, a more bookish life, or a life filled with cultural events. Some may prefer city life, while others rural life. Here there is no rule except what you decide it to be by virtue of what suits you. So it is irrational to simply conform your will to that of others or to live as others want you to live.

Empowering Wisdom from Friedrich Nietzsche:

- *Noble people create their own values (decide what's good or bad) and therefore don't need others' approval.*

In his often-quoted work, *Beyond Good and Evil*, German existentialist, Friedrich Nietzsche, informs you that, "the Noble kind of man," who is the authentic person, "experiences himself as a person who determines value and does not need to have other people's approval … He understands himself as something which in general first confers honour on things, as someone who creates values" (Nietzsche, 1954, ch. 9, sec. 260, p. 579).

Such a person is not part of the herd. He does not do things because others are doing them. Instead, he is himself a "creator of value." This means doing your own independent thinking and acting; coming up with your own solutions to challenges you may face. This does not mean that you should not hear the advice of others. However, authentic people ultimately make their own judgments and do not merely conform for its own sake or to satisfy the expectations of others.

Empowering Wisdom from the Bhagavata Purana:

- *A blind man guided by another blind man misses the right path and falls into a ditch.*

In the *Bhagavata Purana*, an ancient Hindu text, it is explained how following blindly another can lead you astray. In a classic passage, it is said,

> Persons who are strongly entrapped by the consciousness of enjoying material life, and who have therefore accepted as their leader or guru a similar blind man attached to external sense objects, cannot understand that the goal of life is to return home, back to Godhead, and engage in the service of Lord Viṣṇu. As blind men guided by another blind man miss the right path and fall into a ditch, materially attached men led by another materially attached man are bound by the ropes of fruitive labor, which are made of very strong cords, and they continue again and again in materialistic life, suffering the threefold miseries.
>
> (Prabhupada, n.d., canto 7, ch. 5)

You don't need to be a subscriber to the Hindu faith to get the point. Quite understandably, most of us get caught up in the issues of material existence, especially the "threefold miseries" of interpersonal conflicts, your own emotional and physical problems, and acts of nature such as storms, floods, and draughts. So, out of feelings of fear and insecurity about being left alone in this labyrinth of "external sense objects," you depend on another person who is in the same boat as you. This is like the blind leading the blind, and it leads you to lose your way in life, to fail to find the true meaning of life, which is return to the "Godhead" (Heaven) through the acquisition of true knowledge of God.

In the Hindu faith, Lord Viṣṇu is the chief God, who, like the sun, is the source of all light (knowledge and truth), and hence divine inspiration. So, the goal of an enlightened life, much like in Western faiths such as Christianity and Judaism, is to strive to be closer to God, becoming more self-actualized through acquiring knowledge of God. This knowledge can be attained through studying science, philosophy, and the arts. The latter can inspire you to think out of the box, to exercise your own creative juices to confront everyday life without losing track of what matters most, the quest for knowledge and truth, to be closer to God.

If you are a spiritual person, even if you are not deeply religious in the conventional sense, you may find this antidote a powerful lift toward becoming (and feeling) more disposed toward exercising your own creativity in the context of everyday life. Remember, you can be inspired through the quest for knowledge of God (ultimate Truth) without being led blindly (and hence astray) by following the blind!

Exercise 5.11 now asks you to reflect on such wisdom in relation to your dependence on others.

EXERCISE 5.11

1. How do you usually deal with situations in which you have ideas of your own or value perspectives (social, political, practical, etc.) that are not likely to meet with the approval of others from whom you seek approval?

```

```

2. How could you use the counsel offered by Nietzsche, John Stuart Mill, and the Bhagavata Purana to become more authentic?

Self-Respect

Empowering Wisdom from Immanuel Kant:

- *Treat yourself as an end in itself (person), not a "mere means" (object) by asserting your own autonomy and making your own choices.*
- *Your worth and dignity as an autonomous person is unconditional and does not depend on what other people think of you.*

These are the terms the 18th-century German philosopher, Immanuel Kant, used to instruct you to treat yourself (as well as others) as a *person* ("end in yourself") and not as an object ("mere means"). To be a "person" means you are *autonomous*, that is, you have the capacity to make your own decisions and to act independently. This is the opposite of an *object* which cannot act independently but is instead controlled by persons or forces other than itself (Kant, 1964, p. 96).

Because people are autonomous, Kant tells you that they have worth in themselves, unlike objects or things that you can use for a certain purpose, for example, a pen to write with. The worth of the pen depends on this purpose. If the pen runs out of ink, it ceases to have value and can be thrown out. On the other hand, the worth of people does not depend on their serving a certain purpose, for example earning a wage. Instead, the value of a person is *unconditional.*

So, you are treating yourself like an object when you assess your own self-worth on the basis of whether or not you gain the approval of another. However, on the contrary, you are not an object. Your value does not depend on what other people think about you, or what use they have for you (Kant, 1964, p. 96). You are therefore special, irreplaceable, non-objectifiable, and intrinsically worthy regardless of whether you mess up or others approve of you!

Empowering Wisdom from Kristin Neff

- *Be gentle, kind, and understanding with yourself, not critical and judgmental.*
- *Connect with others instead of feeling alone in your suffering.*
- *Hold your pain in balanced awareness, neither ignoring nor exaggerating it.*

As you know, folks who have low self-reliance put themselves down by calling themselves unkind names when they think they were rejected by others (for example, "reject," "loser," etc.). This is the opposite of Self-Respect, which, according to Buddhist, Kristin Neff, requires self-compassion. This involves being kind to yourself, which means being "gentle and understanding with ourselves rather than harshly critical and judgmental." It also means feeling a connection with others rather than feeling alone in your suffering. Finally, it "requires mindfulness—that we hold our experience in balanced awareness, rather than ignoring our pain or exaggerating it" (Neff, 2011).

Having self-compassion is not the same as having high self-esteem because the latter involves rating yourself while the former does not. So, today you may hold yourself in high esteem and tomorrow you may hold yourself in low esteem depending on whether others like or approve of you (Neff, 2011). This is not the unconditional self-acceptance that is essential to Self-Respect.

To become more self-compassionate, Neff suggests doing compassion-based mediation such as loving kindness meditation (Neff, 2011). You will have an opportunity to work on this in working through your cognitive-behavioral plan later in this chapter.

Empowering Wisdom from Aristotle:

- *Love yourself as your own best friend*
- *Wish yourself well for your own sake.*

Aristotle (1941), whose insights into the nature of human happiness are profound and unparalleled, tells you that an essential condition of self-respect is being your own friend.

> For men say that one ought to love best one's best friend, and a man's best friend is one who wishes well to the object of his wish for his sake, even if no one is to know of it; and these attributes are found most of all in a man's attitude towards himself, and so are all the other attributes by which a friend is defined.
>
> (bk. 9, ch. 7, p. 1086)

This means that, as your own best friend, you do not speak damning words against yourself. It is one thing to say you did a very bad thing; but quite another to say you yourself are very bad. The former is consistent with being your own best friend because your best friend would want you to recognize when you made a mistake so you could correct it. But the latter is of no use whatsoever other than to create self-defeating negative emotions such as depression. Nor would your best friend tell you to damn yourself when others disapprove of you; for such a friend would want you to be your own person, and to be capable of rational self-assessment in confronting the inevitability of others' disapproval.

When Aristotle says to *love* yourself, he is not telling you to be selfish, or to violate the rights of others to satisfy yourself. Indeed, for Aristotle, a condition of loving oneself is having respect for others too. Thus, the person who mistreats others is not likely to be a person who truly loves himself. Such an expression of contempt for others amounts to self-contempt turned outward. As such, Aristotle is underscoring the importance of being rational in the treatment of others but also in the treatment of yourself, since, according to Aristotle, your rational self is your true self. This means avoiding needlessly stressing yourself out and thinking and acting rationally. And this you should do, he says, for its own sake, not for ulterior purposes such as pleasing others, for your best friend wishes you well for its own sake.

Exercise 5.12 now gives you an opportunity to do some preliminary reflection on the learned counsel offered by Kant, Neff, and Aristotle.

EXERCISE 5.12

Discuss briefly your own approach to self-regard, and how you could use the counsel offered by Kant, Neff, and Aristotle to become more self-respecting.

Adding Favorite Sages of Your Own

Perhaps you have a favorite sage of your own who you think gives positive advice on how to be more courageous, exercise greater foresight, or become more decisive. Exercise 5.13 gives you an opportunity to add them to the list!

EXERCISE 5.13

1. Do you have a favorite sage of your own who offers empowering wisdom on how to be more courageous; more foresighted; more decisive? If so, formulate this wisdom below. (Even if you don't know the name of the person from whom the advice comes, that's still okay.)

Additional Empowering Wisdom for Decisiveness

Additional Empowering Wisdom for Authenticity

Additional Empowering Wisdom for Self-Respect

TABLE 5.3

Empowering wisdom regarding Decisiveness, Authenticity, and Self-Respect

Decisiveness	Authenticity	Self-Respect
Sartre:	**John Stuart Mill:**	**Kant:**
You are nothing more than the sum of [your] actions and therefore responsible for what you are or become.	Since you are imperfect and learn by experience, try out different modes of living to develop your character as a distinct individual, short of injury to others.	Treat yourself as an end in itself (person), not a "mere means" (object) by asserting your own autonomy and making your own choices.
__You are condemned to be free because you are responsible for everything you do (or don't do).		__Your worth and dignity as an autonomous person is unconditional and does not depend on what other
Epictetus:	__Otherwise, missing is one of the principal ingredients of human happiness, namely your individuality.	people think of you.
Act on your own judgment as though it were a law and disrespectful not to obey it, regardless of what anyone else may think of you.		**Neff:**
		Be gentle, kind, and understanding with yourself, not critical and judgmental.
__Think of yourself as worthy of living as an adult with your own mind.	**Nietzsche:**	__Connect with others instead of feeling alone in your suffering.
The Mills:	Noble people create their own values (decide what's good or bad) and therefore don't need others' approval.	__Hold your pain in balanced awareness, neither ignoring nor exaggerating it.
Don't allow others to enslave your mind.		
Don't be a "willing slave"!		
John Stuart Mill:	**The Bhagavata Purana:**	**Aristotle:**
You have incredible, native powers to perceive, judge, and discriminate. Strengthen them by making your own choices, not merely following others.	A blind man guided by another blind man misses the right path and fall into a ditch.	Love yourself as your own best friend. __Wish yourself well for your own sake.

Compiling a Master List of Empowering Wisdom

Sartre, Epictetus, and Mill have given you some language to formulate their learned counsel that can go on a list of empowering wisdom to inspire Decisiveness. For instance, for each of the formulations in the Decisiveness column of Table 5.3, focus, one at a time, on the formulation with your mind's eye, and key into how it *feels. Does it move you to be more decisive in doing your own thing*!? If yes, keep it on your list of empowering wisdom; if not, take it off or change the language!

Similarly, for each of formulations in the Authenticity column of Table 5.3, focus, one at a time, on the formulation with your mind's eye, and key into how it *feels. Does it make you feel more empowered to be your own person?* If yes, keep it on your list of empowering wisdom; if not, take it off or change the language!

Finally, for each of the formulations in the Self-Respect column of Table 5.3, focus, one at a time, on the formulation with your mind's eye, and key into how it *feels. Does it make you feel more empowered to accept yourself, unconditionally?* If yes, keep it on your list of empowering wisdom; if not, take it off or change the language!

Have you found the counsel formulated in Table 5.3 to have a positive feeling of empowerment? The language used to express this wisdom is an important part of why it can inspire you to feel more empowered.

Exercise 5.14 gives you the opportunity to modify the language as well as the content of your lists.

EXERCISE 5.14

This exercise will help you to develop a *master list of empowering wisdom that is uplifting, consoling, or otherwise empowering for you.*

Please feel free to modify Table 5.3 in responding to the following instructions:

1. For each of the three guiding virtues, place a checkmark in front of each learned counsel you intend to use. Your selections should resonate with you, that is, feel uplifting, consoling, or otherwise empowering to you.

2. If you are not satisfied with the formulation of any of the counsels in Table 5.3, on a separate piece of paper, please rewrite it using language that resonates with you. For example, when I think of Nietzsche's counsel on being a "creator of value," I think of the words "being innovative" and "thinking outside the box." You are encouraged to reformulate or tweak the sages' counsel using any language that is more empowering for you!

3. Please also add any empowering insights to Table 5.3 that you may have formulated in Exercise 5.12. Again, it is important that the language you use is empowering *for you*.

4. Now, congratulate yourself! You now have a master list of wisdom that is empowering for you!

---

6. CREATING A COGNITIVE-BEHAVIORAL PLAN

Are you ready to harness the wisdom of the sages to build a plan of action for overcoming your low self-reliance? Here lies your opportunity to break the shackles of self-oppression that have kept you from being the person you aspire to be. This can be incredibly exciting!

Suppose you have always demanded that everyone like you; however, you are a transgender person who has always been extremely uncomfortable with your birth gender, and have become increasingly despondent over it. While you have considered gender reassignment surgery, you have felt disempowered to go through with it because people would reject you and think you were a "freak."

Recently, however, you have resolved to try to overcome your LSR and are now working on creating a cognitive-behavioral plan which will help you to build your guiding virtues.

To increase your level of Decisiveness, you propose to

- Make an appointment with a surgeon to discuss the procedure.
- Educate yourself about the procedure through online articles.
- Reframe your decision to look into the surgery as a healthy exercise of your rational faculties, and strengthening of your willpower muscle.
- Reframe you rule of rationally and objectively considering whether to undergo the surgery as a law that you would be "impious to transgress."
- Actually go through with whatever you decide rather than procrastinate about it.

To exercise *Authenticity*, you decide to

- Look upon yourself as a "creator of values" and not simply a member of a herd that blindly conforms.
- Reframe the importance of being an individual and not simply a blind conformist as a "principal ingredient of human happiness."
- Resolve not to be like the blind person being led by the blind by prioritizing over others' shortsighted approval, your convictions about personal happiness and being yourself.

To be more *Self-Respecting* you resolve to

- Accept yourself as an "end in yourself," that is as an autonomous (self-determining) person rather than a "mere means" or object to be manipulated by others. Accordingly, you resolve not to think of yourself in derogatory terms such as "freak" which objectify you and flaunt your unconditional worth as a person.
- Be self-compassionate and "gentle and understanding" with yourself about your feelings and desires instead of negatively judging them based on what others might think.
- Love yourself as your own best friend by not stressing yourself out and thinking and acting rationally in the activities of everyday life.

Now it's your turn to build a plan of action based on the learned counsel you have accepted. Exercise 5.15 can help with this!

EXERCISE 5.15

1. Choose a relatively short-term goal from one of the goals you described in Exercise 5.2, which you are now willing to try to achieve. (Recall you were asked to include at least one short-term goal.) Restate this goal in the space provided below:

[blank box]

2. Now, restate the LSR thinking you formulated in Exercise 5.4 that has blocked you from attempting to achieve this goal.

1.

2.

3.

4.

Using your empowering wisdom, the remainder of this exercise will help you to construct the elements of a cognitive-behavioral plan to overcome Conclusion 4 of the above LSR thinking!

3. Using empowering wisdom offered by Sartre, Epictetus, and John Stuart Mill, or any wisdom you may have added in Exercise 5.13 for becoming *more decisive*, what cognitive-behavioral changes would you make to overcome your LSR thinking? For example, what changes would Sartre tell you to make in the way you are presently *thinking* about making decisions? What would you *do* differently according to Sartre? List at least three cognitive-behavioral changes you plan to make based on such advice:

1.

2.

3.

4.

5.

4. Using the counsel offered by the Bhagavada Purana, Nietzsche, and Mill, or any other empowering wisdom you may have added in Exercise 5.13 for becoming *more authentic*, what cognitive-behavioral changes would you make to overcome your LSR thinking? List at least three:

1.

2.

3.

4.

5.

5. Using counsel offered by Kant, Neff, and Aristotle, or any other empowering wisdom you may have added in Exercise 5.13 for becoming *more self-respecting*, what cognitive-behavioral changes would you make to overcome your LSR thinking? List at least three:

1.

2.

3.

4.

5.

6. Now, congratulate yourself! You have just constructed a cognitive-behavioral plan!!

---

7. WORKING ON YOUR COGNITIVE-BEHAVIORAL PLAN

You now have an opportunity to begin to build your habits of Decisiveness, Authenticity, and Self-Respect, instead of defaulting to your self-defeating habit of low self-reliance.

Cognitive–Affective Imagery

You can work on overcoming your LSR thinking by *imagining* yourself in a compromising situation without actually being in it, and then work through your cognitive reframing (refuting your irrational premises, focusing on your virtues and their supporting empowering wisdom). This activity can be a useful preliminary to strengthening your skills in dealing with such situations when you are actually in them. For example, you could imagine yourself screwing up at something that meets with the disapproval of your partner. This is an excellent warm-up exercise for really going through with something that might meet with the disapproval of others.

Exercise 5.16 can help you to get started with practicing some cognitive–affective imagery.

EXERCISE 5.16

1. Choose uplifting language from the Decisiveness column of your master list of key empowering language (see Exercise 5.14) that is especially empowering or uplifting for you. Keep it in the back of your mind at this point.

2. Refer to the LSR thinking you identified in Exercise 5.15, which is blocking a *short-term goal* you also identified in Exercise 5.15.

3. Now, here are instructions for doing cognitive–affective imagery. If you are working with a therapist, the therapist can provide guidance until you get the hang of it and can do it on your own. If you are not being assisted by a therapist, then please read these directions carefully now, memorize them (three steps), and then follow the three-step sequence laid out for you below:

- Step 1: Focus your mind exclusively on your LSR thinking (as identified in Exercise 5.15). Keep going over it in your mind like you did when you first decided you couldn't accomplish your goal. Keep it up until you feel that negative visceral threatening feeling, the clashing of your felt need for approval with the realization that you might not get this approval if you try to achieve your goal. Let yourself resonate with the feeling of powerlessness that emerges, and that "I can't do this!" feeling.

- Step 2: At the peak of feeling this intense negative feeling, shift your focus of mind exclusively to the positive language that you have selected for feeling empowered to become decisive. Let yourself feel the uplift, the empowerment to confront and transcend your anxiety about not getting the approval; toward feeling the freedom to make your own decisions.
- Step 3: Once you have fully brought yourself to resonate with the positivity of the experience, gently shift your attention to reflecting on your experience and what you have learned or discovered from it.

4. Try to reserve a time each day to practice this guided imagery exercise. Next time, however, choose uplifting language from the *Authenticity* column of your master list of key empowering language that is especially empowering or uplifting for you.

5. Similarly, the subsequent day, repeat the exercise except this time choose uplifting language from the *Self-Respect* column of your master list of key empowering language.

6. Practice regularly, shifting between your uplifting language to support *all three* of your guiding virtues.

7. What have you learned or discovered about yourself from your experience practicing your cognitive–affective imagery? Write down your reflections in the space below:

My Reflections about My Experience:

Continue practicing your imagery!!

Loving Kindness Meditation

Practicing self-compassion can be a useful way to build the unconditional self-acceptance of Self-Respect. Loving kindness meditation can be an effective way to accomplish this goal.

Unfortunately, demanding approval from others stifles healthy connections with others, which always involve seeing everyone (yourself included) as being in the same boat; that is, subject to the same inevitabilities of loss, sickness, aging, and death. So, we should have the *same* compassion for everyone, including yourself. Your self-worth is no more dependent on what others think of you than is the worth of others dependent on what you think of them. We are all part of one seamless, unified humanity. Loving kindness meditation can help you to feel this connectivity with others, to feel *equally* unified and loved, instead of putting your self-worth in limbo.

Exercise 5.17 can help you to feel this connectivity and unconditional self-acceptance.

EXERCISE 5.17

1. Please listen to the guided meditation audio recording called "Best Friend Meditation" presented by Lucy Rising (or an find alternative loving kindness, self-compassion, guided mediation if unavailable). This audio + video recording is (at the time of this writing) freely accessible on the following link: http://lucyrising.com/meditations. When you have finished following the presentation, respond to the below questions.

2. Reflect on your *demand* that you get the approval of others to be worthy. How does this demand *feel* when you think of your loving kindness wishes and feelings you extend to yourself and all others?

3. As your own best friend, what are you telling yourself about this demand?

4. When you reflect on your LSR thinking (as described in Exercise 5.15), how does this thinking now feel in relation to the love and compassion you extend to yourself as your own best friend?

Refuting and Reframing

You can helpfully refute and reframe your self-defeating thinking! As discussed in the Introduction to this book, reframing involves placing your negative thinking in a more positive light. Exercise 5.18 will help you to work on practicing refuting and reframing your LSR thinking.

EXERCISE 5.18

1. Refer again to the LSR thinking you identified in Exercise 5.15, which is blocking the short-term goal you also identified in Exercise 5.15. Look carefully at Premise 1 of your LSR thinking, the one that *demands certainty*. In Exercise 5.5, you have already refuted this premise so you can see how irrational it truly is. Think about this refutation until it resonates with you, that is, you get the "I get it" feeling that this premise is truly irrational. If this doesn't happen, then go back to Exercise 5.5 and find a refutation that does resonate with you. Write down your refutation in Table 5.4 in the refutation column for Premise 1.

Now, select some empowering wisdom from one or more of your sages (it could be wisdom you added in Exercise 5.13), and use it to reframe your demand for certainty. Write down this empowering wisdom in Table 5.4 in the reframing column for Premise 1.

2. Just as you have done for Premise 1, refute and reframe Conclusions 3 and 4 of the LSR thinking you identified in Exercise 5.15. Use Table 5.4 below to write down your refutation and reframing for each of these respective conclusions of your LSR thinking.

TABLE 5.4
Refuting and reframing my LSR thinking

Part	Refutation	Reframing
Premise 1		
Conclusion 3		
Conclusion 4		

Engaging in a Shame Attacking Exercise

This type of assignment can help you to work both cognitively and behaviorally on your low self-reliance. Exercise 5.18 provides directions.

EXERCISE 5.19

1. Choose an action to perform that will be likely to draw negative attention to you, that is, something that would lead others to disapprove of you in some way. For example, psychologist

Albert Ellis used to suggest walking down a busy street pulling a banana on a string. You could walk up to a stranger and speak gibberish; or wear an outlandish article of clothing such as a clown suit to a formal dinner. Describe this activity in the space provided below:

2. Next, calendar a time you intend to perform the chosen act. Then, practice refuting it and reframing it using the empowering wisdom from your sages on how to be self-respecting.

3. Next, prior to, during, and after performing the act, practice refuting it and reframing it using your learned counsel.

4. After performing the action, reflect on your experience in the space provided below. How did you feel when you were engaging in the act? What if anything did you learn from your experience? What if anything did you learn about yourself?

Congratulations on completing your shame attacking exercise! Feel free to repeat it as many times as you like!

Getting Some Bibliotherapy

If you are working with a therapist, your therapist may recommend a movie that can help you to gain inspiration for becoming more decisive, authentic, and self-respecting. In any event, one such movie is *Mona Lisa Smiles,* starring Julia Roberts and Kirsten Dunst, and directed by Mike Newell (2003). The film is set in the 1950s at an all-women's school (Wellesley College) where the students merely assume their education is but a precursor to becoming a wife and mother. Just see how a decisive, authentic, and self-respecting role model, a teacher (played by Julia Roberts) can provide incredible inspiration to be your own person!

The little book titled, *Growing in Love: 21 Ways to Become Less Dependent & More Authentic*, by James Leonard Park (1998), available free online, can give you further empowering counsel on overcoming your LSR thinking, and replacing it with ideas that promote Authenticity.

If you like to read, I also recommend the classic, *The Art of Love* by Eric Fromm (2006), which can give you a lift toward cultivating mutuality in intimate, loving relationships. In this little book, Fromm speaks of love as an art which, like other arts, requires practice. "[M]ature love," he says, "is a union underlying the condition of preserving one's integrity, one's individuality … In love, the paradox occurs that two beings become one and yet remain two" (Fromm, 2006, p. 19). Sound familiar? This idea of human connectedness is at the core of your loving kindness meditation, which you did in Exercise 5.17.

EXERCISE 5.20

1. Select a movie or literary work that has the theme of overcoming dependency on others to become more authentic. If one of the suggestions provided here interests you, then feel free to pursue it as your bibliotherapy.

Alternatively, if you are working with a therapist then you may find it useful to discuss other possibilities with the therapist. If you are using this *Workbook* as a self-help tool, you are also free to find an alternative that inspires Authenticity.

2. Once you have viewed (or read) your bibliotherapy, write your reflections in the space provided below. What words would you use to describe the feelings it evoked? Has it helped to prepare you for your own personal goals that you have described in Exercise 5.2?

Acting on Your Goal

This is the final stage of your process of working on your cognitive-behavioral plan. It involves doing all the things you listed in your cognitive-behavioral plan, which you developed in Exercise 5.15, which includes *acting* on your goal. For example, if you have always wanted to change your hairstyle and dress in a way that pleases you, even if it's not likely to please your partner, then this is the time to express your Authenticity; and if you have been vacillating about writing that novel, thinking that nobody would like it, then this is the time to be decisive and put pen to paper; and stop thinking of yourself as the quintessential loser, and start defining yourself through your actions! Finally, continue practicing your guided imagery, meditation, and refuting and reframing of any of the self-defeating lines of thinking at the root of your low self-reliance.

Exercise 5.21 provides instructions.

EXERCISE 5.21

1. Review the cognitive-behavioral items on your behavioral plan created in Exercise 5.15.

2. Refute Premise 1 and Conclusions 3 and 4 of your LSR thinking and reframe them using your empowering wisdom for exercising Decisiveness, Authenticity, and Self-Respect as developed in Exercise 5.15.

3. Implement each of the behavioral elements in your plan, which includes acting on your goal. Keep in mind that "action" can also include *not* doing things you were previously intimated to do for fear of being rejected if you refused, for example, not engaging in sex acts you do not want to perform.

3. Continue to refute and reframe your LSR thinking, and keep up your loving kindness meditation, even after you act on your goals. This can help support and build your new habits as you plan further goals and implement them.

4. Provide your reflections below about your experience in implementing your cognitive-behavioral plan.

5. This is an incredible milestone, so congratulate yourself!

Working on Your Other Goals

In Exercise 5.2, you described at least three goals that you would like to fulfill but have been blocked by your low self-reliance. Now that you have worked through your first, short-term goal, you can continue working to fulfill the other goals you described, or you can even add new goals.

The process is the same, and you have already gone through it in addressing your short-term goal. So, you now possess knowledge of this process, and you are also on your way to cultivating your virtues and accomplishing your goals. Here is a summary of the process:

1. Formulate your LSR thinking (Exercise 5.4).
2. Refute Premise 1 and Conclusions 3 and 4 of this thinking (Exercise 5.5).
3. Embrace your guiding virtues (Exercises 5.6 through 5.9).
4. Get empowering wisdom from the sages on pursuing the virtues (Exercises 5.10 through 5.14).
5. Use this learned counsel to construct a cognitive-behavioral plan (Exercise 5.15).
6. Work on your cognitive-behavioral plan (Exercises 5.16 through 5.21).

Having worked through the exercises in this chapter, you are well on your way to attaining greater and greater freedom and fulfillment in life as you become less and less dependent on the approval of others for self-validation. Clearly, building your guiding virtues of Decisiveness, Authenticity, and Self-Respect is a lifelong commitment. Keep working through the above six steps regularly. If you falter, no problem. You are human, after all. Get back in the saddle. You will prevail!

REFERENCES

Aristotle. (1941). *Nicomachean ethics.* In McKeon, R. (Ed.). *The Basic Works of Aristotle.* Random House.

Epictetus. (1948). *The Enchiridion.* Higgins, T.W. (Trans.). Liberal Arts Press. Retrieved from www.gutenberg.org/files/45109/45109-h/45109-h.htm

Fromm, E. (2006). *The Art of Love.* Harper Collins.

Kant, I. (1964). *Groundwork of the metaphysics of morals.* Trans. Paton, H.J., Harper & Row.

Mill, J.S. & Mill, H.T. (1869). *The subjection of women.* Longmans, Green, Reader, and Dyer. Retrieved from www.gutenberg.org/files/27083/27083-h/27083-h.htm

Mill, J.S. (1859). *On liberty.* Walter Scott Publishing Co. Retrieved from www.gutenberg.org/files/34901/34901-h/34901-h.htm

Neff, K. (May 27, 2011). Why self-compassion trumps self-esteem. *Greater Good Magazine.* Retrieved from https://greatergood.berkeley.edu/article/item/try_selfcompassion

Newell, M. [Director] (2003). *Mona Lisa Smile.* Columbia Tristar / Sony Pictures Entertainment. Retrieved from www.imdb.com/title/tt0304415/?ref_=vp_back

Nietzsche, F. (1954). *Beyond good and evil.* Trans. Helen Zimmern. In *The philosophy of Nietzsche.* Random House. ch. 9, sec. 260, 579.

Park, J.L. (1998). *Growing in love: 21 ways to become less dependent and more authentic.* Existential Books. Retrieved from https://s3.amazonaws.com/aws-website-jamesleonardpark---freelibrary-3puxk/GIL.html

Prabhupada, S. (n.d.). *Bhagavata purana.* Retrieved from https://vedabase.io/en/library/sb/7/

Sartre, J.P. (2007). *Existentialism is a humanism,* Carol.Macomber (Trans.). Yale University Press.

Yiğitoğlu, G.T. & Keskin, G. (2019). Relationship between dysfunctional beliefs and stress coping methods in drug-addicted patients: A sample of Turkey. *Indian Journal of Psychiatry,* 61.5, 508–519. www.indianjpsychiatry.org/article.asp?issn=0019-5545;year=2019;volume=61;issue=5;spage=508;epage=519;aulast=Yigitoglu

6

Overcoming Your Obsessive Thinking

As you have seen in the introduction to this chapter, obsessive *can't*stipation is a cognitive type of *can't*stipation that sustains unwanted thoughts ("I can't stop thinking about this horrible thought!"). This can keep you in a vicious cycle of painful anxiety that can seriously stifle your personal happiness.

1. GOALS OF THE CHAPTER:

Accordingly, the goals of this chapter are to:

1. Increase awareness of your obsessive thinking and the language you are using to sustain it.
2. Refute this thinking.
3. Identify guiding virtues that counteract your obsessive thinking.
4. Identify empowering wisdom from great sages on how to seek these virtues.
5. Use this learned counsel to construct a cognitive-behavioral plan for increasing your virtues.
6. Work on your plan, including exercising control over such unwanted thoughts.

2. THE NATURE OF OBSESSIVE THINKING

This type of *can't*stipation is associated with chronic anxiety about whether the thoughts in question are realistic. This can take up a lot of time in the course of your day, biting severely into your ability to engage in constructive, fulfilling activities.

To boot, obsessive *can't*stipation can lead you to engage in rituals to ward off the bad thoughts. This could be a certain thought activity such as counting; or it could involve a checking activity such as checking and rechecking a locked door to make certain it is locked.

In general, there are two types of obsessions, (1) moral and (2) existential. Moral obsessions involve obsession over morally bad thoughts such as the possibility of killing someone. Existential obsessions involve thoughts about bad things happening to you or to someone else whom you love.

DOI: 10.4324/9781003035282-7

Morally Obsessive Thinking

For example, the thinking that sustains moral obsessions can look like this:

1. I must be certain that I won't stab my husband to death with a steak knife.
2. But I have this thought that I might really do it!
3. So, it's not certain I won't really do it.
4. So, this could mean I'm a *horrible person*.
5. So, I can't stop thinking about it!

As you can see, you tell yourself in Premise 1 that you must be certain you won't stab your husband to death with a steak knife. But then because, in Premise 2, you tell yourself that you have the thought of doing it, you conclude in 3 that it's *not certain* you won't really do it. This uncertainty feels threatening to you *as a person*, which leads you to damn yourself ("horrible person").

The idea here is that if you have the thought about doing this act, you *might* actually do it; for why else would such a thing have occurred to you in the first place! So, in 4, you further conclude that you might be a *horrible person*; for what kind of person would *not* be certain she wouldn't do such a horrible thing!

So, in 5, you tell yourself you just can't let this go and must continually keep checking this thought over and over to *make sure* you wouldn't actually do it. But this keeps you perpetually in a vicious circle because the more you check it out, the more you keep telling yourself that you are not certain you wouldn't do it!

In desperation you might try to do some sort of ritual to ward off the thinking, but as long as you are committed to the premises of your morally obsessive thinking, these rituals will only compound the problem, not make it go away.

The problem lies first in the *perfectionistic demand* you are making about being certain you wouldn't do such a bad thing; and second, in the language you are using to *damn yourself* for having the thought of doing it ("horrible person"). But are you really a "horrible person" to have such a thought, or just an imperfect human being who had this unwanted thought? Other possible words people might use to damn themselves include:

- "monster"
- "devil"
- "pervert"
- "murderer"
- "lunatic"
- "psychopath"
- "demon."

Other common examples of moral obsessions that can key into such thinking and language include:

- killing a pedestrian while driving
- doing something "sinful" (violative of your religion)
- committing suicide by overdosing on a drug
- destroying someone else's property
- engaging in inappropriate sex acts
- screaming profanities in the presence of others, and
- contaminating others with a disease.

Existentially Obsessive Thinking

For example, the thinking that sustains existential obsessions can look like this:

1. I must be certain I won't get very sick and die.
2. But I have this thought of this happening to me.
3. So, I am not certain it won't really happen to me.
4. So, it's *awful* this could really happen to me.
5. So, I can't stop thinking about it.

As you can see, in Premise 1, you demand certainty that you won't get very sick and die. But because you have the thought of this happening to you in 2, you conclude in 3 that you're not certain it won't really happen. Indeed, the very thought of it somehow makes the possibility a real thing! So, in 4 you catastrophize about this possibility that you could get sick and die by calling it "awful." Then, since it is such an awful possibility you conclude that you can't stop thinking about it. You must keep checking it over and over to really see if it can really happen. This uncertainty, however, is not eliminated through your rumination but instead creates a vicious cycle where the more you ruminate over it, the more you keep confirming the possibility of it actually happening.

So, you might, as in the case of moral obsessions, engage in rituals to try to escape the viciousness of this cycle. But it doesn't work because the thinking that fuels it is still intact and playing out over and over in your mind.

The problem is that you are *demanding* certainty that such a bad thing not happen to you; and then when you conclude that it is a real possibility, this uncertainty *feels* utterly threatening to you, so you catastrophize about the negative possibility ("It's awful") and then, to satisfy your demand for certainty, you tell yourself that you can't stop thinking about it until you eliminate the uncertainty. But, again, it won't go away unless you eliminate the thinking that perpetuates your vicious cycle of obsession!

Further examples of *catastrophic language* you may use to rate this uncertainty include:

- "horrible"
- "unthinkable"
- "intolerable"
- "unbearable"
- "the pits"
- "dreadful"
- "nightmarish"
- "sickening."

Other examples of existential obsessions driven by such thinking are these:

- getting viciously attacked by a dog
- something bad happening to a loved one
- eating or drinking something that is contaminated
- things being messy or out of order, and
- having forgotten to turn off the stove (even though you checked it several times).

Exercise 6.1 is an icebreaker to help you get more in touch with the feelings going on inside you when you tell yourself you can't stop thinking about the unwanted thoughts.

EXERCISE 6.1

Write down your answers to the following questions in the space provided. Use separate pieces of paper if necessary. If you don't ever have moral obsessions, you can skip question 2; if you don't have existential obsessions, you can skip question 3.

1. When you have an obsessive thought, how do you feel about the fact that you are having this thought?

2. If a *moral* obsession, what do you tell yourself about *yourself*? Why do you tell yourself this about yourself? How do you *feel* about yourself?

3. If an *existential* obsession, what do you tell yourself about the *thought* of this bad thing happening? Does the mere thought of its happening upset you? Explain.

4. When the thought keeps repeating in your mind, how do you feel? What, if anything, do you do to try to deal with this feeling?

5. Are you satisfied with the way you try to deal with it? Explain.

The Self-Defeating Nature of Your Obsessive Thinking

Unfortunately, your obsessive thinking creates intense anxiety, which you may tend to resolve by concluding, "I can't stop the thought." The self-defeating result of this thinking is that you keep yourself ruminating about the thought and it takes its toll on your personal and interpersonal happiness.

3. EXAMINING *YOUR* OBSESSIVE THINKING

In this section you will have the opportunity to examine your own obsessive thinking. So, what does *your* obsessive thinking look like? Exercises 6.2 through 6.4 will help you to answer this question.

EXERCISE 6.2

Please briefly describe some obsessive thoughts (at most five) you tend to have and would like not to have. At least one of these thoughts should be one that you presently are obsessing over and would especially like to work on. Your obsessions can be moral or existential, or both.

1.

2.

3.

4.

5.

EXERCISE 6.3

1. If your list of obsessive thoughts includes *moral* obsessions, make a list of some of the self-damning language you tend to use when you have these obsessions.

Your Disempowering, Self-Damning Language List

With the above filled in, you have a list of at least some of the self-damning terms you tend to use to disempower yourself in the case of moral obsessions. These are words that you will need to retire from your vocabulary!

2. If your list of obsessive thoughts includes *existential* obsessions, make a list of some of the catastrophic language you tend to use when you have these obsessions.

Your Disempowering, Catastrophic Language List

EXERCISE 6.4

Next, for each of the cases you listed in Exercise 6.2, write down your obsessive thinking (chain of reasoning leading you to say you can't) using the language you identified in Exercise 6.3. To formulate the thinking in *moral* obsessions on your list (if any) please follow the *moral* obsession template provided below. To formulate the thinking in *existential* obsessions on your list (if any) please follow the *existential* obsession template also provided below.

Moral Obsession Template:

1. I must be certain that I won't/didn't [enter obsessive thought here].
2. But I have this thought that I might really do it!
3. So, it's not certain I won't really do it.
4. So, this could mean I'm [enter self-damning term here].
5. So, I can't stop thinking about it!

For example, suppose you have the obsessive thought of raping one of your colleagues at work. Then your morally obsessive thinking would look like this:

1. I must be certain that I won't <u>rape my colleague</u>.
2. But I have this thought that I might really do it!
3. So, it's not certain I won't really do it.
4. So, this could mean I'm <u>a pervert</u>.
5. So, I can't stop thinking about it!

Existential Obsession Template:

1. I must be certain it won't/didn't happen that [enter an unwanted event].
2. But I have this thought of this happening.
3. So, I am not certain it won't really happen.
4. So, it's [enter a catastrophic term] that this could really happen.
5. So, I can't stop thinking about it.

For example, suppose you have the obsessive thought of your heart failing, despite having no medical evidence that it is. Then your existentially obsessive thinking would look like this:

1. I must be certain it won't happen that <u>my heart is failing</u>.
2. But I have this thought of this happening.
3. So, I am not certain it won't really happen.
4. So, it's <u>horrible</u> that this could really happen.
5. So, I can't stop thinking about it.

Now it's your turn to formulate *your* dependency thinking:

Case	Your Obsessive Thinking
1.	1. 2. 3. 4. 5.
2.	1. 2. 3. 4. 5.
3.	1. 2. 3. 4. 5.
4.	1. 2. 3. 4. 5.

Case	Your Obsessive Thinking
5.	1.
	2.
	3.
	4.
	5.

Refuting Your Obsessive Thinking

Now that you have formulated the thinking you are doing to obsessively *can't*stipate yourself, it's time to look at this thinking carefully to showing how irrational it truly is. This step is known as *refutation* in cognitive-behavior therapy. It can help you to appreciate exactly why your thinking is irrational!

To illustrate, consider again one of the previous examples from Exercise 6.4:

1. I must be certain that I won't rape my colleague.
2. But I have this thought that I might really do it!
3. So, it's not certain I won't really do it.
4. So, this could mean I'm a pervert.
5. So, I can't stop thinking about it!

Using the above reasoning as an example, Table 6.1 provides examples of some rational questions you can ask yourself in refuting the irrational parts of your dependency thinking. These irrational parts are Premise 1 and Conclusions 4 and 5.

It's now time for you to refute your own obsessive thinking! Exercise 6.5 will assist.

TABLE 6.1
Examples of refutation of Premise 1 and Conclusions 3 and 4 of obsessive thinking

Part of Your Obsessive Thinking to Be Refuted	Ask Yourself This Question to Refute Given Part of Your Thinking
1. I must be certain that I won't rape my colleague.	*Where is it written that I must be certain I won't commit this act?*
	Answer: Nowhere except in my head! I don't have to be *certain* to have reasonable belief I wouldn't do something like this.
Premise 1 again	*Am I even being consistent when I demand that I must be certain I won't do such a thing while no one has absolute certainty?*
	Answer: I don't believe anyone else has such certainty, so why am I a special case. Most people seem to function quite well without having certainty they would not do bad things, so why do I think I must have such assurance to function well?
4. So, this could mean I'm a pervert.	*Do I think others are "perverts" because they lack certainty they would not rape one of their colleagues?*
	Answer: No! I am negatively judging myself according to a stricter standard than that by which I judge others. And this standard is not even realistic!
Conclusion 4 again	*What are the practical consequences of calling myself a pervert?*
	Answer: I merely create self-defeating anxiety without serving any useful purpose.

TABLE 6.1
(Continued)

Part of Your Obsessive Thinking to Be Refuted	Ask Yourself This Question to Refute Given Part of Your Thinking
5. So, I can't stop thinking about it!	*Is it really that I can't or is it rather that I am choosing not to?*
	Answer: Unless I lack free will like some preprogrammed machine, I *can* stop thinking about it!
Conclusion 5 again	*What are the practical consequences of telling myself I can't stop thinking about it?*
	Answer: I keep myself in a state of suspended anxiety without doing anything constructive to stop thinking about it, and move on with my life!

EXERCISE 6.5

Asking yourself the questions provided in Table 6.1 (as relevant), refute Premise 1, and Conclusions 4 and 5 of each of the obsessive thinking chains you have constructed in Exercise 6.4. Write down the irrational premise or conclusion and your respective refutation in the columns provided in Table 6.1A.

TABLE 6.1A
Refutations of my obsessive thinking

My Obsessive Thinking	My Refutation
Chain 1:	
Premise 1:	Refutation of Premise 1:
Conclusion 4:	Refutation of Conclusion 4:
Conclusion 5:	Refutation of Conclusion 5:
Chain 2:	
Premise 1:	Refutation of Premise 1:
Conclusion 4:	Refutation of Conclusion 4:
Conclusion 5:	Refutation of Conclusion 5:
Chain 3:	
Premise 1:	Refutation of Premise 1:
Conclusion 4:	Refutation of Conclusion 4:
Conclusion 5:	Refutation of Conclusion 5:

TABLE 6.1A

(Continued)

My Obsessive Thinking	My Refutation
Chain 4:	
Premise 1:	Refutation of Premise 1:
Conclusion 4:	Refutation of Conclusion 4:
Conclusion 5:	Refutation of Conclusion 5:
Chain 5:	
Premise 1:	Refutation of Premise 1:
Conclusion 4:	Refutation of Conclusion 4:
Conclusion 5:	Refutation of Conclusion 5:

4. EMBRACING YOUR GUIDING VIRTUES

By working on building certain "virtues" you can overcome your obsessive thinking. These guiding virtues include Serenity (Peace of Mind), Self-Respect, and Respect for Life. Before proceeding, please carefully review the definitions of each of these virtues in Table 6.2.

Notice that these virtues are ideals. This means that they can never be attained perfectly, so they set goals to strive for over the course of your lifetime. As such, backsliding or falling short of the progress you hoped for are par for the course. Just keep at it and you will keep getting better and better!

Following is an overview of each of these virtues along with exercises to help you get started!

Serenity

Serenity is a state of peace of mind which counteracts obsessive thinking by allowing you to let go of intrusive thoughts without evaluating and checking them, over and over again.

TABLE 6.2

Definitions of your guiding virtues

Guiding Virtue	Description
1. *Serenity*	Allowing thoughts to freely enter and exit conscious awareness without catastrophizing, damning, or demanding perfection in conceiving, pondering, or dismissing them.
3. *Respect for Life*	Acceptance of life as possessing worth and meaning despite the inevitability of problems of living.
4. *Self-Respect*	Unconditional, self-acceptance based on a deep philosophical understanding of human worth and dignity.

Serene people are other-regarding and tend to have positive feelings for others. They are comfortable with probability rather than certainty, and therefore do not demand certainty or otherwise attempt to control what is beyond their control. They are comfortable with the fact that not everything is always neat and orderly, that bad things are inevitable, but this does not make the world itself a bad place. To the contrary, they perceive the imperfections in the world as opportunities to make constructive changes. As such, they see human imperfection in themselves and others as opportunities to learn and grow, intellectually, emotionally, and spiritually. They see aging, illness, loss, and death as conditions acceptance of which is requisite to enjoying life, rather than becoming obsessed with these possibilities to the detriment of personal and interpersonal happiness.

How serene are you? Exercise 6.6 can help to address this question.

EXERCISE 6.6

1. How comfortable are you with such things as aging, illness, loss, and death? In the space provided, give two or three examples of how you deal with such things.

2. When things are not neat or orderly, how do you feel? How do you generally deal with disorderliness?

3. Do you tend to be more concerned with your own feelings or those of others? Give an example or two.

4. How do you feel about the uncertainty of bad things happening? How do you generally deal with such possibilities? Give at least one example.

5. Do you consider yourself a perfectionist? Explain.

Respect for Life

Respect for Life also supports and is supported by Serenity by virtue of accepting life despite problems of living. Indeed, people who have Respect for Life view problems of living as inevitable parts of meaningful and worthwhile lives. Such individuals accept that living involves taking risks and provides no guarantees. As such, when bad things happen, as they will, such individuals tend to avoid globally catastrophic or damning judgments about their lives ("My life sucks"), realizing that what's true of a part of life is not necessarily true of the whole.

Some who have respect for their lives may perceive the intrinsic worth of their lives in terms of being a gift from God, and thus a sin to waste or damn it. Some who are not especially religious may perceive the worth of their lives in terms of its potential to provide personal and interpersonal happiness through the interpersonal relationships forged, development of intellectual and moral virtues, helping others, good works, and lasting pleasure, among other aspects of human well-being. In any event, people who respect their lives tend not to waste them on meaningless or self-defeating activities including ruminating about bad thoughts, realizing that their lives are too precious to spend like this.

Exercise 6.7 can help you get clearer about how life-respecting you are.

EXERCISE 6.7

1. Do you value your life? If so, what makes your life valuable to you? If not, why not?

2. When things go wrong in your life, how do you generally manage it? What is your general attitude about your life in such situations?

3. How much of your life, generally speaking, is spent on things you would, from an objective perspective, regard as wasteful or self-defeating? Explain.

Self-Respect

Self-Respect is distinct from Respect for Life although these virtues are mutually supportive. A person may exaggerate the problems of life while still being reasonably comfortable with themselves, although people who are able to deal well with the stresses of life generally have more self-respect. For example, they may be able to more effectively handle rejection by others, realizing that the latter is an inevitable part of living.

Self-Respect is also supported by Serenity by virtue of allowing self-doubts to freely enter and exit consciousness without self-damnation or feeling compelled to ruminate about them. People who are self-respecting do not globally damn themselves when they make mistakes, but instead distinguish between the deed and the doer, welcoming constructive criticism aimed at helping them to do better in the future. As such, they *unconditionally* accept themselves, which means they do not question their self-worth. This, in turn, means that they do not perceive their self-worth as diminished by mistakes in judgment. Nor do they see their self-worth in terms of their achievements or the approval of others. So, they do not see failure or loss of approval as reasons to question their self-worth. As such, they tend not to suffer anxiety about messing up or falling out of favor with others. Nor do they see their status as moral agents as a function of what thoughts pass in and out of their minds. Instead, they realize that as imperfect beings, their thoughts, emotions, and deeds need not be perfect for them to retain their worth and dignity as persons.

Exercise 6.8 can help you become clearer about how self-respecting *you* are.

EXERCISE 6.8

1. Do you ever have self-doubts? If so, under what circumstances? Give at least two examples.

2. Do you ever use any globally damning language to rate yourself (for example, "failure," "stupid," etc.)? If so, under what circumstances?

3. When you make mistakes, fail at something important to you, have bad thoughts, or encounter strong disapproval or criticism from others, how do you usually deal with the situation? What do you tell yourself about yourself?

4. Do you demand perfection of yourself? If so, under what circumstances? How do you think of yourself when you fall short of your demand?

Now, let's get to work on your virtues (Serenity, Respect for Life, and Self-Respect) starting with some preliminary self-reflections in Exercise 6.9.

EXERCISE 6.9

1. How do you think embracing these virtues could change your life?

2. Do you know anyone who embraces these virtues? How does this impact their lives and the lives of those around them?

3. Would you like to be more like these people? Why, or why not?

5. EMPOWERING WISDOM FROM THE STAGES ON PURSUING THE VIRTUES

So how can you become more serene, life-respecting, and self-respecting? Below are some reflections about these virtues from some of the world's greatest thinkers. This can help you formulate some powerful antidotes to your obsessive thinking!

Serenity

Empowering Wisdom from Plato:

- *God in heaven is the greatest, best, fairest, most perfect, and the material world, in which you reside, is but an imperfect copy.*

Imagine, you stop telling yourself that you must have certainty and that feeling that you need to be certain evaporates in thin air. So, now the thought of getting a fatal disease pops into your mind. You think about it and say to yourself, "Well I don't know for sure if it will happen or not. But that's outside my control. I am reasonably careful in taking care of myself. That's all I can do. So goodbye idea. I don't need to think about you."

This is what the ancient Greek philosopher Plato would tell you to do. According to this wise gentleman, the material world is a world where you can't be sure of anything because things are constantly changing. Of course, you can have reasonable beliefs or opinions about things; but you will only drive yourself up a tree if you look for certainty this side of heaven. So today there is no cure for a disease; fast forward a few years and there is a cure; then there may be a mutation of the disease, and no longer the same cure. Medical science takes one giant step forward and nature throws a monkey wrench into it. So demanding certainty in this world of ours is like trying to squeeze water out of a stone. It's futile!

The way Plato sees it, you are trying to find heaven on earth, which is a mistake. "[T]he world," he says, "has been framed in the likeness of that which is apprehended by reason and mind and is unchangeable, and must therefore of necessity, if this is admitted, be a copy of something." So, the world is an imperfect copy of an ideal world, that of heaven. As such, the only perfect being is "God who is the image of the intellectual, the greatest, best, fairest, most perfect, the one *only* begotten heaven" (Plato, 1892, italics added). In heaven you can be certain. Here on earth, there are possibilities. But this need not give you pause because these possibilities are endless and include exciting opportunities to affect welcome change!

Empowering Wisdom from Epictetus:

- *The future is* not *within your power to control.*
- *Your thoughts* are *within your power to control.*

Greco-Roman philosopher, Epictetus, joins Plato's choir to admonish you not to try to control things that are not in your control. Can you control what you think? Yes! Can you control how you feel? Yes! Can you control your own actions? Yes!

But can you control the future? It is in your power *to try*! So, you bring an umbrella along on a rainy day and expect it to keep you dry. Well maybe it will, but maybe it won't. A windy rain turns the umbrella inside out and you get soaked to the bone! Was it reasonable to bring the umbrella? Yes, and it was in your power to bring along that umbrella of yours; but if you *demand certainty* that you stay dry, you will have overstepped your powers. Give it up, says Epictetus, and accept that your powers of control are confined to your own thoughts, feelings, and actions. And if you let go of this demand, you will, he says, "never incur anything which you shun." On the other hand, "if you shun sickness, or death, or poverty, you will run the risk of wretchedness [anxiety].” So, the antidote to your anxiety is quite clear: “Remove [the habit of] aversion, then, from all things that are not within our power, and apply it to things undesirable which are within our power” (Epictetus, 1948). It's quite liberating to give up this demand! Let it go, admonishes Epictetus, and take a load off!

Empowering Wisdom from Alan Watts:

- *Let go your demand for certainty and become open to truth whatever it turns out to be.*

When you demand certainty, you wall yourself off from truth. In effect, you tell yourself there is only one thing that can and must happen. But herein lies a blatant contradiction with reality because reality does not come in only one flavor—the one you want. So, if you demand certainty that bad things not happen, or even that you won't end up doing something you may regret, you are hiding your head in the sand, attempting to escape confronting the truth.

So, instead of hiding from the truth by demanding certainty, you can instead confront it by having faith. It is on these terms that contemporary Buddhist philosopher, Alan Watts, defines what it means to have faith:

> Faith … is an unreserved opening of the mind to the truth, whatever it may turn out to be. Faith has no preconceptions; it is a plunge into the unknown. Belief clings, but faith lets go.
>
> (p. 24)

When you demand certainty, you wall yourself off from the truth, which is the opposite of having faith. To demand certainty is like saying “I don't trust anything or anyone, including my own ability to deal with what may happen.” According to Watts, this is also anti-religious. For, being religious does not mean being closed to the future but rather open to the truth.

So, if you demand that bad things not happen (to yourself or others you love), you exercise no faith in your capacity to deal with whatever happens. Likewise, if you demand that you not do anything morally bad, you exercise no faith *in yourself*.

From a Western perspective, this is also to turn a blind eye on God who is All Loving and Good. In demanding certainty, you effectively assume the power of God to create reality by fiat. This is the opposite of having faith in God!

Empowering Wisdom from Thich Nhat Hanh:

- *Let go of “I,” “me,” and “mine” to embrace your true self.*

Another Buddhist view that can be particularly useful in dealing with moral obsessions, but also with existential obsessions, is that your idea of *yourself*, or what you refer to as “I” or “me,” is illusory. “This will harm *me*”; “I must be certain *I* won't do bad things”; “Bad things must not happen to *me*.” In each of these statements, you assume that there is a permanent, independently existing thing called *I*, *me*, or *myself* behind the fleeting images and feelings that flow through a state of consciousness. On the contrary, says the Buddhist, there is just this flow of images and feelings, so no *thing* that could be harmed, do bad things, or happen to it. This may sound very strange since our brains construct this notion of self out of the perception of images and ideas. So, there isn't a further permanent, independent thing called myself behind the impermanent flow of images and ideas.

According to Buddhist monk, Thich Nhat Hanh (1966),

> The idea of self is the hidden idea that there is something called “self,” “me,” or “mine.” It's an idea that “I,” “me,” exist, and that there are things belonging to “me” “Me” and “mine.”

However, it is precisely this assumption, he warns, that is at "the center of all our grasping, of all our imagining, of all our wrong perceptions" (Hanh, 1966). If there is no underlying independent self, then there is no point to *self*-damning when this illusory self does something wrong. Of course, there can be constructive change for the future because change is really what reality is. New images and feelings can replace old ones as the flow of ideas and images continues.

This expansive flow of ideas, says Hanh, is your "true self." The "I" and "me" refer to a deceptive "small self." According to Hanh,

> We are imprisoned in our small selves, thinking only of some comfortable conditions for this small self, while we destroy our large self. If we want to change the situation, we must begin by being our true selves."

This "true self" consists of our coalescence and unity with all living beings, human and non-human alike, as well as all other interdependent parts of nature such as the earth, minerals, heat, rivers, consciousness, without which no selves could exist. You, me, all of us "inter-exist." We exist in relation to one grand unified reality. Citing the English poet, Sir Edwin Arnold, Watts puts the point succinctly: "Foregoing self, the universe grows I" (Watts, 1951, p. 110). By focusing exclusively on yourself as an independent thing, you miss reality and lose your (all-inclusive) "true self"!

So let go of this "small self," stop clinging to it and making demands about something that does not have a permanent, independent existence in the first place. Embrace, instead, your "true self" which is your all-encompassing "large self." This can be a powerful antidote to the suffering generated by making demands on an illusory self. If it doesn't exist as a separate being, it doesn't *need* to be anything!

This detachment from your "small self" helps to create feelings of unity with the conscious states beyond those ascribed to you. There is then no longer dogged obsession with me versus you; no longer *selfishness*; no point to defending *me* against *you*. Instead, there is a universal collectivity of consciousness. No partitions! As discussed later in this chapter, in the section on "Creating a Cognitive-Behavioral Plan," *mindfulness* meditation can prove useful in aspiring toward this goal.

EXERCISE 6.10

Discuss briefly your present approach to trying to deal with your obsessions and how you could use the counsel offered by Plato, Epictetus, Watts, and Hanh to become more serene.

Respect for Life

Empowering Wisdom from Vicktor Frankl:

- *Embrace Tragic Optimism by finding personal meaning or purpose in your suffering.*
- *Turn your suffering into a human achievement and accomplishment.*
- *Derive from your guilt opportunity to change yourself for the better.*
- *Derive from life's finiteness incentive to take responsible action.*

Imagine you are in the infamous "death camp" Auschwitz during the Holocaust, surrounded by the scent of burning flesh, seeing, every day, your fellow prisoners being led away into ovens and gas chambers. This was the world of Austrian existentialist and Holocaust survivor, Viktor Frankl, who founded the therapy he called "Logotherapy."

Frankl (1984) maintains that you can still be optimistic even under such oppressive, painful conditions. He calls this "tragic optimism," which occurs when there is pain, guilt, and death (p. 161).

For many of us, any type of optimism under such conditions may, at first blush, seem unthinkable. However, according to Frankl (1984), human beings have a special capacity for

(1) turning suffering into a human achievement and accomplishment;
(2) deriving from guilt the opportunity to change oneself for the better; and
(3) deriving from life's transitoriness an incentive to take responsible action.

(pp. 161–162)

These things are possible if you have found a purpose, reason, or meaning in terms of which you reframe reality. Once you have found this meaning, it has the capacity to not only make you happy but also help you to cope with suffering. Such a meaning or purpose, however, needs to resonate with you. One size does not fit all. What may work for me in a certain difficult situation may not work for you, and vice versa.

Frankl gives the example of an elderly patient of his whose beloved wife had passed away and had gone into depression. Frankl asked this patient how his wife would have felt if he had died before she died. The patient responded that she would have suffered greatly. Frankl then pointed out that he had spared his wife this great suffering by surviving her. So, the patient found meaning in this tragedy. His surviving his wife was not in vain after all for it had saved his beloved wife great pain (Frankl, 1984, p. 135).

In this situation there was tragedy (pain, guilt, and death), yet the patient was able to conjure a "tragic optimism" as a result of reframing his situation according to a previously unrealized purpose or meaning.

Much better than wallowing in pain, guilt, death! Likewise, there is a much better alternative to obsessing about the *possibilities* of tragedy. This is to find a meaning and purpose that can alleviate your anxiety. So, you keep ruminating about dying young because your father died young. This puts a damper on your living. But you can reframe the death of your father as a wakeup call to take responsibility for your life and do positive things with it while you have the precious time. Perhaps your father was a very industrious person and was actively involved in activities he loved doing when he died. His death gave you a positive model to emulate: A life rich with activity, doing what you love right up until the curtain comes down; tragic because it ended earlier than usual, yet still an optimistic way to end a life well lived. So, instead of futilely struggling to escape tragedy (by ruminating on its possibility), respect your life by embracing your capacity to find new purposes and meanings to reframe it.

Empowering Wisdom from William James:

- *Have faith that things will work out and, as a result, they will!*

Many religious folks believe that their lives are worthwhile because, despite all the struggles here on earth, there is another world where there is redemption and bliss. The more scientific and less religious folks may pessimistically view such a way of reaping value from life by pointing to the lack of empirical evidence to substantiate the existence of such a world. Of course, even if it isn't certain, *it's still possible* there is another such world, right? But this possibility, while not a certainty, may be all you really need to keep a positive attitude, even during hard times!

According to William James, the great American pragmatist,

> This life is worth living ... since it is what we make it, from the moral point of view, and we are determined to make it from that point of view, so far as we have anything to do with it, a success.
>
> (James, 1896, p. 60)

James calls this "self-verifying faith." By virtue of believing that there is some ultimate purpose, your life *automatically* takes on serious worth for you. Deny it and you may find yourself obsessing over the shitty things that might happen to you in this life. Believe in divine forgiveness and your obsessive thoughts about doing something morally bad lose their sting, since you are in the care of an almighty loving God who has your back. In this case, if it *feels* good, it really is good, since it can save you from the abyss of anxiety that destroys your quality of life. So, if it works to make your life worth living, use it. At the end of the day, according to James, that is what truly counts!

Empowering Wisdom from John Hick:

- *Without danger or difficulty there'd be no Courage or Fortitude; no Generosity, Kindness, the agape aspect of Love, Prudence, Unselfishness, or any other life enhancing virtues.*

If you think that a life that contains suffering must be a bad life and that therefore you need to obsess over the possibility of bad things happening, or even about your doing something bad, then think twice, admonishes the contemporary philosopher and theologian, John Hick. To the contrary, he maintains, human suffering, whether a result of nature or misdeeds of human beings, not only does not make your life bad, but arguably can make it better. Sound strange? Well, without suffering, says Hick (1973), ethical concepts like virtue, and even right or wrong, would be devoid of meaning:

> Courage and fortitude would have no point in an environment in which there is, by definition no danger or difficulty. Generosity, kindness, the *agape* aspect of love, prudence, unselfishness, and all other ethical notions which presuppose life in an objective environment could not even be formed. Consequently, such a world, however well it might promote pleasure, would be very ill adapted for the development of the moral qualities of human personality. In relation to this purpose it might be the worst of all possible worlds!
>
> (pp. 41–42)

If people never did anything morally wrong, there would be no virtue of repentance. If there were no diseases or other natural threats to human life, there would be no medical sciences or other applied sciences. It would indeed be a sterile universe, and you would lead a very boring existence!

EXERCISE 6.11

1. How does the possibility of bad things happening such as loss, illness, death, or human misdeeds, including your own, affect your view about the value of your own life?

2. How could the counsel provided by Frankl, James, and Hick improve your respect for your life?

Self-Respect

Empowering Wisdom from Epicurus:

- *Exercise "sober reasoning" to promote "absence of pain in the body and of trouble in the soul."*
- *Secure "health of body and tranquility of mind" as "the sum and end of a happy life."*

It is beyond debate that self-degradation creates painful emotions such as depression, intense guilt, and anxiety. Fortunately, ancient Greek sage, Epicurus (n.d.), has provided a useful antidote to such emotional stress aimed at boosting the amount of pleasure you reap from living. This is to stop putting yourself down, which means not obsessing about bad things you aren't sure you won't do in the future (moral obsession).

First, according to Epicurus, the beginning and end of a happy life is pleasure, which is, he says, "the absence of pain in the body and of trouble in the soul"; which means no obsessing. When you suffer no physical or mental pain, there is "no need to go in search of something that is lacking."

So, how can you enjoy such a life of pleasure? Epicurus' answer: "[D]irect every preference and aversion toward securing health of body and tranquility of mind, seeing that this is the sum and end of a happy life." Such a happy life, admonishes Epicurus,

> is not an unbroken succession of drinking-bouts and of merrymaking, not sexual love, not the enjoyment of the fish and other delicacies of a luxurious table, which produce a pleasant life; it is *sober reasoning*, searching out the grounds of every choice and avoidance, and banishing those beliefs through which the greatest disturbances take possession of the soul.

A key to accomplishing this goal is accordingly to pass over pleasures "when a greater annoyance ensues from them." For example, overdoing a food you like can make you sick.

Getting high on an addictive drug to feel better can create only temporary relief at the expense of an addiction problem or harmful side-effects, thereby creating more pain in the long run. In contrast, Epicurus recommended pleasures like building friendships (he emphasized the importance of having friends), or doing things that can give you mental pleasure, like the theatre, art, or music; or which can keep your body (as well as your mind) in shape, such as athletics and working out.

Second, Epicurus cautions you that "the future is neither wholly ours nor wholly not ours, so that neither *must* we count upon it as quite certain to come nor despair of it as quite certain not to come" (italics added). Accordingly, stop causing "trouble in your soul" by demanding certainty about the future! If you stop demand certainty, you won't feel the need to obsess.

So, Epicurus' prescription for your moral obsessions (or your existential ones) is to exercise "sober reasoning" (prudence) in choosing pleasures conducive to tranquility and absence of physical pain; avoiding things that produce greater mental or physical disturbances in the long run. This includes not putting yourself down or catastrophizing about possible bad things!

Empowering Wisdom from Jean-Paul Sartre:

- *You are, before all else, something that projects itself into a future, and is conscious of doing so unlike a patch of moss, fungus, or cauliflower.*

You are a conscious, self-aware, feeling being, who is capable of creating plans of action to change his life in the future. Thus, French Existentialist, Jean-Paul Sartre (2007) submits that

> man has more dignity than a stone or a table … What we mean to say is … that man is, before all else, something that projects itself into a future, and is conscious of doing so. Man is indeed a project that has a subjective existence, rather unlike that of a patch of moss, a spreading fungus, or a cauliflower.

(p. 23)

So, you are really a quite incredibly complex being, a being who is self-aware and projects itself into the future through a plan of action. And you have the freedom (and responsibility) to use this special capacity to make something of yourself through your plan of action set in motion. Indeed, what Sartre is telling you is that you *are* a plan of action conscious of itself.

Now you can, of course, treat yourself like "a cauliflower" by putting yourself down; and you can imitate a patch of moss by vegetating (read: obsess about who you really are instead of defining who you really are by doing things). Yes, you can turn yourself into whatever you want, but at the end of the day it will be you who bears the responsibility.

Empowering Wisdom from Saint Thomas Aquinas:

- *Your unique ability to reason, unlike any other creature, is an imprint of the divine light, making you special among all of God's creations.*

If you are a believer in the Judeo-Christian God, then you can think of yourself as a child of God whose human faculty of "natural reason itself is a participation of the divine light" (Aquinas, 1947, I, Q. 12, Art. 11); that is, this special capacity of yours for reasoning, which is unique to humankind, is a finite and imperfect copy (an imprint) of God's infinite wisdom.

Aristotle, who influenced St. Thomas, put the point very eloquently. "The activity of God," he said,

> which surpasses all others in blessedness, must be contemplative [the activity of knowing through the power of reason]; and of human activities, therefore, that which is most akin to this must be most of the nature of happiness. This is indicated, too, by the fact that the other animals have no share in happiness, being completely deprived of such activity.
>
> (Aristotle, 1941, bk. 10, ch. 8, p. 1107)

From this point of view, you possess unconditional worth and dignity. You are very special, indeed!

So, would God approve of your degrading and tormenting yourself through your obsessions? Of course not! This is not to say you could not learn from your mistakes. Indeed, this is why you have reason in the first place, namely, to work toward constructive change so you can get closer to God by becoming more knowledgeable, and thus more like God (albeit imperfectly).

Empowering Wisdom from Immanuel Kant:

- *Treat yourself as an end in itself (a person), not as a mere means (an object).*

If you are not a believer in God (atheist or agnostic) you may find the 18th-century German philosopher, Immanuel Kant, a better fit to inspire Self-Respect. Approaching human worth and dignity from a more secular perspective, Kant (2018) reminds you of a fundamental distinction between objects and persons. "Rational beings," he says, "are called persons, because their very nature points them out as *ends in themselves*, that is as something which must not be used *merely as means*" (p. 724).

You are a person, not an object. Objects have value only because they have particular uses. Your flash drive has value only because it can store data. If it ceases to perform this function, it loses its worth and can be discarded. You, on the other hand, retain your value regardless of whether you perform a given function, for example, regardless of whether you are an active member of the workforce. This value persists because, unlike your flash drive, you are a rational, self-determining agent. This means that you can make your own decisions and make claims on others to respect your right of self-determination. This, in turn, means others need to get your permission before they decide things that are within the province of your own self-determination. For example, a doctor needs to get your informed consent before performing a medical procedure on you. You are therefore special, having a right of self-determination, and therefore a right to make claims on others to treat you with respect.

According to Kant, being treated with respect also applies to yourself as well as others. You should also never treat *yourself* like an object or thing by damning yourself when you cease to act or perform in a way that you find unacceptable. Your value as a person does not wane with such unsatisfactory performance.

So, what if you had a bad thought! This does not make you a *bad person* who deserves to be tortured. It does not mean that you cease to be worthy of respect. Indeed, this right to be respected and treated as a self-determining agent is *unconditional*, and therefore does not depend on how well or poorly you fulfill a certain purpose, goal, or function. You are not an object to be trashed when you fail to satisfy standards either you set for yourself, or others set for you.

So, keep in mind the distinction between "ends in themselves" (persons) and "mere means" (objects), and accordingly stop treating yourself like an object by damning yourself, and, instead, as a person deserving of respect.

Empowering Wisdom from The Dalai Lama, Thich Nhat Hanh, and Erich Fromm:

- *If you want others to be happy, practice compassion. If you want to be happy, practice compassion.*
- *Build a home inside by accepting yourself and learning to love and heal yourself.*
- *Affirm your own life, happiness, growth and freedom.*
- *If you can only love others, you cannot love at all.*

If you are obsessing, especially over whether you would really do something very bad, the first thing you may be inclined to do is to go after your own jugular. "What kind of person am I even to think of doing such a thing let alone do it!" And then begins the litany of demeaning language that only adds fuel to your feelings of self-contempt.

Well, Buddhists have long admonished us to exercise compassion for all others, including yourself. Instead of putting yourself down, try a little tenderheartedness, just what you would expect others to show you when you are having a difficult time, and what you would show them during their difficult times. "There I go again tormenting myself. I want so much to be sure I wouldn't do such a thing. I must really care if I feel so strongly about this. But I am using this caring quality to torture myself, which is the opposite of what I should be doing with it. I wish myself better than this. I wish myself peace and happiness. Let me be peaceful and content."

In his co-authored book, *The Art of Happiness*, the Dalai Lama (2009) emphasizes that you are not likely to have unconditional acceptance of yourself if you do not have compassion and exhibit kindness for others. "There is," he states, "an inextricable link between one's personal happiness and kindness, compassion, and caring for others. And this is a two-way street: increased happiness leads to greater compassion, and increased compassion leads to greater happiness" (p. 258). So, the Dalai Lama is entreating you to turn a compassionate eye to others, for the sake of others as well as yourself. "If you want others to be happy, practice compassion. If you want to be happy, practice compassion" (p. 58). Both your happiness and that of others require you to have compassion for others.

Conversely, if you do not have compassion and love for yourself, you are not going to have compassion and love for others. "You can't offer happiness until you have it for yourself," Hanh (2014) admonishes. "So build a home inside by accepting yourself and learning to love and heal yourself" (p. 14).

Thich Nhat Hanh's astute counsel is also eloquently confirmed by social psychologist Erich Fromm (2006):

[M]y own self must be as much an object of my love as another person. *The affirmation of one's own life, happiness, growth, freedom is rooted in one's capacity to love* i.e. in care, respect, responsibility, and knowledge. If an individual is able to love productively, he loves himself too; if he can love *only* others, he cannot love at all.

(pp. 55–56, emphasis in original)

So, get ready to "affirm [your] own life, happiness, growth and freedom"! Stop damning yourself for having bad thoughts; or damning your life when bad things happen, or you think that they may. Extend this compassion to others too by affirming their "lives, happiness, growth and freedom."

EXERCISE 6.12

Discuss briefly, in the space provided below, your own approach to Self-Respect, and how you could use the counsel offered by Epicurus, Sartre, Aquinas, Kant, The Dalai Lama, Hanh, and Fromm to become more self-respecting.

Adding Favorite Sages of Your Own

Perhaps you have a favorite sage of your own whom you think gives positive advice on how to be more serene, life-respecting, and self-respecting. Exercise 6.13 below gives you an opportunity to add them to the list!

EXERCISE 6.13

1. Do you have a favorite sage of your own who offers empowering wisdom on how to be more serene, life-respecting, and self-respecting? If so, describe this learned counsel below. (Even if you don't know the name of the person from whom the advice comes, that's still okay.)

Additional Empowering Wisdom for Serenity

Additional Empowering Wisdom for Respect for Life

Additional Empowering Wisdom for Self-Respect

Compiling a Master List of Empowering Wisdom

Plato, Epictetus, Watts, and Hanh have provided some language to formulate their learned counsel that can go on a list of empowering wisdom to inspire Serenity. For instance, for each of the formulations in the Serenity column of Table 6.3, focus, one at a time, on the formulation with your mind's eye, and key into how it *feels. Does it make you feel more empowered to let go of your obsessiveness?* If yes, put it on your list of empowering language; if not, take it off or change the language!

Similarly, for each of the formulations in the Respect for Life column of Table 6.3, focus, one at a time, on the formulation with your mind's eye, and key into how it *feels. Does it make you feel more open toward accepting your life?* If yes, keep it on your list of empowering language; if not, take it off or change the language!

Finally, for each of the formulations in the Self-Respect column of Table 6.3, focus, one at a time, on the formulation with your mind's eye, and key into how it *feels. Does it make you feel more inclined to accept yourself?* If yes, keep it on your list of empowering language; if not, take it off or change the language!

Have you found the counsel formulated in Table 6.3 to have a positive feeling of empowerment? The language used to express this wisdom is an important part of why it can feel empowering.

Exercise 6.14 gives you the opportunity to modify the language as well as the content of your lists.

TABLE 6.3

Empowering wisdom regarding Serenity, Respect for Life, and Self-Respect

Serenity	Respect for Life	Self-Respect
Plato:	**Frankl:**	**Epicurus:**
God in heaven is the greatest, best, fairest, most perfect, and the material world, in which you reside, is but an imperfect copy.	Embrace Tragic Optimism by finding personal meaning or purpose in your suffering.	Exercise sober reasoning to promote absence of pain in the body and of trouble in the soul.
Epictetus:	__Turn your suffering into a human achievement and accomplishment.	Secure "health of body and tranquility of mind" as the sum and end of a happy life.
The future is not within your power to control.	__Derive from your guilt opportunity to change yourself for the better.	**Sartre:**
__Your thoughts are within your power to control.	__Derive from life's finiteness incentive to take responsible action.	You are, before all else, something that projects itself into a future, and is conscious of doing so unlike a patch of moss, fungus, or cauliflower.
Watts:	**James:**	**Aquinas:**
Let go your demand for certainty and become open to truth whatever it turns out to be.	Have faith that things will work out and, as a result, they will!	Your unique ability to reason, unlike any other creature, is an imprint of the divine light, making you special among all of God's creations.
Thich Nhat Hanh:	**Hick:**	**Kant:**
Let go of "I," "me," and "mine" to embrace your true self.	__Without danger or difficulty there'd be no Courage or Fortitude; no Generosity, Kindness, the agape aspect of Love, Prudence, Unselfishness, or any other life enhancing virtues.	Treat yourself as an end in itself (a person), not as a mere means (an object).
		Dalai Lama:
		If you want others to be happy, practice compassion. If you want to be happy, practice compassion.
		Thich Nhat Hanh:
		Build a home inside by accepting yourself and learning to love and heal yourself.
		Fromm:
		Affirm your own life, happiness, growth and freedom.
		__If you can only love others, you cannot love at all.

EXERCISE 6.14

This exercise will help you to develop a *master list of empowering wisdom that is uplifting, consoling, or otherwise empowering for you.*

Please feel free to modify Table 6.3 in responding to the following instructions:

1. For each of the three guiding virtues, place a checkmark in front of each learned counsel you intend to use. Your selections should resonate with you, that is, feel uplifting, consoling, or otherwise empowering to you.

2. If you are not satisfied with the formulation of any of the counsels in Table 6.3, on a separate piece of paper, please rewrite it using language that resonates with you. For example, when I think of Hanh's counsel on embracing your "true self," I think of the words "universal self" and "unity." You are encouraged to reformulate or tweak the sages' counsel using any language that is most empowering for you!

3. Please also add any empowering insights to Table 6.3 that you may have formulated in Exercise 6.12. Again, it is important that the language you use is empowering *for you*.

4. Now, congratulate yourself! You now have a master list of wisdom that is empowering for you!

6. CREATING A COGNITIVE-BEHAVIORAL PLAN

Are you ready to harness the wisdom of the sages to build a plan of action for overcoming your obsessive *can'ts*tipation? Here is your opportunity to break the shackles of self-oppression that have kept you chained to your obsessions. This can be incredibly exciting!

Suppose you have the obsessive thought of doing something irresponsible or negligent that could seriously harm or kill your four-year-old child, for example like not stopping her from running out into the busy street and getting hit by an oncoming car; or leaving her unstrapped in her car seat; or not taking her to the doctor when she is seriously ill. As a mom you have always tried to protect your child and have considered her a "precious gift from God"; but now these persistent thoughts of doing such morally abominable things has raised "serious doubts" in your mind about whether you are actually capable of doing such things and therefore about your own worthiness as a mom and as a human being. "What kind of monster could be capable of doing such things to her own baby."

These thoughts have prevented you from enjoying spending time with your little girl and have begun to strain your relationship with her. Even when you tell her how much you love her, you can hear yourself saying to yourself, "Do you really love her?"

However, you are now working on a cognitive-behavioral plan to overcome your morally obsessive *can'ts*tipation.

To gain more *Serenity*, you propose to

- Stop focusing so much on I, me, and mine, and instead on others besides yourself. So you decide to do volunteer work to help impoverished people.
- Work on letting go your demand for certainty by becoming open to the truth, regardless of whether you like it or not.
- Have greater "faith" or "trust" in your self to deal with reality as it is, not as what you demand it to be.
- Reframe the future as outside your control and instead accept your thoughts as within your control.
- Reframe the physical world, including yourself, as an imperfect, flawed, and uncertain copy of God in Heaven which is "greatest, best, fairest, and most perfect."

To exercise *Respect for Life*, you decide to

- Reframe the thoughts you are experiencing constructively, as an instruction to yourself about what *not* to do, for example, not forgetting to strap your child securely into her car seat.
- Look upon the thoughts as a sign of how fragile life is, your own as well as your daughter's, and therefore to affirm the value of life by continuing to build a positive relationship with your daughter.
- See your suffering as a mark of how much love you truly have for your daughter. After all, if even the thought of harming your daughter upsets you so much, then how strong indeed must be your love for her!
- Have faith in yourself that you will overcome these thoughts.

To be more *Self-Respecting* you resolve to

- See yourself, not simply as a malfunctioning object whose sole purpose is to take care of your child, but instead as an "end in yourself," a being whose value is unconditional regardless of what you think, feel, or do.

- Exercise "sober reasoning" to avoid emotionally disturbing yourself such as damning yourself for having bad thoughts.
- Affirm your "own life, happiness, growth and freedom" as a condition of your love for others including your child.
- Reframe your image of yourself as a child of God, who possesses an "imprint of the divine light."

Now it's your turn to build a plan of action based on the learned counsel you have embraced. Exercise 6.15 will help with this!

EXERCISE 6.15

1. Choose an obsessive thought you described in Exercise 6.2 that you are presently having and want especially to work on. (Recall you were asked to include at least one such thought in your list of cases.) Restate this thought in the space provided below:

2. Now, restate the obsessive thinking you formulated in Exercise 6.4 that has prevented you from overcoming this obsession.

1.

2.

3.

4.

5.

Using your empowering wisdom, the remainder of this exercise will help you to construct the elements of a cognitive-behavioral plan to overcome Conclusion 5 of the above obsessive thinking!

3. Using the learned counsel offered by Plato, Epictetus, Watts, and Thich Nhat Hanh, or any other empowering wisdom you may have added in Exercise 6.13 for becoming *more serene*, what cognitive-behavioral changes would you make to overcome your obsessive *can't*stipation? For example, what changes would Hanh tell you to make in the way you conceive the idea of yourself? List at least three cognitive-behavioral changes you plan to make based on the advice of these sages:

1.

2.

3.

4.

5.

4. Using the learned counsel offered by Frankl, James, Hick, or any other empowering wisdom you may have added in Exercise 6.13 for becoming *more life respecting*, what cognitive-behavioral changes would you make to overcome your obsessive *can't*stipation? List at least three:

1.

2.

3.

4.

5.

5. Using the learned counsel offered by Epicurus, Sartre, Kant, Aquinas, the Dalai Lama, Thich Nhat Hanh, and Fromm, or any other empowering wisdom you may have added in Exercise 6.13 for becoming *more self-respecting*, what cognitive-behavioral changes would you make to overcome your obsessive thinking? List at least three:

1.

2.

3.

4.

5.

6. Now, congratulate yourself! You have just constructed a cognitive-behavioral plan!!

---

7. WORKING ON YOUR COGNITIVE-BEHAVIORAL PLAN

You will now have an opportunity to begin to build your habits of Serenity, Respect for Life, and Self-Respect instead of defaulting to your self-defeating habit of obsessive *can'ts*tipation.

Cognitive–Affective Imagery

You can work on overcoming your obsessive thinking by first focusing on the feelings associated with your obsessive thinking and then changing your focus to the empowering wisdom associated with positive feelings. With practice, this can, in turn, help to neutralize the negative feelings associated with your obsessive thinking and help you to cultivate your guiding virtues.

To illustrate, using the previous example, you can practice your imagery by letting yourself first have the thought that triggers your obsession, namely that of doing something that risks your child's life. In this state you would then let yourself *feel* the conflict arising from demanding that you never do such a thing, and the thought of your doing such a thing. Amid this painful feeling of uncertainty of whether you could actually do such a thing to your child, you shift your attention to your guiding virtue of Serenity and focus your attention now on the language of your empowering wisdom, allowing yourself to experience the uplifting or consoling feelings the latter evokes. For instance, applying Frankl's philosophy of "tragic optimism," you could construct a new positive, personal meaning to the suffering triggered by the thought of harming your child. Thus, you might reframe it as a sign of how much you truly love your child. You suffer precisely because the thought of harming someone you love so dearly is painful.

Here the aim is to practice until you reverse the negative polarity of the thought that triggers your obsessive thinking! Exercise 6.16 can help you to get started with practicing some cognitive–affective imagery on your own obsessive thinking.

EXERCISE 6.16

1. Choose empowering wisdom from the Serenity column of your master list of empowering wisdom (see Exercise 6.14) that is especially empowering for you. Keep it in the back of your mind at this point.

2. Refer to the obsessive thinking you identified in Exercise 6.15 that you are presently having and want to work on.

3. Now, here are instructions for doing your cognitive–affective imagery. If you are working with a therapist, the therapist can provide guidance until you get the hang of it and can do it on your own. If you are not being assisted by a therapist, then please read these directions carefully now, memorize them (three steps), and then follow the three-step sequence laid out . for you below:

- Step 1: Focus your mind exclusively on your obsessive thinking (as identified in Exercise 6.15). Keep going over it in your mind like you did when you first decided you couldn't accomplish your goal. Keep it up until you feel that negative visceral threatening feeling, the clashing of your felt need for certainty with the realization that you do not have this certainty. Let yourself resonate with the feeling of powerlessness to stop checking for certainty.
- Step 2: At the peak of feeling this intense negative feeling, shift your focus of mind exclusively to the empowering wisdom that you have selected for feeling empowered to become serene. Let yourself feel the empowering feelings it creates to confront and overcome your anxiety about not having certainty; and the feeling of freedom to stop the obsession.
- Step 3: Once you have fully brought yourself to resonate with the positivity of the experience, gently shift your attention to reflecting on your experience and what you have learned or discovered from it.

4. Try to reserve a time each day to practice this guided imagery exercise. Next time, however, choose empowering wisdom from the *Respect for Life* column of your master list of empowering wisdom that is especially empowering for you.

5. Similarly, the subsequent day, repeat the exercise except this time choose empowering wisdom from the *Self-Respect* column of your master list of empowering wisdom.

6. Practice regularly, shifting between your empowering wisdom to support *all three* of your guiding virtues.

7. What have you learned or discovered about yourself from your experience practicing your cognitive–affective imagery? Write down your reflections in the space provided below.

My Reflections about My Experience:

Keep practicing!!

Exposure and Response Prevention

Many folks with obsessive thinking also have *compulsions*, which are things you may do (called "rituals") to try to stop your obsessive thinking. For example, maybe you start to count or tap your foot as a way to try to get rid of your bad thought. Maybe you wash your hands excessively when you touch something dirty and start to obsess about it. Of course, this doesn't work to alleviate your anxiety in the long run and instead reinforces your obsessive thinking by signaling to your brain that there is something catastrophic going on which needs immediate attention. It sends you into a "fight or flight" mode that only compounds your obsessive *can't*stipation. So, the goal here is to practice having the intrusive thought *without* engaging in the ritual—without counting, tapping your foot, washing your hands over and over again, or whatever else you may do.

This will take a commitment from you, and it will be hard to do at first. But it gets easier the more you get used to stopping your ritual. This is because a part of your brain (the ventral striatum), which is responsible for purposive action, changes its neural passages. This part of the brain has dopamine receptors so when you actually accomplish your goal of not engaging in your ritual, it will feel good! This is how you can get into a new habit of *not* performing your ritual when you have obsessive thinking. This can also help to support your work on getting rid of your obsessive *can't*stipation because it sends the message that there is no catastrophe going on that needs immediate attention!

Exercise 6.17 can help you to practice your response prevention. Please work this exercise *only if* you feel compelled to perform a ritual in response to your obsessive thinking,

---

EXERCISE 6.17

In practicing Exercise 6.16, did it help you to stop performing your ritual? If yes, great! Continue to do Exercise 6.16 as your response prevention exercise. If not, then you should also practice the following Exposure and Response Prevention (ERP) exercise in addition to (but not in place of) the cognitive–affective imagery you worked on in Exercise 6.16.

1. Think again of the thought that triggers your obsessive thinking and let yourself go through this thinking until you feel powerless to get this thought out of your mind. If you need to do something to get the thought into your head, such as touching something dirty, then go ahead and do it.

2. At this point you will also feel compelled to go into your ritual. *But don't perform it!* Instead, work cognitively on your obsessive thinking until your anxiety diminishes. There are a few options, here, and they are all helpful. One is to focus on your demand for certainty and refute it. "It is plainly impossible to be certain about anything in this world. If I had to be certain something bad wouldn't happen, I wouldn't do anything at all, and, even then, I couldn't be certain nothing bad would happen. So, this demand is absurd and I will just let it go."

Another option is to add some empowering wisdom to your refutation. "Only God in heaven, who is 'the greatest, best, fairest, most perfect' (as Plato would say) has certainty. But I have faith that things will work out in the end anyway."

Another option is to do some mindfulness meditation. This option is addressed in the next section of this chapter.

3. Work cognitively on your demand until you feel your anxiety level substantially decrease. Regardless of whether your anxiety diminishes, do *not* perform your ritual for at least 30 minutes. Next time you perform this ERP exercise increase your response time by waiting an

additional 15 minutes. The next time, increase it 15 minutes more, and so on for each subsequent session. Eventually, you will succeed at eliminating your ritual!

As mentioned, this takes a commitment on your part. But it is well worth the effort! You *can* do this!

4. Arrange a convenient time to practice your ERP exercise every day until you no longer feel compelled to perform your ritual. Don't get discouraged if you backslide. Just keep working on it!

5. In the space provided below, record you experience working on this exercise after you have succeeded in getting rid of your compulsion or after the first week of working on it, whichever comes first. How successful have you been in stopping your ritual so far? Has it gotten any easier for you to stop it? Update your response to this question each week (if necessary). Feel free to use additional paper to record your experience.

Mindfulness Meditation

In mindfulness meditation, you are an observer of your intrusive thought, not an evaluator or interpreter of it. Your goal is to train yourself to detach from the thought, not to evaluate it (catastrophize about it, damn yourself for thinking it, or any other manner of judging it). Key to attaining this skill is to let go of your *demand for certainty*. So, there is the thought you are having. You simply observe or watch it, without demanding that you know for certain whether it is a true thought, and hence without evaluating it. It is simply a thought, plain and simple. It carries no baggage. It can pass out of your consciousness as easily as it has entered when you no longer see it as something you *must* be certain about.

Exercise 6.18 provides guidance in cultivating this skill.

EXERCISE 6.18

1. Please listen to the following Yoga meditation presentation, "Guided Meditation for Intrusive Thoughts, OCD, & Anxiety" presented on YouTube by Malia Yoga (or find an alternative guided meditation for intrusive thoughts if unavailable). Here is the YouTube link: www.youtube.com/watch?v=GTriRU6PYNA

2. After listening to the presentation at least once, replay it while allowing your intrusive thought to freely enter your consciousness, without performing any ritual. Then allow yourself to gently push this thought out of consciousness as freely as it entered. Remember, as the presentation emphasizes, key to overcoming the obsessive thinking that keeps your thought recycling is letting go your demand for certainty.

3. Describe in the space provided below this first experience using meditation to deal with your obsessive thinking. How successful have you been so far in reducing your level of anxiety? How successful have you been at letting go your demand for certainty during meditation? What implications of this mindfulness activity do you see for reducing or eliminating your obsessiveness?

4. Continue to work daily on using meditation to allow your intrusive thought to freely enter and leave your consciousness. Do this at first while listening to video presentation, but then, once you feel you have the hang of it, practicing your skill without the aid of the presentation.

5. After practicing for two weeks, describe in the space provided below your experience practicing mindfulness meditation to deal with your obsessive thinking. What changes, if any, have you experienced, since beginning your mindfulness practice?

Congratulations on using mindfulness meditation to deal with your obsessive thinking!

Compassion-Based Meditation

One important aspect of mindfulness meditation is that, by virtue of being nonjudgmental, it can help you to detach from the "I," "me," and "mine" of obsessive thinking. If you are just an observer, the thought is not about you or yours; so there is no longer any basis for damning yourself or catastrophizing about bad things happening to *you*. Indeed, there is empirical evidence that mindfulness meditation can reduce self-referential processing in the brain while increasing other regarding processing (Shi & He, 2020).

Another type of meditation that further supports other-regarding brain processing is "loving kindness" meditation, a form of compassion-based meditation. This type of meditation, as discussed in the Introduction to this *Workbook*, involves sending a message of loving kindness to all living beings, including but not restricted to yourself. This can help you to widen your idea of self to include others. This is the sense of your "true self" referenced by Thich Nhat Hanh. As such, this type of meditation can be especially useful if you have moral obsessions as well as self-referential existential obsessions ("Something bad might happen to *me*!") because it takes focus off *you* exclusively, apart from others. It can also be useful in supporting Self-Respect because you also send yourself a message of loving kindness.

Exercise 6.19 can give you practice in this type of meditation.

EXERCISE 6.19

1. Please listen to the guided meditation audio recording called "Loving Kindness Meditation" presented by Kristin Neff. This audio recording is (at the time of this writing) freely accessible from the following link: https://self-compassion.org/guided-self-compassion-meditations-mp3-2/ (If unavailable locate an alternative loving kindness guided meditation.)

When you have finished following the audio recording, respond to the below questions.

2. Reflect on your obsessive thinking. How does this thinking now feel in relation to the grander scope of your connectedness with all living beings?

3. When you think about giving up your obsessive thought, letting it go, how does this feel?

4. Keep in mind that the more you practice your loving kindness meditation the better you will get at it!

Refuting and Reframing

A key step in implementing your cognitive-behavioral plan is refuting and reframing your obsessive thinking. In so doing you will have cleared the way to engage in constructive behavioral change without being obstructed by your obsessive thinking. Exercise 6.18 will help you to work on practicing refuting and reframing your obsessive thinking.

EXERCISE 6.20

1. Refer to the obsessive thinking you identified in Exercise 6.15, which is keeping your from letting go the obsessive thought you also identified in Exercise 6.15. Look carefully at Premise 1 of your obsessive thinking, the one that *demands certainty*. In Exercise 6.5, you have already refuted this premise so you can see how irrational it truly is. Think about this refutation until it resonates with you, that is, you get the "I get it" feeling that this premise is truly irrational. If this doesn't happen, then go back to Exercise 6.5 and find a refutation that does resonate with you. Write down your refutation in Table 6.4 in the refutation column for Premise 1.

Now, select some empowering wisdom from one or more of your sages (it could be wisdom you added in Exercise 6.13), and use it to reframe your demand for certainty. Write down this empowering wisdom in Table 6.4 in the reframing column for Premise 1.

TABLE 6.4
Refuting and reframing my obsessive thinking

Part	Refutation	Reframing
Premise 1		
Conclusion 3		
Conclusion 4		
Conclusion 5		

2. Just as you have done for Premise 1, refute and reframe Conclusions 3 and 4 of the obsessive thinking you identified in Exercise 6.15. Use Table 6.4 to write down your refutation and reframing for each of these respective conclusions of your obsessive thinking.

Congratulations! You have now refuted and reframed your obsessive thinking!

Getting Some Bibliotherapy

Ready to do some bibliotherapy?

Below, are some things to read or listen to that can help inspire Serenity, Respect for Life, and Self-respect. If you are working with a therapist, your therapist may add to this list, or recommend alternative bibliotherapy for you.

In her online blog, "Tiny Buddha," Lori Deschene (n.d.) offers several Buddhist recommendations for overcoming your demand for certainty. These include:

1. Replacing expectations with plans.
2. Becoming a feeling observer.
3. Preparing for different possibilities.
4. Getting confident about your coping and adapting skills.
5. Utilizing stress reduction techniques preemptively.
6. Focusing on what you can control.
7. Practicing mindfulness.

This very readable blog succinctly supports the activities recommended here for implementing your cognitive-behavioral plan. To get the details please check out this blog.

You have already picked up some learned counsel from Viktor Frankl "for cultivating Respect for Life. These and much more can be found in Frankl's classic book, *Man's Search for Meaning* (Frankl, 1984, p. 9). This relatively short book begins by recounting the time Frankl spent in a Nazi concentration camp during the Third Reich. Frankl draws from his experience in the camp to show you how you can have the power to cope with even such tragic conditions if you are open to finding new meanings to your suffering. This book can help you put your life into perspective especially if you suffer from existential obsessions.

Another book that embodies Frankl's philosophy is *Tuesdays with Morrie* by Mitch Albom (2002) in which Albom talks about his weekly visits with his former professor, Morrie Schwartz, a Brandeis University sociology professor dying from ALS (Lou Gehrig's Disease). Morrie talks about many life issues that are often the subjects of existential obsessions such as aging, death, the suffering of others, and regrets. In confronting these subjects, Morrie poignantly shows how giving up the demand for certainty and learning to respect life as it is, not as it must be, enabled him to attain great Serenity and Respect for Life in his last days. I highly recommend checking out this classic book if you struggle with existential issues about death and dying.

If you have moral obsessions, then I highly recommend listening to Albert Ellis' lecture on *Unconditionally Accepting Yourself and Others*, available as an audio recording. This lecture delivered by Ellis in the colorful language he is known for, presents a vivid idea of what it means to have Self-Respect (Ellis, 2005).[1]

As you have seen, obsessive thinking is fueled by a perfectionistic demand for certainty. This is why you may benefit by checking out my self-help book, *Making Peace with Imperfection: Discover your Perfectionism Type, End the Cycle of Criticism, and Embrace Self-Acceptance* (2019). This book covers ten different types of perfectionism, including certainty perfectionism. It also contains exercises you can do to further support your present efforts to let go of your demand for certainty.

EXERCISE 6.21

Select at least two of the presented bibliotherapy options provided above and work through them. After you have worked through them, enter your reflections in the space provided below on whether and in what ways they were useful for you in addressing your obsessive *can't*stipation. Feel free to use additional paper if necessary.

Acting on Your Cognitive-Behavior Plan

This is the final stage of your process of working on your cognitive-behavioral plan. It involves doing all the things you listed in your cognitive-behavioral plan, which you developed in Exercise 6.15. For example, as a way to gain greater Serenity you planned to stop focusing so much on "I," "me," and "mine," and instead on others besides yourself. In particular, you planned to do volunteer work to lend aid to poor people. So now that you have been practicing mindful and compassion-based meditation, you have prepared yourself to embrace such a wider sense of self that transcends the "I," "me," and "mine" of obsessive thinking. And now is the time to act on this newfound sense of self!

Exercise 6.22 provides instructions for so doing.

EXERCISE 6.22

1. Review the cognitive-behavioral items on your cognitive-behavioral plan created in Exercise 6.15.

2. As developed in Exercise 6.20, review your refutation and reframing of Premise 1 and Conclusions 4, 5, and 6 of your obsessive thinking.

3. Now you are ready to implement each of the tasks in your cognitive-behavioral plan. Keep in mind that this can include *not* doing some things, for example, not engaging in rituals, not focusing on yourself, not restricting the constructive activities in your life, etc. Be patient

and work through both cognitive and behavioral elements of the plan. With your cognitive-behavioral skills you have been working on in this chapter, you are in an excellent position to overcome you obsessive thinking!

4. Continue to refute and reframe your obsessive thinking (Exercise 6.20); cognitive–affective imagery (Exercise 6.16); exposure and response prevention (Exercise 6.17); mindfulness meditation (Exercise 6.18); and compassion-based meditation (Exercise 6.19). This can help to support and build your new virtuous habits going forward!

5. Provide your reflections below about your experience in implementing your cognitive-behavioral plan.

```



```

6. This is an incredible milestone, so, once again, congratulate yourself!

Working on Other Obsessions

For any other moral or existential obsessions you may presently have or tend to have (based on what you indicated in Exercise 6.2), or whatever other obsessions you may develop in the future, the process for addressing them is the same six-step approach you have just worked through. So, you now possess knowledge of this process, and you are well on your way to cultivating your guiding virtues and supporting empowering wisdom to counteract and neutralize obsessive thinking.

Here is a summary of the process:

1. Formulate your obsessive thinking (Exercise 6.4).
2. Refute Premise 1 and Conclusions 4 and 5 of this thinking (Exercise 6.5).
3. Embrace your guiding virtues (Exercises 6.6 through 6.9).
4. Get empowering wisdom from the sages on pursuing the virtues (Exercises 6.10 through 6.14).
5. Use this learned counsel to construct a cognitive-behavioral plan (Exercise 6.15).
6. Work on your cognitive-behavioral plan (Exercises 6.16 through 6.22).

Having worked through the exercises in this chapter, you are well on your way to attaining greater and greater freedom and fulfillment in life as you become less and less burdened by obsessive thinking. Clearly, building your guiding virtues of Serenity, Respect for Life, and Self-Respect is a lifelong commitment. Keep working through the above six steps regularly. If you falter, no problem. You are human, after all. Get back in the saddle. You will prevail!

NOTE

1 A portion of this recording is also presently accessible online as a free video (Ellis, 2013).

REFERENCES

Albom, M. (2002). *Tuesdays with Morrie: An old man, a young man, and life's greatest lesson.* Broadway Books.

Aquinas, T. (1947). *Summa theologica* (Trans. Fathers of the English Dominican Province). Benziger Bros.

Aristotle (1941). *Nicomachean Ethics.* In McKeon, R. (Ed.), *The basic works of Aristotle.* Random House.

Cohen, E.D. (2019). *Making peace with imperfection: Discover your perfectionism type, end the cycle of criticism, and embrace self- acceptance.* Impact Publishers.

Dalai Lama. (2009). *The art of happiness: A handbook for living.* Penguin Publishing Group. Kindle edition.

Deschene, L. (n.d.). 7 ways to deal with uncertainty so you can be happier and less anxious. Tiny Buddha. Retrieved from 7 Ways to Deal with Uncertainty So You Can Be Happier and Less Anxious (tinybuddha.com).

Ellis, A. (2013). Unconditionally accepting yourself. REBT Info / REBT Training. Online Video. Retrieved from https://rebtinfo.com/dr-ellis-on-unconditional-self-acceptance-video/

Ellis, A. (2005). *Unconditionally accepting yourself and others.* Audiotape. https://store.albertellis.org/products/unconditionally-accepting-yourself-and-others

Epictetus. (1948). *The Enchiridion.* Higgins, T.W. (Trans.). Liberal Arts Press. Retrieved from www.gutenberg.org/files/45109/45109-h/45109-h.htm

Epicurus. (n.d.). Letter to Menoeceus, trans. Hicks, R.D. Retrieved from http://classics.mit.edu/Epicurus/menoec.html

Frankl, V.E. (1984). *Man's search for meaning.* Simon & Shuster, Inc.

Fromm, E. (2006). *The Art of Love.* Harper Collins.

Hanh, T.N. (2014). *How to love.* Parallax Press. Kindle Edition.

Hanh, T.N. (1966). The sun my heart. In Kotler, A. (Ed.), *Engaged Buddhist reader.* Parallax Press, pp. 162–170. Retrieved from www2.hawaii.edu/~freeman/courses/phil394/The%20Sun%20My%20Heart.pdf

Hick, J. H. (1973). *Philosophy of religion.* Prentice-Hall, Inc.

James, W. (1896). *Is life worth living?* S. Burns Weston. Retrieved from https://archive.org/details/islifeworthlivin00jameuoft/mode/2up

Kant, I. (2018) *Fundamental principles of the metaphysic of morals.* Project Gutenberg, Kindle edition.

Plato (1892). Timaeus. In Jowett, B. (trans.), *The dialogues of Plato,* 3rd edition revised and corrected. Retrieved from https://oll.libertyfund.org/title/plato-dialogues-vol-3-republic-timaeus-critias#lf0131-03_head_034

Sartre, J.P. (2007). *Existentialism is a humanism,* Carol Macomber (Trans.). Yale University Press.

Shi, Z. & He, L. (2020). Mindfulness: Attenuating self-referential processing and strengthening other-referential processing. *Mindfulness,* 11, 599–605. https://doi.org/10.1007/s12671-019-01271-y

Watts, A. (1951). *The wisdom of insecurity.* Knopf Doubleday Publishing Group.

Index

Note: Page numbers in **bold** type indicate tables.

For Product Safety Concerns and Information please contact our EU
representative GPSR@taylorandfrancis.com
Taylor & Francis Verlag GmbH, Kaufingerstraße 24, 80331 München, Germany